How to File For Divorce in New York

HOW TO FILE
FOR DIVORCE
IN NEW YORK

with forms

Second Edition

———

Brette McWhorter Sember
Edward A. Haman
Attorneys at Law

Sphinx Publishing
A Division of Sourcebooks, Inc.
Naperville, IL

Second Edition, 2001

Published by: **Sphinx® Publishing, A Division of Sourcebooks, Inc.®**

<u>Naperville Office</u>
P.O. Box 4410
Naperville, Illinois 60567-4410
(630) 961-3900
FAX: 630-961-2168

This publication is designed to provide accurate and authoritative information in regard to the subject matter covered. It is sold with the understanding that the publisher is not engaged in rendering legal, accounting, or other professional service. If legal advice or other expert assistance is required, the services of a competent professional person should be sought.

From a Declaration of Principles Jointly Adopted by a Committee of the
American Bar Association and a Committee of Publishers and Associations

This product is not a substitute for legal advice.

Disclaimer required by Texas statutes.

Library of Congress Cataloging-in-Publication Data

Sember, Brette McWhorter, 1968-
    How to file for divorce in New York / Brette McWhorter Sember, Edward A. Haman.--
2nd ed.
      p. cm. -- (Self-help law kit with forms)
    Includes index.
    ISBN 1-57248-141-2
    1. Divorce--Law and legislation--New York (State)--Popular works. 2. Divorce--Law
and legislation--New York (State)--Forms.   I. Haman, Edward A. II. Title. III. Series.

KFN5126.Z9 S46 2001
346.74701'66--dc21

                                               2001016087

Printed and bound in the United States of America.
VHG Paperback — 10 9 8 7 6 5 4 3 2 1

CONTENTS

Using Self-Help
Law Books

Before using a self-help law book, you should realize the advantages and disadvantages of doing your own legal work and understand the challenges and diligence that this requires. .

The Growing Trend

Rest assured that you won't be the first or only person handling your own legal matter. For example, in some states, more than seventy-five percent of the people in divorces and other cases represent themselves. Because of the high cost of legal services, this is a major trend and many courts are struggling to make it easier for people to represent themselves. However, some courts are not happy with people who do not use attorneys and refuse to help them in any way. For some, the attitude is, "Go to the law library and figure it out for yourself."

We write and publish self-help law books to give people an alternative to the often complicated and confusing legal books found in most law libraries. We have made the explanations of the law as simple and easy to understand as possible. Of course, unlike an attorney advising an individual client, we cannot cover every conceivable possibility.

Cost/Value Analysis

Whenever you shop for a product or service, you are faced with various levels of quality and price. In deciding what product or service to buy, you make a cost/value analysis on the basis of your willingness to pay and the quality you desire.

When buying a car, you decide whether you want transportation, comfort, status, or sex appeal. Accordingly, you decide among such choices as a Neon, a Lincoln, a Rolls Royce, or a Porsche. Before making a decision, you usually weigh the merits of each option against the cost.

When you get a headache, you can take a pain reliever (such as aspirin) or visit a medical specialist for a neurological examination. Given this choice, most people, of course, take a pain reliever, since it costs only pennies; whereas a medical examination costs hundreds of dollars and takes a lot of time. This is usually a logical choice because it is rare to need anything more than a pain reliever for a headache. But in some cases, a headache may indicate a brain tumor and failing to see a specialist right away can result in complications. Should everyone with a headache go to a specialist? Of course not, but people treating their own illnesses must realize that they are betting on the basis of their cost/value analysis of the situation. They are taking the most logical option.

The same cost/value analysis must be made when deciding to do one's own legal work. Many legal situations are very straight forward, requiring a simple form and no complicated analysis. Anyone with a little intelligence and a book of instructions can handle the matter without outside help.

But there is always the chance that complications are involved that only an attorney would notice. To simplify the law into a book like this, several legal cases often must be condensed into a single sentence or paragraph. Otherwise, the book would be several hundred pages long and too complicated for most people. However, this simplification necessarily leaves out many details and nuances that would apply to special or unusual situations. Also, there are many ways to interpret most legal questions. Your case may come before a judge who disagrees with the analysis of our authors.

Therefore, in deciding to use a self-help law book and to do your own legal work, you must realize that you are making a cost/value analysis. You have decided that the money you will save in doing it yourself outweighs the chance that your case will not turn out to your satisfaction. Most people handling their own simple legal matters never have a problem, but occasionally people find that it ended up costing them more to have an attorney straighten out the situation than it would have if they had hired an attorney in the beginning. Keep this in mind while handling your case, and be sure to consult an attorney if you feel you might need further guidance.

LOCAL RULES   The next thing to remember is that a book which covers the law for the entire nation, or even for an entire state, cannot possibly include every procedural difference of every jurisdiction. Whenever possible, we provide the exact form needed; however, in some areas, each county, or even each judge, may require unique forms and procedures. In our state books, our forms usually cover the majority of counties in the state, or provide examples of the type of form which will be required. In our national books, our forms are sometimes even more general in nature but are designed to give a good idea of the type of form that will be needed in most locations. Nonetheless, keep in mind that your state, county, or judge may have a requirement, or use a form, that is not included in this book.

You should not necessarily expect to be able to get all of the information and resources you need solely from within the pages of this book. This book will serve as your guide, giving you specific information whenever possible and helping you to find out what else you will need to know. This is just like if you decided to build your own backyard deck. You might purchase a book on how to build decks. However, such a book would not include the building codes and permit requirements of every city, town, county, and township in the nation; nor would it include the lumber, nails, saws, hammers, and other materials and tools you would need to actually build the deck. You would use the book as your guide, and then do some work and research involving such matters as whether you need a permit of some kind, what type and grade of wood are available in your area, whether to use hand tools or power tools, and how to use those tools.

Before using the forms in a book like this, you should check with your court clerk to see if there are any local rules of which you should be aware, or local forms you will need to use. Often, such forms will require the same information as the forms in the book but are merely laid out differently or use slightly different language. They will sometimes require additional information.

CHANGES IN
THE LAW

Besides being subject to local rules and practices, the law is subject to change at any time. The courts and the legislatures of all fifty states are constantly revising the laws. It is possible that while you are reading this book, some aspect of the law is being changed.

In most cases, the change will be of minimal significance. A form will be redesigned, additional information will be required, or a waiting period will be extended. As a result, you might need to revise a form, file an extra form, or wait out a longer time period; these types of changes will not usually affect the outcome of your case. On the other hand, sometimes a major part of the law is changed, the entire law in a particular area is rewritten, or a case that was the basis of a central legal point is overruled. In such instances, your entire ability to pursue your case may be impaired.

To help you with local requirements and changes in the law, be sure to read the section in Chapter 2 on "Legal Research."

Again, you should weigh the value of your case against the cost of an attorney and make a decision as to what you believe is in your best interest.

INTRODUCTION

Going through a divorce is probably one of the most common, and most traumatic, encounters with the legal system. Paying a divorce lawyer can be one of the most expensive bills to pay, and at a time when you are least likely to have extra funds. In a contested divorce case it is not uncommon for the parties to run up legal bills of over $10,000; and horror stories abound of lawyers charging substantial fees with little progress to show for it. This book is designed to enable you to obtain a divorce without hiring a lawyer. Even if you do hire a lawyer, this book will help you to work with him or her more effectively, which can also reduce the legal fee.

This is not a law school course, but a practical guide to get you through "The System" as easily as possible. Legal jargon has nearly been eliminated. For ease of understanding, this book uses the term *spouse* to refer to your husband or wife (whichever applies), and the terms *child* and *children* are used interchangeably.

Please keep in mind that different judges and courts in different counties may have their own particular (if not peculiar) procedures, forms, and ways of doing things. The court clerk's office can often tell you if they have any special forms or requirements. Court clerks cannot give legal advice, but they can tell you what their court or judges require.

The first two chapters of this book will give you an overview of the law and the legal system. Chapter 3 will help you decide if you want an attorney. Chapter 5 will help you evaluate your situation and give you an idea of what to expect if you decide to go through with a divorce. The remaining chapters will show you what forms you need, how to fill out the forms, and what procedures to follow. You will also find two appendices in the back of the book. Appendix A contains selected portions of the New York law and court rules dealing with property division, maintenance (alimony), and child support. Although these provisions are discussed in the book, it is sometimes helpful to read the law exactly as it is written.

Appendix B contains the forms you will complete. You will not need to use all of the forms. Depending upon your situation, this book will tell you which forms you need.

Be sure to read "An Introduction to Legal Forms" in Chapter 6 before using any of the forms in this book.

MARRIAGE "INS AND OUTS"

Several years (or maybe only months) ago, you made a decision to get married. This chapter will discuss, in a very general way, what you got yourself into, how to get out, and whether you really want to get out.

MARRIAGE

Marriage is frequently referred to as a contract. It is a legal contract and, for many, it is also a religious contract. This book will deal only with the legal aspects. The wedding ceremony involves the bride and groom reciting certain vows, which are actually mutual promises about how they will treat each other. There are also legal papers signed, such as a marriage license and a marriage certificate. These formalities create certain rights and obligations for the husband and wife. Although the focus at the ceremony is on the emotional and romantic aspects of the relationship, the legal reality is that financial and property rights are being created. These financial and property rights and obligations cannot be broken without a legal proceeding.

Marriage will give each of the parties certain rights in property, and it creates certain obligations with respect to the support of any children they have together (or adopt). Unfortunately, most people do not fully realize that these rights and obligations are being created until it comes time for a divorce.

New York does not recognize homosexual marriage or common law marriage. A *common law* marriage is where a couple are deemed to be married by virtue of living together for a certain period of time. They proclaim themselves to be husband and wife; however, they have never complied with the legal requirements for marriage, such as obtaining a marriage license, taking vows, and filing a marriage certificate.

DIVORCE

A divorce is the most common method of terminating or breaking the marriage contract. In New York, a divorce is sometimes referred to as a *matrimonial proceeding.* You will see this term used in some of the forms. In a divorce, the court declares the marriage contract broken, divides the parties' property and debts, decides if either party should receive alimony (known as *maintenance* in New York), and determines the custody, support, and visitation with respect to any children the parties may have.

GROUNDS FOR DIVORCE

In New York, there must be a specific reason (called *grounds*) for a court to grant a divorce. The spouse asking for the divorce is called the *plaintiff* and must be able to prove that he or she is legally entitled to a divorce from the other spouse, called the *defendant*. There are only five legally acceptable reasons for a divorce:

1. **Cruel and inhuman treatment.** This is where the defendant has treated the plaintiff cruelly and inhumanly, either physically, mentally, or emotionally, in such a way that it is unsafe for them to live together. Although this is the legal standard, most plaintiffs who seek a divorce based upon cruel and inhuman treatment use the following description in their court papers: "The Defendant called the Plaintiff names, provoked arguments, and withheld affection, making it unsafe and improper for the parties

to continue to reside together." Any further detail is usually not required. This description fits almost any divorcing couple and is the most commonly used grounds for divorce in New York.

2. **Adultery.** This only applies to adultery committed by the defendant. This is extremely hard to prove since there must be evidence other than the testimony of the spouses. The plaintiff must provide evidence and testimony from witnesses that prove that the defendant engaged in sexual intercourse with another person while married to the plaintiff.

3. **Imprisonment.** The defendant must be imprisoned for three or more years during the marriage.

4. **Abandonment.** The defendant must have abandoned the plaintiff at least one year ago and must not have returned. Essentially, this means he or she moved out. The plaintiff must be able to testify that the abandonment occurred without provocation (this means that the plaintiff did not tell, or ask, the defendant to move out), and the plaintiff must have asked the defendant to return and the defendant did not return.

5. **Living separate and apart.** The couple has lived apart for at least one year, either under a valid Separation Agreement or Judgment of Separation. During that period of time, the parties cannot live together and cannot have sexual intercourse.

ANNULMENT

ANNULMENT VS.
DIVORCE

The basic difference between a *divorce* and an *annulment* is that a divorce says, "this marriage is broken," and an annulment says, "there never was a marriage." An annulment is more difficult and often more complicated to prove, so it is not used very often. Annulments are only possible in a few circumstances, usually where one party deceived the other. If you decide that you want an annulment, you should consult an attorney. If you are seeking an annulment for religious reasons and need to go through a church procedure (rather than, or in addition to, a legal procedure), you should consult your priest, minister, or rabbi. A divorce is generally easier to get than an annulment.

GROUNDS FOR ANNULMENT

Annulments can only be granted in the following six circumstances:

1. One of the parties was too young to get married. In New York, both parties must be at least eighteen years old to get married (there are a few exceptions, such as where the under-age person has parental consent and is between sixteen and eighteen, or where the under-age person has the consent of a parent and a Supreme or Family Court Judge and is between fourteen and sixteen). Only the under-age person can seek the annulment and only if the parties did not freely cohabit (live together).

2. One of the parties did not understand he or she was entering into marriage, usually due to mental retardation or mental illness.

3. Due to an incurable physical incapacity, one of the parties is physically unable to consummate the marriage.

4. One of the parties agreed to the marriage while under force, duress or fraud. *Duress* means the person was being threatened or was under some kind of pressure so that he or she did not voluntarily enter into the marriage. An example of *fraud* is where one party married the other in order to have the right to inherit from him or her, with no intention to ever live together as husband and wife.

5. One of the parties has suffered from an incurable mental illness for five or more years.

6. One of the parties was already married to another person who was still alive at the time of the marriage. This might occur if one party re-married, mistakenly believing his divorce was final. Intentional bigamy is also an example.

If your spouse wants to stop an annulment, there are several arguments he or she could make to further complicate the case. This area of the law is not as well defined as divorce. Annulments are much less common than divorces. The annulment procedure can be extremely complicated, and should not be attempted without consulting a lawyer.

LEGAL SEPARATION

In New York, a legal separation is like getting a divorce while remaining married in name only. A legal separation is created in one of two ways:

1. when a couple signs a Separation Agreement and files it with the court, or

2. when a court issues a Judgment of Separation.

SEPARATION
AGREEMENTS

The Separation Agreement or Judgment of Separation divides all of the property, assets, and debts of the marriage; and specifies custody, visitation, maintenance, and child support. However, the couple legally remains married. After a couple has been legally separated for one year, the Separation Agreement or Judgment of Separation can be "converted" to a divorce. All of the terms of the Separation Agreement or Judgment of Separation become the terms of the Judgment of Divorce.

To become legally separated with a Separation Agreement, you and your spouse must sign a Separation Agreement and file it with the court clerk. One year after filing the Separation Agreement, you can proceed with your divorce (unless you begin to live together again since filing the Separation Agreement).

JUDGMENT OF
SEPARATION

To obtain a Judgment of Separation, one of you must begin a court action for separation. This basically follows the same procedure as an action for divorce, but substitutes the word "separation" for the word "divorce" in the court papers. As with a divorce, you need to have certain reasons, or grounds, to get a Judgment of Separation. There are only four legally acceptable grounds for a Judgment of Separation:

1. Cruel and inhuman treatment.

2. Adultery.

3. Imprisonment.

4. Abandonment.

As you can see, these are the same grounds you need to prove in order to get a divorce. Therefore, if your spouse will not agree to work out a Separation Agreement, it is a waste of time to seek a Judgment of Separation when you can simply seek a Judgment of Divorce with the same procedure and the same grounds.

Do You Really Want a Divorce?

Getting a divorce will have an impact on several aspects of your life, and can change your entire life-style. Before you begin the process of getting a divorce, you need to take some time to think about how it will affect your life. This section will help you examine these things, and offer alternatives in the event you want to try to save your relationship. Even if you feel absolutely sure that you want a divorce, you should still read this section so you are prepared for what may follow.

LEGAL DIVORCE

Legal divorce is simply the breaking of your matrimonial bonds and the termination of your marriage contract and partnership. Going through a court system procedure, and having to deal with your spouse as you go through it, creates tremendous stress. However, when compared to the other aspects of divorce, the legal divorce does not last as long. On the other hand, the legal divorce can be the most confrontational and emotionally explosive stage. There are generally three matters to be resolved through the legal divorce:

1. The divorce of two people: Basically, this gives each the legal right to marry someone else.

2. The division of their property (and responsibility for debts).

3. The care and custody of their children.

Although it is theoretically possible for the legal divorce to be concluded within a few weeks or months, the legalities may continue for years, mostly caused by the emotional aspects leading to battles over the children.

SOCIAL AND
EMOTIONAL
DIVORCE

Your divorce will continue to have a tremendous impact on your social and emotional lives long after you are legally divorced. These impacts include:

Lack of companionship. Even if your marriage is one of the most miserable, you may still notice at least a little emptiness or loneliness after the divorce. It may not be that you miss your spouse in particular, but just miss another person being around.

Grief. Divorce may be viewed as the death of a marriage, or maybe the funeral ceremony for the death of a marriage. And like the death of anyone or anything you have been close to, you will feel a sense of loss. This aspect can take you through all of the normal feelings associated with grief. You will get angry and frustrated over the years you have "wasted." You will feel guilty because you "failed to make the marriage work." You will find yourself saying, "I can't believe this is happening to me." And, for months or even years, you will spend a lot of time thinking about your marriage. It can be extremely difficult to put it all behind you, and to get on with your life.

The single's scene: dating. You may find that you are dropped from friends' guest lists as your current friends, who are probably all married, no longer find that you, as a single person, fit in with their circle. If you want to avoid solitary evenings before the TV, you'll find yourself trying to get back into the "single's scene." This can be very difficult, especially if you have custody of the kids. And the dating scene is (or at least should be) entirely changed with the ever-present threat of AIDS and other communicable diseases.

FINANCIAL
DIVORCE

Many married couples are just able to make ends meet. After getting divorced there are suddenly two rent payments, two electric bills, etc. For the spouse without custody, there is also child support to be paid. For at least one spouse, and often for both, money becomes even tighter than it was before the divorce. Also, once you have divided up your property, each of you will need to replace the items the other person got to keep.

DIVORCE AND CHILDREN

The effect upon your children, and your relationship with them, can often be the most painful and long-lasting aspect of divorce. Your relationship with your children may become strained as they work through their feelings of blame, guilt, disappointment and anger. This strain may continue for many years. You and your children may even need professional counseling. Also, as long as there is child support and visitation involved, you will be forced to have at least some contact with your ex-spouse.

ALTERNATIVES TO DIVORCE

By the time you have purchased this book, and read this far, you have probably already decided that you want a divorce. However, if what you have just read and considered has made you want to make a last effort to save your marriage, there are a few things you can try. These are only very basic suggestions. Details, and other suggestions, can be offered by professional marriage counselors.

Talk to your spouse. Choose the right time (not when your spouse is trying to unwind after a day at work, or is trying to quiet a screaming baby), and talk about your problems. Try to establish a few ground rules for the discussion, such as:

☞ Talk about how you feel, instead of making accusations that may start an argument.

☞ Each person listens while the other speaks (no interrupting).

☞ Each person must say something that he or she likes about the other, and about the relationship.

As you talk you may want to discuss such things as where you would like your relationship to go, how it has changed since you got married, and what can be done to bring you closer together.

Change your thinking. Many people get divorced because they will not change something about their outlook or their life-style. Then, once they get divorced, they find they've made that same change they resisted for so long. For example, George and Wendy were unhappy in their marriage. They did not seem to share the same life-style. George felt overburdened with responsibility and bored. He wanted Wendy to be more independent and outgoing, to meet new people, to handle the household budget, and to go out with him more often. But Wendy was more shy and reserved, wasn't confident in her ability to find a job and succeed in the "business world," and preferred to stay at home. Wendy wanted George to give up some of his frequent nights "out with the guys," to help with the cooking and laundry, to stop leaving messes for her to clean up, and to stop bothering her about going out all the time. But neither would try change, and eventually all of the "little things" built up into a divorce.

After the divorce, Wendy was forced to get a job to support herself. Now she has made friends at work, she goes out with them two or three nights a week, she's successful and happy at her job, and she's quite competent at managing her own budget. George now has his own apartment, and has to cook his own meals (something he finds he enjoys), and do his own laundry. He has also found it necessary to clean up his own messes and keep the place neat, especially if he's going to entertain guests. George has even thought about inviting Wendy over for dinner and a quiet evening at his place. Wendy has been thinking about inviting George out for a drink after work with her friends.

Both George and Wendy have changed in exactly the way the other had wanted. It's just too bad they did not make these changes before they got divorced. If you think some change may help, give it a try. You can always go back to a divorce if things do not work out.

Counseling. Counseling is not the same as giving advice. A counselor should not be telling you what to do. A counselor's job is to assist you in figuring out what you really want to do. A counselor's job is mostly to ask questions that will get you thinking. Actually, just talking things out with your spouse is a form of self-counseling. The only problem is that it is difficult to remain objective and non-judgmental. You both need to be able to calmly analyze what the problems are, and discuss possible solutions.

Very few couples seem to be able to do this successfully, which is why there are professional marriage counselors. As with doctors and lawyers, good marriage counselors are best discovered by word of mouth. You may have friends who can direct you to someone who helped them. You can also check with your family doctor or your clergyman for a referral, or even check the telephone Yellow Pages under "Marriage and Family Counselors" or some similar category. You can see a counselor either alone or with your spouse. It may be a good idea for you to see a counselor even if you are going through with the divorce.

Another form of individual counseling is talking to a close friend. Just remember the difference between counseling and advice giving! Do not let your friend tell you what you should do.

Trial separation. Before going to the time, expense, and trouble of getting a divorce, you and your spouse may want to try just getting away from each other for awhile. This can be as simple as taking separate vacations, or as complex as actually separating into separate households for an indefinite period of time. This may give each of you a chance to think about how you will like living alone, how important or trivial your problems are, and how you really feel about each other.

Mediation. If you and your spouse agree you want a divorce, but can not agree about dividing your property and debts, custody, or child support, but do not wish to have a judge make these decisions, mediation is an alternative. A *mediator* is a therapist or attorney who works with a couple and helps them make those decisions themselves. A mediator helps the couple create a separation agreement. One spouse then converts it to a divorce after a year. Many people prefer to use mediation as opposed to a court procedure because they are able to come to a resolution that fits their lives, not one imposed by a court. Mediation is often less expensive than a contested court procedure. If you choose to mediate, be aware that there is no licensing or certification of mediators in New York state, so be sure your mediator is trained and experienced. You can contact the New York State Council on Divorce Mediation (800-894-2646) for a referral to a reputable mediator in your area. See Chapter 4 for more information on this.

THE LEGAL SYSTEM 2

This chapter will give you a general introduction to the legal system. There are things you need to know in order to obtain a divorce (or help your lawyer get the job done), and to get through any encounter with the legal system with a minimum of stress. These are some of the realities of our system. If you do not learn to accept these realities, you will experience much stress and frustration.

THEORY VS. REALITY

Our legal system is a system of rules. There are basically three types of rules:

1. *Rules of Law:* These provide the basic substance of the law, such as a law telling a judge how to go about dividing your property.

2. *Rules of Procedure:* These tell how matters are to be handled in the courts, such as requiring court papers to be in a certain form, delivered to the other party in a certain manner, or filed within a certain time.

3. *Rules of Evidence:* These require facts to be proven in a certain way.

The theory is that these rules allow each side to present evidence most favorable to that side, and an independent person or persons (the judge or jury) will be able to figure out the truth. Then certain legal principles will be applied to that "truth," which will give a fair resolution of the dispute between the parties. These legal principles are supposed to be relatively unchanging so that we can all know what will happen in any given situation and can plan our lives accordingly. This will provide order and predictability to our society. Any change in the legal principles is supposed to occur slowly, so that the expected behavior in our society is not confused from day-to-day. Unfortunately, the system does not really work this way. What follows are only some of the problems in the real legal system.

The System Is Not Perfect

Contrary to how it may seem, legal rules are not made just to complicate things and confuse everyone. They are attempts to make the system fair and just. They have been developed over hundreds of years, and in most cases they do make sense. Unfortunately, our efforts to find fairness and justice have resulted in a complex set of rules. The legal system affects our lives in important ways, and it is not a game. However, it can be compared to a game in some ways. The rules are designed to apply to all people, in all cases. Sometimes the rules do not seem to give a fair result in a certain situation, but the rules are still followed. Just as a referee can make a bad call, so can a judge. There are also cases where one side wins by cheating.

Judges Don't Always Follow the Rules

It is a shocking discovery for many young lawyers. After spending three years in law school learning legal theory and countless hours preparing for a hearing, and having all of the law on your side, you find that the judge is not going to pay any attention to legal theories and the law. Many judges are going to make a decision simply on what they think seems fair under the circumstances. This concept is actually being taught in some law schools now. Unfortunately, what "seems fair" to a particular judge may depend upon his or her personal ideas and philosophy. For example, there is nothing in the divorce laws that gives one parent priority in child custody; however, a vast majority of judges believe that a child is generally better off with his or her mother. All other things being equal, these judges will still find a way to justify awarding custody to the mother.

THE SYSTEM IS OFTEN SLOW

Even lawyers get frustrated at how long it can take to get a case completed. Whatever your situation, things will take longer than you expect. Patience is required to get through the system with a minimum of stress. Do not let your impatience or frustration show. No matter what happens, keep calm and be courteous.

NO TWO CASES ARE ALIKE

Just because your friend's case went a certain way does not mean yours will have the same result. The judge can make a difference, and more often the circumstances will make a difference. You can't assume you will be ordered to pay the same amount of child support just because your co-worker makes the same income as you and has the same number of children. There are usually other circumstances your co-worker doesn't tell you about, and possibly doesn't understand.

HALF OF THE PEOPLE "LOSE"

Remember, there are two sides to every legal issue, and there is usually only one winner. Especially if you let the judge decide, do not expect to have every detail go your way.

DIVORCE LAW AND PROCEDURE

This section will give you a general overview of the law and procedures involved in getting a divorce. To most people, including lawyers, the law appears very complicated and confusing. Fortunately, many areas of the law can be broken down into simple and logical steps. Divorce is one of those areas.

Law and the legal system are often compared to games, and just like games, it is important to know the players:

THE PLAYERS

The judge. The judge has the power to decide whether you can get divorced, how your property will be divided, which of you will get custody of the children, and how much the other will pay for child support. The judge is the last person you want to make angry with you. In general, judges have large caseloads and like it best when your case can be concluded quickly and without hassle. This means that the more you and your spouse agree upon, and the more complete your paperwork is, the better the judge will like it. Most likely, your only direct contact with the judge will be at the final hearing, which may last as little as five minutes. (See Chapter 6 for more about how to deal with the judge.)

The judge's secretary. The judge's secretary sets the hearings for the judge, and can frequently answer many of your questions about the procedure and what the judge would like or require. Once again, you do not want to make an enemy of the secretary. This means that you do not call her frequently and do not ask too many questions. A few questions are okay, and you may want to start off saying that you just want to make sure you have everything in order for the judge. You'll get much farther by being nice rather than by arguing.

The judge's law clerk. The judge's law clerk is an attorney who assists the judge and often holds pre-trial conferences to help the parties reach a settlement. The law clerk can answer some of your questions about the law, but cannot give you legal advice. The law clerk generally knows how the judge will decide many issues and if a law clerk suggests a settlement, you are usually wise to accept it.

The matrimonial referee. Uncontested divorces are not heard by a judge, but by an attorney employed by the court called a referee. Treat the referee with the same respect you show a judge because he or she is acting as a judge.

The court stenographer. The court stenographer records everything that is said at a court appearance. Be sure to get his or her card because you will need to purchase a transcript from him or her after the case is over.

The court clerk. Where the secretary usually only works for one judge, the court clerk handles the files for all of the judges. The clerk's office is the central place where all of the court files are kept. The clerk files your court papers and keeps the official records of your divorce. Most people who work in the clerk's office are friendly and helpful. While they cannot give you legal advice (such as telling you what to say in your court papers), they can help explain the system and the procedures (such as telling you what type of papers must be filed). The clerk has the power to accept or reject your papers, so you don't want to anger the clerk either. If the clerk tells you to change something in your papers, just change it. Don't argue or complain.

Lawyers. Lawyers serve as guides through the legal system. They guide their own client, while trying to confuse, manipulate, or out-maneuver their opponent. In dealing with your spouse's lawyer (if he or she has one) try to be polite. You won't get anywhere by being antagonistic. Generally the lawyer is just doing his job to get the best situation for his client. Some lawyers are truly nasty people. These lawyers simply cannot be reasoned with, and you shouldn't try. If your spouse gets one of these lawyers, it is a good idea for you to get a lawyer also. Chapter 3 will provide more information to help you decide if you need a lawyer.

The courts. Divorce cases (also known as *matrimonial* cases) are heard in Supreme Court. Each county in New York has a Supreme Court with at least one judge. If you decide to file for divorce, you will do so in Supreme Court. The Court of Appeals and the Appellate Division Courts are courts where only appeals are heard.

New York has a Family Court in each county, which hears cases that are about child abuse and neglect, juvenile delinquency, some adoptions, family offenses (domestic violence), and cases that are only about custody, visitation and child or spousal support without being part of a divorce. People who are already divorced, people who are still married and not seeking a divorce, or people who are not married but have children together can all go to Family Court. Prior to filing for divorce, you can go to Family Court and get orders directing custody, child support, and spousal support (similar to maintenance). Family Court is very user-friendly. The clerks will help you fill out the forms and many people do not use attorneys.

This book. This book will serve as your map of the trail through the legal system. In most cases, the dangers along the way are relatively small. If you start getting lost, or the dangers seem to be getting worse, you can always hire a lawyer to jump to your aid.

THE LAW   The law relating to divorce, as well as to any other area of law, comes from two sources:

1. The New York Statutes, which are the laws passed by the New York Legislature; and

2. The past decisions of New York courts.

This book is designed so you won't need to look up the law. However, a portion of the New York statutes, relating to property division, maintenance, and child support, can be found in Appendix A of this book.

Residency Requirement

One basic law you need to be aware of is that in order to get divorced in New York, you must fall into one of the following four categories:

1. At least one spouse must have lived in New York for two years prior to filing for divorce.

2. At least one spouse must have lived in New York for one year prior to filing for divorce and either:

   a. the parties were married in New York; **or**

   b. the parties have lived together in New York at some point during the marriage.

3. At least one spouse has lived in New York for one year prior to filing for divorce and the grounds for divorce happened in New York.

4. Both parties currently live in New York and the grounds for divorce happened in New York.

The second source of law, the past decisions of the New York courts, are much more difficult to locate and follow. For most situations the law is clearly spelled out in the statutes, and the past court decisions are not all that important. However, if you wish to learn more about how to find these court decisions, see the section on "Legal Research" later in this chapter.

The law is really very simple in most divorce cases. You will need to show the following four things:

1. A reason, or *grounds*, for a divorce to be granted.

2. How your property and debts should be divided between you and your spouse.

3. Who should have custody of your children and how they should be supported.

4. If there should be any maintenance (alimony), and if so, how much?

THE PROCEDURE
The procedural requirements come from the New York Statutes. The basic uncontested divorce process may be viewed as a five-step process:

1. File court papers asking the judge to grant a divorce (which includes dividing your property and deciding the caretaking of the children).

2. Notify your spouse that you are filing for divorce.

3. File papers explaining the grounds for the divorce, your financial situation and what you are asking the court to do about assets, debts, custody, and child support.

4. Attend a hearing or file an affidavit.

5. Have the judge sign a judgment granting the divorce.

The uncontested divorce procedure is the simplest way to obtain a divorce in New York. Uncontested means you and your spouse are in agreement or that your spouse does not respond to the papers you file. We'll now look at these steps in a little more detail. Later chapters will tell you how to carry out these steps.

Verified Complaint and Summons with Notice. The Verified Complaint is the basic form in which you ask the court to grant you a divorce, divide your property, and decide other matters such as maintenance, child custody and visitation, and child support. (see form 7, p.187.) The Summons with Notice is a request for your spouse to respond to your request for a divorce. (see form 4, p.183.) The Summons with Notice also describes the categories of things you are asking the court to decide and what grounds you will be proving, as described in your Verified Complaint. Full instructions for the Summons with Notice are provided in later chapters. Once the Verified Complaint and the Summons with Notice are completed, they are taken to the court clerk to be filed.

Notifying your spouse. After you've prepared the Summons with Notice, you need to officially *serve it on* (i.e., have it delivered to) your spouse. Even though your spouse may already know that you are filing for divorce, you still need to have him or her officially notified. This is done by having a copy of your Summons with Notice delivered to your spouse. The manner in which this must be carried out will be explained in detail later.

Other papers. After you have properly notified your spouse, and he or she either has not responded or has indicated his or her agreement, there are several other forms that must be completed and filed with the court clerk. These forms are contained in Appendix B and explained in detail later.

The Hearing or Affidavit. Once the papers are completed, filed, and accepted by the court clerk, you may either testify at a hearing or submit a written statement (called an *affidavit*) containing your testimony. This is described later in greater detail.

The Referee's Report and Judgment of Divorce. A *referee* will review your paperwork or listen to your testimony, and issue a Finding of Fact and Conclusions of Law (Referee's Report), which is a recommendation about whether to grant the divorce, how your property should be divided, who should have custody of your children, and how your children are to be supported. (see form 22, p.236.) If it applies in your case, a decision on maintenance payments will also be made. A judge will accept the Referee's Report and sign the Judgment of Divorce. (see form 23, p.244.) You will prepare both the Referee's Report and the Judgment of Divorce, and submit them to the court. These forms are explained in detail later in the book. Once the Judgment of Divorce is signed by the judge, you are officially divorced.

LEGAL RESEARCH

NEW YORK
STATUTORY
CODE

This book has been designed so that you don't need to do research. However, if you want to find out more about the divorce law in New York, or if you run into a complication that requires you to get more information, this section will give you some guidance.

The main source of information on New York divorce law is the *New York Statutory Code*. This is a set of books which contain the laws passed by the New York Legislature. It is updated yearly. A set can usually be found at the public library, although check to be sure they have the most recent set. The most likely set you will find will be titled *McKinney's Consolidated Laws of New York Annotated*, which is discussed more below. This set of books is divided by subject, such as "Civil Procedure Law & Rules," "Estates, Powers and Trusts Law," "General Obligations," etc. Divorce law is found in the volumes on "Domestic Relations Law."

In addition to the laws passed by the legislature, law is also made by the decisions of the judges in various cases each year. To find this *case law* you will need to go to a law library. Each county has a law library connected with the court, so you can ask the court clerk where the law library is located. Also, law schools have libraries which may be open to the public. Don't be afraid to ask the librarian for assistance. They cannot give you legal advice, but they can tell you where the books are located.

ANNOTATED
STATUTES

McKinney's Consolidated Laws of New York Annotated are numerous volumes which contain the New York statutes. Each section of the statutes is followed by summaries (called *annotations*) of court cases which discuss that section of the statutes.

NEW YORK DIGEST	The *New York Digest* is a set of books which give summaries of cases, and the place where you can find the court's full written opinion. Information in the digest is arranged alphabetically by subject. Find the chapter on "Divorce," then find the headings of the subject you want, such as "child support," "maintenance," "property division," etc.
CASE REPORTERS	Case reporters are books containing court decisions. *New York Reports* (abbreviated as N.Y.), *New York Supplement* (N.Y.S.), and *North Eastern Reporter* (N.E.) publish Court of Appeals decisions (the highest court in New York). *Appellate Division Reports* (A.D.) and *New York Supplement* (N.Y.S.) publish cases from the Appellate Division (courts that are directly below the Court of Appeals). *New York Miscellaneous Reports* (Misc.) publishes trial court decisions. All of these reporters have newer and older versions. The newer versions have "2d" after their abbreviation. If the digest gives you a reference to *Bliss v. Bliss*, 66 N.Y.2d 382 (1985), this tells you that you can find the case called *Bliss v. Bliss*, in volume 66 of *New York Reports 2d Series*, on page 382, and that the case was decided by the court in 1985.
NEW YORK JURISPRUDENCE	*New York Jurisprudence* is a legal encyclopedia. You simply look up the subject you want ("Dissolution of Marriage"), in alphabetical order, and it gives you a summary of the law on that subject. It will also refer to specific court cases, which can then be found in the reporters.
NEW YORK COURT RULES AND REGULATIONS	The *New York Court Rules and Regulations* are the rules applied in various courts in New York. You would be primarily concerned with the Uniform Trial Court Rules.
OTHER SOURCES	Other books you may want to ask for at the law library are:

- ☞ *New York Matrimonial Practice*, by Willard H. DaSilva, published by West Group.
- ☞ *New York Practice Guide: Domestic Relations*, published by Matthew-Bender.
- ☞ *West's McKinney's Forms*, which is a set of books that contain forms for all types of legal matters.

LAWYERS 3

DO YOU NEED A LAWYER?

Whether you need an attorney will depend upon many factors, such as how comfortable you feel handling the matter yourself; whether your situation is more complicated than usual; how much opposition you get from your spouse; and whether your spouse has an attorney. You may also want to hire a lawyer if you encounter a judge with a hostile attitude, or if your spouse gets a lawyer who wants to fight. There are no court appointed lawyers in divorce cases, so if you want an attorney you will have to hire one, or qualify for assistance from a legal aid society.

A very general rule is that you should consider hiring an attorney whenever you reach a point where you no longer feel comfortable representing yourself. This point will vary greatly with each person, so there is no easy way to be more definite. You should probably get an attorney if your spouse has a pension you want to receive part of; your spouse owns a business; your spouse earned a degree during the marriage; your spouse is in the military; your spouse has ever been violent towards you; you fear for your safety or that of your children; you are seeking a large or lifetime maintenance payment; you want your spouse to be responsible for a large amount of debt; you and your spouse cannot agree about custody; or your spouse is contesting the divorce.

Rather than asking if you *need* a lawyer, a more appropriate question is: "Do you *want* a lawyer?" We will now discuss some of the "pros" and "cons" of hiring a lawyer, and some of the things you may want to consider in making this decision.

One of the first questions you will want to consider, and most likely the reason you are reading this book, is: How much will an attorney cost? Attorneys come in all ages, shapes, sizes, sexes, racial and ethnic groups—and price ranges. For a very rough estimate, you can expect an attorney to charge anywhere from $150 to $1,000 for an uncontested divorce, and from $800 and up for a contested divorce. Lawyers usually charge an hourly rate for contested divorces, ranging from about $75 to $300 per hour. Most new (and therefore less expensive) attorneys would be quite capable of handling a simple divorce, but, if your situation became more complicated, you would probably prefer a more experienced lawyer. As a general rule, you can expect it to cost more than what you think it will cost at the beginning.

ADVANTAGES TO
HIRING A
LAWYER

The following are some of the advantages to hiring a lawyer:

☛ Judges and other attorneys may take you more seriously. Most judges prefer both parties to have attorneys. They feel this helps the case move in a more orderly fashion, because both sides will know the procedures and relevant issues. Persons representing themselves often waste a lot of time on matters that have absolutely no bearing on the outcome of the case.

☛ A lawyer will serve as a "buffer" between you and your spouse. This can lead to a quicker passage through the system, by reducing the chance for emotions to take control and confuse the issues. You will not have to deal directly with your spouse at all.

☛ Attorneys prefer to deal with other attorneys for many of the same reasons as listed above. However, if you become familiar with this book, and conduct yourself in a calm and proper manner, you should have no trouble. (Proper courtroom manners will be discussed in Chapter 6.)

☛ You can let your lawyer worry about all of the details. By having an attorney you need only become generally familiar with the contents of this book, as it will be your attorney's job to file the proper papers in the correct form, and to deal with the court clerks, the judge, the process server, your spouse, and your spouse's attorney.

☛ Lawyers provide professional assistance with problems. In the event your case is complicated, or suddenly becomes complicated, it is an advantage to have an attorney who is familiar with your case. It can also be comforting to have a lawyer to turn to for advice and to have your questions answered.

ADVANTAGES TO
REPRESENTING
YOURSELF

The following are some advantages to representing yourself:

☛ You save the cost of a lawyer.

☛ Sometimes judges feel more sympathetic toward a person not represented by an attorney. Sometimes this results in the unrepresented person being allowed a certain amount of leeway with the procedure rules.

☛ The procedure may be faster. Two of the most frequent complaints about lawyers received by the bar association involve delay in completing the case, and failure to return phone calls. Most lawyers have a heavy caseload, which sometimes results in cases being neglected for various periods of time. If you are following the progress of your own case you will be able to push it along the system diligently.

☛ Selecting any attorney is not easy. As the next section shows, it is hard to know whether you are selecting an attorney with whom you will be happy.

MIDDLE
GROUND

You may want to look for an attorney who will be willing to accept an hourly fee to answer your questions and give you help as you need it. This way you will save some legal costs, but still get some professional assistance.

Selecting a Lawyer

Selecting a lawyer is a two-step process. First you need to decide which attorney to make an appointment with, then you need to decide if you want to hire that attorney.

FINDING LAWYERS

The following are some suggestions to help you locate lawyers for further consideration.

☞ Ask a friend. A common, and frequently the best, way to find a lawyer is to ask someone you know to recommend one to you. This is especially helpful if the lawyer represented your friend in a divorce, or other family law matter.

☞ Lawyer referral service. You can find a referral service by looking in the yellow pages phone directory under "Attorney Referral Services" or "Attorneys." This is a service, usually operated by a bar association, which is designed to match a client with an attorney handling cases in the area of law the client needs. The referral service does not guarantee the quality of work, nor the level of experience or ability, of the attorney. Finding a lawyer this way will at least connect you with one who is interested in divorce and family law matters, and probably has some experience in this area. There are now some private lawyer referral services, which do offer some guarantees regarding the lawyers on their referral lists. The New York State Bar Association Referral Service can be reached at 800-342-3661. There may be another service run by your county's bar association as well.

☞ Yellow pages. Check under the heading for "Attorneys" in the yellow pages phone directory. Many of the lawyers and law firms will place display ads indicating their areas of practice, and educational backgrounds. Look for firms or lawyers that indicate they practice in areas such as "divorce," "family law," or "domestic relations."

☞ Ask another lawyer. If you have used the services of an attorney in the past for some other matter (for example, a real estate closing, traffic ticket or a will), you may want to call and ask if he or she could refer you to an attorney whose ability in the area of family law is respected.

EVALUATING A
LAWYER

From your search, select three to five lawyers worthy of further consideration. Your first step will be to call each attorney's office, explain that you are interested in seeking a divorce, and ask the following questions:

☛ Does the attorney (or firm) handle this type of matter?

☛ How much will it cost? (Don't expect to get a definite answer, but they may be able to give you a range or an hourly rate. You will probably need to talk to the lawyer for anything more detailed.)

☛ How soon can you get an appointment?

If you like the answers you get, ask if you can speak to the attorney. Some offices will permit this, but others will require you to make an appointment. Make the appointment if that is what is required. Once you get in contact with the attorney (either on the phone or at the appointment), ask the following questions:

☛ How much will it cost?

☛ How will the fee be paid?

☛ How long has the attorney been in practice?

☛ How long has the attorney been in practice in New York?

☛ What percentage of the attorney's cases involve divorce cases or other family law matters? (Don't expect an exact answer, but you should get a rough estimate that is at least twenty percent.)

☛ How long will it take? (Don't expect an exact answer, but the attorney should be able to give you an average range and discuss things which may make a difference).

If you get acceptable answers to these questions, it's time to ask yourself the following questions about the lawyer:

☛ Do you feel comfortable talking to the lawyer?

☛ Is the lawyer friendly toward you?

☞ Does the lawyer seem confident in himself or herself?

☞ Does the lawyer seem to be straight-forward with you, and able to explain things so you understand?

If you get satisfactory answers to all of these questions you probably have a lawyer you will be able to work with. Most clients are happiest with an attorney with whom they feel comfortable.

WORKING WITH A LAWYER

In general, you will work best with your attorney if you keep an open, honest and friendly attitude. You should also consider the following suggestions.

ASK QUESTIONS

If you want to know something or if you do not understand something, ask your attorney. If you do not understand the answer, tell your attorney and ask him or her to explain it again. There are many points of law that many lawyers do not fully understand, so you should not be embarrassed to ask questions. Many people who say they had a bad experience with a lawyer either did not ask enough questions, or had a lawyer who would not take the time to explain things to them. If your lawyer isn't taking the time to explain what he's doing, it may be time to look for a new lawyer.

GIVE YOUR
LAWYER
COMPLETE
INFORMATION

Anything you tell your attorney is confidential. An attorney can lose his license to practice if he reveals information without your permission. So do not hold back. Tell your lawyer everything, even if it doesn't seem important to you. There are many things that seem unimportant to a non-attorney, but can change the outcome of a case. Also, don't hold something back because you are afraid it will hurt your case. It will definitely hurt your case if your lawyer doesn't find out about it until he hears it in court from your spouse's attorney. But if he knows in advance, he can plan to eliminate or reduce damage to your case.

BE PATIENT
Listen to what your lawyer tells you about the law and the system. It will do you no good to argue because the law or the system does not work the way you think it should. For example, if your lawyer tells you that the judge cannot hear your case for two weeks, don't try demanding that he set a hearing tomorrow. By refusing to accept reality, you are only setting yourself up for disappointment. And remember: It's not your attorney's fault that the system isn't perfect, or that the law doesn't say what you would like it to say.

ACCEPT REALITY
As difficult as it may be, try to be patient with the system (which is often slow as we discussed earlier), as well as with your attorney. Do not expect your lawyer to return your phone call within an hour. He may not be able to return it the same day either. Most lawyers are very busy, and over-worked. It is rare that an attorney can maintain a full caseload and still make each client feel as if he is the only client.

TALK TO THE SECRETARY
Your lawyer's secretary can be a valuable source of information. Often the secretary will be able to answer your questions, and you won't get a bill for the secretary's time.

LET YOUR ATTORNEY DEAL WITH YOUR SPOUSE
It is your lawyer's job to communicate with your spouse, or with your spouse's lawyer. Many lawyers have had clients lose or damage their cases when the client decides to say or do something on their own. If your spouse calls you, you can always say: "You need to have your lawyer call my lawyer."

BE ON TIME
Be on time to appointments with your lawyer, and to court hearings. If you are late to a meeting with your lawyer, you may still be charged for the time. If you are late to a court hearing, the consequences can be even more severe.

KEEP YOUR CASE MOVING
Many lawyers operate on the old principle of "The squeaking wheel gets the oil." Work on a case tends to get put off until a deadline is near, an emergency develops, or the client calls. Many lawyers take more cases than can be effectively handled in order to earn the income they desire. Your task is to become a squeaking wheel that doesn't squeak too much. Whenever you talk to your lawyer ask the following questions:

☞ What is the next step?

☞ When do you expect it to be done?

☞ When should I talk to you next?

If you do not hear from the lawyer when you expect, call him the following day. Don't remind him that he didn't call; just ask how things are going.

FIRING YOUR LAWYER

If you can no longer work with your lawyer, it is time to either go it alone or get a new attorney. You will need to send your lawyer a letter stating that you no longer desire his or her services, and are discharging him or her from your case. Also state that you will be coming by his or her office the following day to pick up your file. The attorney does not have to give you his or her own notes or other work he or she has in progress, but he or she must give you the essential contents of your file (such as copies of papers already filed or prepared and billed for, and any documents that you provided). If he or she refuses to give you your file, for any reason, contact The New York State Bar Association about filing a complaint, or *grievance*, against the lawyer. Of course, you will need to settle any remaining fees charged for work that has already been done by the lawyer.

MEDIATORS AND MEDIATION 4

FINDING A MEDIATOR

A *mediator* is a professional trained in conflict resolution who can help you and your spouse work out a separation agreement without lawyers or going to court. The New York State Council on Divorce Mediation, at **http://www.nysmediate.org,** can help you find a trained mediator in your area. If you already have an attorney, ask him or her for a referral to a mediator. Mediators advertise in the phone book and your local bar association may be able to give you a list of mediators in your area.

EVALUATING A MEDIATOR

Once you get the name of a recommended mediator, schedule a free consultation for you and your spouse. Meet with the mediator and ask lots of questions.

- ☞ What kind of training did he or she receive?

- ☞ Does he or she have experience in the field of divorce mediation? (there are many other kinds mediators who specialize in other areas)

- ☞ Is he or she a lawyer, therapist or other professional?

☞ How many years has he or she been practicing mediation?

☞ Is he or she a member of any mediation organizations?

☞ How is the fee determined?

☞ How many sessions will be necessary?

☞ How often can he or she see you for the sessions? (generally you want to have a session at least every two weeks, just to keep the ball rolling)

You will want to also consider the mediator's personality type. Do both you and your spouse feel comfortable? Do you feel that you will be able to discuss private and personal issues with the mediator? It is important that you find a mediator you trust. Mediation is not all business and paperwork. A good mediator will encourage the couple to discuss their feelings and talk about personal issues. It is often the case that couples battle over property or custody when unresolved issues between them are the real problem. A mediator will not solve your problems, but will instead help you face them and put them behind you as you work out the details of ending your marriage. He or she is like a guide who leads you through the maze of your feelings. Make sure you find a guide you trust not to get you lost.

GETTING YOUR SPOUSE TO GO TO MEDIATION

Often one spouse wants to go to mediation and the other is resistant. Don't be surprised if your spouse rejects the idea of mediation at first. Some people mistakenly think it is a kind of therapy or other mental health situation. Get some brochures from a mediator and give them to your spouse. Suggest that he or she read about mediation on the Internet. Explain that mediation will be less expensive than if you let lawyers handle the divorce. Tell your spouse you are not out to cheat him or her and that you do not think divorce should be about one person winning and the other losing. Explain that mediation is the best way to resolve custody and visitation. Mediation allows the parents to decide how they will share time with their children. Talk about how a judge will not know your children, nor make decisions based on their personalities and needs.

Ask your spouse to just attend a free consultation with the mediator if nothing else. Most people are convinced after meeting with a mediator.

What to Expect in Mediation

Many people mistakenly think that mediation will be quick and easy. This is usually not the case. Each mediator handles cases differently, but in general you can expect to spend a lot of time in the beginning filling out forms and providing information. Next your mediator will spend some time discussing the law with you, to make sure you both understand what your options are. At this point, some mediators suggest that each person talk with an attorney to find out what the attorney thinks would happen in court. This lets you know what your alternatives are and can often be an incentive to continue in mediation.

The mediator will guide you through one issue at a time. You and your spouse will be encouraged to talk openly and honestly about your opinions and feelings, however, all mediators make sure that such discussions do not turn into shouting matches and always are careful that the people do not intimidate or frighten each other. There may be issues that you cannot resolve right away. The mediator will move on to other topics and come back to the difficult decisions later. Don't give up just because something cannot be solved the first time. Some things take time to resolve.

The mediator does not make any decisions for you. He or she instead tries to help you and your spouse reach decisions together. This involves communication and compromise. Mediators not only work out the details of the divorce, but also help parents develop a new relationship together as parenting partners. It is important that parents be able to communicate and make decisions together after a divorce, without allowing bitterness or anger to infect the children. Mediators make sure that parents have a good groundwork for future decision-making before they leave mediation.

It is important to note that mediation is a completely voluntary process and that either spouse is free to leave at any time. It is also important to understand that there are couples that are not appropriate for mediation. These include marriages in which there is domestic violence, substance abuse or mental illness.

There are alternative methods of mediation available for difficult situations. Some mediators work in teams and will co-mediate with a couple who cannot bear to sit in the same room together. Other mediators will incorporate therapy into the process to help people cope with difficult problems.

Once you have worked through all of the issues involved in your divorce and have made decisions about maintenance, custody, child support, asset and debt division, your mediator will draw up an agreement. Some mediators draw up a non-binding agreement, which is then sent to one of the spouse's attorneys to be legalized, while others will draw up a binding separation agreement. Be sure you completely understand everything before you sign anything.

WORKING WITH A MEDIATOR

You can choose to go to a mediator at any point in your divorce proceedings. Some couples start in court and then realize that the situation is uncomfortable and potentially very expensive.

When you go to mediation you should not expect the mediator to solve your problems for you. A mediator is in the room to help you and your spouse communicate. While it is sometimes easier to talk to the mediator, you should remember that you are there to communicate with your spouse.

You should never lie to your mediator. You only harm yourself if you distort the facts in mediation. If your spouse finds out about your lie, it is likely that the mediation will be over and you will be back in court with your fate in the hands of a judge.

Remember that the mediator, even if he or she is an attorney, is not your attorney and cannot give you specific legal advice. Mediators give legal information, but are not supposed to evaluate your situation and give advice. If you want some advice about your situation, see an attorney on your own.

Many people come to mediation with a bottom line in mind. They talk to a lawyer, find out what likely result they can get in court and then go to mediation knowing they will not settle for less than that. This can be helpful, but it can also stop you from making compromises that will benefit you. Remember to look at the big picture.

Some mediators will allow or encourage your teenage children to participate in the portion of the mediation that deals with custody. It is important to consider the wishes of your children and this is a way that allows you to give them a voice in the decision.

PAYING FOR MEDIATION

When you come to the first session, the mediator will ask how you will share the expense of the mediation. Some couples share the cost, while others agree that one spouse will pay for it. Be sure to discuss this with your spouse before you go. If you cannot agree, the mediator can help you reach an agreement.

Mediation is almost always less expensive than a contested divorce with two attorneys. However, if you and your spouse are in agreement about everything, there may be no need to go to a mediator. Instead you can file for an uncontested divorce without paying for a mediator or attorney.

EVALUATING YOUR SITUATION 5

The following things should be done or considered before you begin the divorce process.

RELATIONS WITH YOUR SPOUSE

First, you should evaluate your situation with respect to your spouse. Have you both agreed to get a divorce? If not, what kind of reaction do you expect from him or her? Your expected reaction can determine how you proceed. If your spouse reacts in a rational manner, you can probably use the uncontested procedure. But if you expect an extremely emotional, even violent, reaction, you will need to take steps to protect yourself, your children, and your property; and can expect to use the contested procedure. (Also, be sure to read the section on "Protecting Yourself, Your Children, and Your Property" in Chapter 13).

You were warned on the back cover of this book not to let your spouse find this book, and it was for a very good reason. Unless you and your spouse have already decided together to get a divorce, you don't want your spouse to know you are thinking about filing for divorce. This is a defense tactic, although it may not seem that way at first. If your spouse thinks you are planning a divorce, he or she may do things to prevent you from getting a fair result. These things include withdrawing money from bank accounts, hiding information about income, and hiding assets. So do not let on until you have collected all of the information you will need and are about to file with the court, or until you are prepared to protect yourself from violence, if necessary.

> **Caution:** Tactics such as withdrawing money from bank accounts and hiding assets are potentially dangerous. If you try any of these things you risk looking like the "bad guy" before the judge. This can result in anything from having disputed matters resolved in your spouse's favor, to being ordered to produce the assets (or be jailed for contempt of court).

Theoretically, the "system" would prefer you to keep evidence of the assets (such as photographs, sales receipts, or bank statements), to present to the judge if your spouse hides them. Then your spouse will be the bad guy and risk being jailed. However, once your spouse has taken assets, and hidden them, or sold them and spent the money, even a contempt order may not get the money or assets back. If you determine that you need to get the assets in order to keep your spouse from hiding or disposing of them, be sure you keep them in a safe place, and disclose them on your Statement of Net Worth. (see form 10, p.195.) Do not dispose of them. If your spouse claims you took them, you can explain to the judge why you were afraid that your spouse would dispose of them and that you merely got them out of his or her reach.

FINANCIAL INFORMATION

It is extremely important that you collect all of the financial information you can get. This information should include originals or copies of the following:

❑ Your most recent income tax return (and your spouse's if you filed separately).

❑ The most recent W-2 tax forms for yourself and your spouse.

❏ Any other income reporting papers (such as interest, stock dividends, etc.).

❏ Your spouse's most recent paystub, hopefully showing year-to-date earnings (otherwise try to get copies of all paystubs since the beginning of the year).

❏ Deeds to all real estate; and titles to cars, boats, or other vehicles.

❏ Your and your spouse's will.

❏ Life insurance policies.

❏ Stocks, bonds or other investment papers.

❏ Pension or retirement fund papers and statements.

❏ Health insurance card and papers.

❏ Bank account or credit union statements.

❏ Your spouse's social security number, driver's license number, date and place of birth and your date and place of marriage.

❏ Names, addresses and phone numbers of your spouse's employer, close friends and family members.

❏ Credit card statements, mortgage documents, and other credit and debt papers.

❏ A list of vehicles, furniture, appliances, tools, etc., owned by you and your spouse. (See the next section in this chapter on "Property and Debts" for forms and a detailed discussion of what to include).

❏ Copies of bills or receipts for recurring, regular expenses, such as electric, gas or other utilities, car insurance, etc.

❏ Copies of bills, receipts, insurance forms, or medical records for any unusual medical expenses (including for recurring or continuous medical conditions) for yourself, your spouse or your children.

❏ Receipts or a list of child care, educational, and extra-curricular expenses for your children.

❏ Any other papers showing what you and your spouse earn, own, or owe.

Make copies of as many of these papers as possible, and keep them in a safe and private place (where your spouse will not find them). Try to make copies of new papers as they come in, especially as you get close to filing court papers, and as you get close to a court hearing.

WHICH GROUNDS TO USE

You will need to decide which grounds for divorce to use. First, review the grounds for divorce described in Chapter 1, then read the following.

IMPRISONMENT

If your spouse was imprisoned for three or more years during your marriage, you may use imprisonment as your grounds. Your spouse must have been in prison during the last five years in order for you to use this as grounds. For example, if your spouse was in prison for four years, but that was ten years ago, you are not eligible.

ABANDONMENT

In order to use the grounds of abandonment, your spouse must have abandoned you more than one year ago; the abandonment must have been without provocation; and you must have asked your spouse to return and he or she would not. If all of these conditions are met, abandonment would be an appropriate grounds to use.

ADULTERY

Even if your spouse did commit adultery, you probably should not use adultery as your grounds for divorce, because adultery is difficult to prove. It does not matter if you saw it first-hand, or if your spouse admits it. This is not enough evidence. Generally, if your spouse committed adultery, you can use cruel and inhuman treatment as your grounds for divorce, with the adultery as an example of the cruel and inhuman treatment.

CRUEL AND INHUMAN TREATMENT

If you know your divorce is going to be uncontested, or if you and your spouse have few assets and no children, cruel and inhuman treatment is probably the simplest grounds to use. Simply use the language described in Chapter 1. (Only if it's true, of course). It is important that the conduct you describe occurred within the last five years.

SEPARATION
AGREEMENT

A Separation Agreement may be your best choice if you and your spouse have assets and debts, or have children and child support is likely, because the two of you can work out these decisions and then spell them out clearly and fully in a Separation Agreement. You can then wait one year after signing and filing the Separation Agreement and seek a divorce based upon the separation. Everything in the Separation Agreement becomes your Judgment of Divorce. You may also wish to work out a Separation Agreement and then, instead of waiting one year, go ahead and seek a divorce immediately using other grounds. Again, all the terms of the Separation Agreement will become the terms of your Judgment of Divorce. The only difference is that you must prove the other grounds you use, and you will be divorced sooner.

JUDGMENT OF
LEGAL
SEPARATION

There is no point in seeking a Judgment of Legal Separation. It requires one of the same grounds as divorce, so you may as well just use that grounds to file for divorce.

PROPERTY AND DEBTS

PROPERTY

This section is designed to help you get a rough idea of where things stand regarding the division of your property, and to prepare you for completing the court papers you will need to file. The following sections will deal with the questions of your debts, and child support, custody and visitation. If you are still not sure whether you want a divorce, these sections may help you to decide. You always want to use current information.

This section basically assists you in completing the Property Inventory. (see form 1, p.180.) This form is a list of all of your property, and key information about that property. First, you need to understand how property is divided. Trying to determine how to divide assets and debts can be difficult. Under New York's equitable distribution law, *equitable distribution* means the assets and debts of the marriage are divided in a way that is fair, but not necessarily equal. Assets and debts are separated into two categories: *marital property* (meaning it is both yours and your spouse's), and *separate property* (meaning it is yours or your spouse's alone). In making this distinction the following rules apply:

1. If the asset or debt was acquired after the date you were married, it is presumed to be a marital asset or debt. It is up to you or your spouse to prove otherwise.

2. A separate asset or debt is one that was acquired before the date of your marriage. It is also a separate asset if you acquired it during the marriage through a gift or inheritance (as long as it wasn't a gift from your spouse), or property that you acquired as compensation for personal injuries; for example, a settlement you received in a worker's compensation case or a settlement you received for injuries from a car accident. Income from separate property is also separate property; for example, rent you receive during the marriage from an investment property you had before you got married. If you exchange one of these separate assets or debts after you are married, the replacement asset or debt is still separate. For example: You had a $6,000 car before you got married. After the marriage, you traded it for a different $6,000 car. The new car is still separate property. Finally, you and your spouse may sign a written agreement that certain assets and debts are to be considered separate or marital.

3. Marital assets and debts are those acquired during your marriage, even if they were acquired by you or your spouse individually. This includes the increase in value of a separate asset during the marriage, but only if the increase in value occurred because of something the non-owner spouse did (for example if your spouse remodeled an apartment building you own and this caused it to increase in value), or due to the use of marital funds to pay for or improve the property. All rights accrued during the marriage in pension, retirement, profit-sharing, insurance, and similar plans are marital assets. It is also possible for one spouse to make a gift of separate property to the other spouse, thereby making it marital property.

4. Real estate that is in both names is considered marital property, and it's up to the spouse claiming otherwise to prove it.

5. Finally, whether an asset or debt is marital or separate, and the value of any asset, is determined as of the date of the Separation Agreement, or the date the Summons was filed, whichever is first.

PROPERTY
INVENTORY
(form 1)

The Property Inventory (form 1), Debt Inventory (form 2) and the instructions that follow, call for a rather specific, detailed listing of property and debt items. Some of these will be grouped together and listed as a single amount in the Statement of Net Worth. (see form 10, p.195.) However, it is still a good idea to have a more detailed list, such as that provided by using form 1 and form 2. You will notice that form 1 is divided into nine columns. (see form 1, p.180.) These columns are designated as follows:

Column (1): "S." You will check the box in this column if that piece of property is "separate" property, as described above.

Column (2): "Description." In this column you will describe the property. A discussion regarding what information should go in this column will follow.

Column (3): "ID#." This column is used to write in the serial number, account number, or other number that will help clearly identify that piece of property.

Column (4): "Value." This is for the current market value of the property.

Column (5): "Balance Owed." This will show how much money is owed on the property, if any.

Column (6): "Equity." Subtract the "Balance Owed" from the "Value." This will show how much the property is worth to you (your *equity*).

Column (7): "Owner H-W-J." This column will show the current legal owner of the property. "H" designates the husband, "W" the wife, and "J" is for jointly owned property (in both of your names).

Column (8): "H." This column will be checked for those pieces of property you expect the husband will keep.

Column (9): "W." This column is for the property you expect the wife will keep.

Use columns (1) through (7) to list your property, including the following:

Cash. List the name of the bank, credit union, etc., and the account number, for each account. This includes savings and checking accounts, and certificates of deposit (CDs). The balance of each account should be listed in the columns entitled VALUE and EQUITY. (Leave the "Balance Owed" column blank.) Make copies of the most recent bank statements for each account.

Stocks and bonds. All stocks, bonds or other *paper investments* should be listed. Write down the number of shares and the name of the company or other organization which issued them. Also copy any notation such as *common* or *preferred* stock or shares. This information can be obtained from the stock certificate itself, or from a statement from the stock broker. Make a copy of the certificate or the statement.

Real estate. List each piece of property you and your spouse own. The description might include a street address for the property, a subdivision name and lot number, or anything that lets you know what piece of property you are referring to. There probably will not be an ID number, although you might use the county's tax number. Real estate (or any other property) may be in both of your names (joint), in your spouse's name alone, or in your name alone. The only way to know for sure is to look at the deed to the property. (If you cannot find a copy of the deed, try to find mortgage papers or payment coupons, homeowners insurance papers, or a property tax assessment notice). The owners of property are usually referred to on the deed as the *grantees*. In assigning a value to the property, consider the market value, which is how much you could probably sell the property for. This might be what similar houses in your neighborhood have sold for recently. You might also consider how much you paid for the property, or how much the property is insured for. ***Do not*** use the tax assessment value, as this is usually considerably lower than the market value.

Vehicles. This category includes cars, trucks, motor homes, recreational vehicles (RVs), motorcycles, boats, trailers, airplanes, and any other means of transportation for which the State requires a title and registration. Your description should include the following information (which can usually be found on the title or on the vehicle itself):

☛ The year it was made.

☛ The make, which is the name of the manufacturer, such as "Ford," "Honda," "Chris Craft," etc.

☛ The model of the vehicle, for example, Mustang, LTD, or Aerostar. The model may be a name, a number, a series of letters, or a combination of these.

☛ The serial number is most likely found on the vehicle, as well as on the title or registration.

Make a copy of the title or registration. Regarding a value, you can go to the public library and ask to look at the *blue book* for cars, trucks or whatever it is you're looking for. A blue book (which may actually be yellow, black, or any other color) gives the average values for used vehicles. Your librarian can help you find what you need. Another source is the classified advertising section of a newspaper to see the current selling price of similar vehicles. You might also try calling a dealer to see if he can give you a rough idea of the value. Be sure you take into consideration the condition of the vehicle.

Furniture. List all furniture as specifically as possible. You should include the type of piece (such as sofa, coffee table, etc.), the color, and if you know it, the manufacturer, line name or the style. Furniture will not usually have a serial number, although if you find one be sure to write it on the list. Just estimate a value, unless you just know what it's worth.

Appliances, electronic equipment, yard machines, etc. This category includes such things as refrigerators, lawn mowers and power tools. Again, estimate a value, unless you are familiar enough with them to simply "know" what they are worth. There are too many different makes, models, accessories and age factors to be able to figure out a value otherwise. These items will probably have a make, model and serial number on them. You may have to look on the back, bottom or other hidden place for the serial number, but try to find it.

Jewelry and other valuables. You don't need to list inexpensive "costume" jewelry. And you can plan on keeping your own personal watches, rings, etc. However, if you own an expensive piece you should include it in your list, along with an estimated value. Be sure to include silverware, original art, gold, coin collections, etc. Again, be as detailed and specific as possible.

Life insurance with cash surrender value. This is any life insurance policy that you may cash in or borrow against, and therefore has value. If you can not find a cash surrender value in the papers you have, you can call the insurance company and ask.

Other "big ticket" items. This is simply a general reference to anything of significant value that does not fit in one of the categories already discussed. Examples might be a portable spa, an above-ground swimming pool, golf clubs, guns, pool tables, camping or fishing equipment, or farm animals or machinery.

Pensions and military benefits. The division of pensions, and military and retirement benefits, can be a complicated matter. Whenever these types of benefits are involved and you cannot agree on how to divide them, you will need to consult an attorney or a CPA to determine the value of the benefits and how they should be divided. Be sure to read the section in Chapter 13 on "Pension Plans." To divide these plans, complicated and highly technical paperwork must be completed and submitted to the court and the employer involved. You will need an attorney who is experienced in this area to handle the paperwork.

What not to list. You will not need to list your clothing and other personal effects. Pots and pans, dishes and cooking utensils ordinarily do not need to be listed, unless they have some unusually high value.

Once you have completed your list, go back through it and try to determine who should end up with each item. The ideal situation is for both you and your spouse to go through the list together, and divide things up fairly. However, if this is not possible, you will need to offer a reasonable settlement to the judge. Consider each item, and make a checkmark in either column (8) or (9) to designate whether that item should go to the husband or wife. You may make the following assumptions:

☛ Your separate property will go to you.

☛ Your spouse's separate property will go to your spouse.

☛ You should get the items that only you use.

☛ Your spouse should get the items only used by your spouse.

☛ The remaining items should be divided, evening out the total value of all the marital property, and taking into consideration who would really want that item.

To somewhat equally divide your property (we're only talking about marital property here), you first need to know what the total value of your property is. First of all, do not count the value of the separate items. Add the remaining amounts in the "Equity" column of form 1, which will give you an approximate value of all marital property.

When it comes time for the hearing, you and your spouse may be arguing over some or all of the items on your list. This is when you'll be glad that you made copies of the documents relating to the property on your list. Arguments over the value of property may need to be resolved by hiring appraisers to set a value; however, you'll have to pay the appraiser a fee. Dividing your property will be discussed further in later chapters. (See Chapter 10 for information on dividing property in contested cases.)

DEBTS   This section relates to the Debt Inventory, which will list your debts. (see form 2, p.181.) Although there are cases where, for example, the wife gets a car but the husband is ordered to make the payments, generally whoever gets the property also gets the debt owed on that property. This seems to be a fair arrangement in most cases.

DEBT
INVENTORY
(form 2)

On form 2 you will list each debt owed by you or your spouse. As with separate property, there is also separate debt. This is any debt incurred before you were married, that is yours alone. Form 2 contains a column for "S" debts, which should be checked for each separate debt. You will be responsible for your separate debts, and your spouse will be responsible for his or hers.

> **Warning:** If you and your spouse are jointly responsible for a debt, you are not relieved of your obligation to pay just because your spouse agrees to pay (or is ordered to pay) the debt in the divorce proceeding. If your spouse doesn't pay, the creditor can still come after you for payment. You would then need to take your spouse to court to get him or her to reimburse you.

To complete the Debt Inventory (see form 2, p.181), list each debt as follows:

Column (1):   "S." Check if this is a separate debt, as described above.

Column (2):   "Creditor." Write in the name and address of the creditor (the bank, company or person the debt is owed to).

Column (3):   "Account No." Write in the account, loan or mortgage number.

Column (4) :   "Notes." Write in any notes to help identify what the loan was for (such as "Christmas gifts," "Vacation," etc.).

Column (5):   "Monthly Payment." Write in the amount of the monthly payment.

Column (6) :   "Balance Owed." Write in the balance still owed on the loan.

Column (7):   "Date." Write in the date (approximately) when the loan was made.

Column (8):   "Owner H-W-J." Note whether the account is in the husband's name "H", the wife's name "W", or jointly in both names "J".

Columns (9) & (10): "H" and "W." These columns note who will be responsible for the debt after the divorce. As with your property, each of you will keep your separate debts, and the remainder should be divided taking into consideration who will keep the property the loan was for and equally dividing the debt. (See Chapter 10 for information on dividing debts in contested cases.)

CHILD SUPPORT

Once again, the judge will probably go along with any agreement you and your spouse reach, as long as he or she is satisfied that the child will be adequately cared for. In New York, when a court decides child support, the Child Support Standards Act is used to determine the amount based upon the combined income of you and your spouse and the number of children you have. However, you and your spouse are able to "opt out" of the Act (that is, not use the Act to determine the amount of your child support) by reaching an agreement about child support on your own. If you do so, you must give the court a good reason for doing so and the amount you agree on must be reasonable.

The amount of child support cannot be less than $300 per year or $25 per month (this is not per child; it applies no matter how many children you have). If you choose to "opt-out," you must consider the factors listed under "Step 11, (c) Additional Factors," beginning on the fourth page of the Child Support Worksheet, and you must state to the court that you have considered them. (see form 13, p.223.) If you already have a Family Court order for child support, this order will be incorporated into your divorce and you do not need to complete a child support worksheet.

The following information and the Child Support Worksheet will help you get an idea of the proper amount of child support. Because you need to file a child support worksheet with the court, use the one in this book. (see form 13, p.223.) Here you are only trying to get a rough idea of the amount of child support to expect. Later, after you have more accurate income information, you will complete the final copy to file with the court clerk. As you prepare your form to file, you will refer back to this section for instructions on completing the form. The information on form 13 will also help you to fill out part of the Statement of Net Worth. (see form 10, p.195.) Where an agreement on child support cannot be reached, the following procedure will be used:

HOW CHILD
SUPPORT IS
DETERMINED

Generally there are two factors used to determine the proper amount of support to be paid: (1) the needs of the child, and (2) the financial ability of each parent to meet those needs. New York has simplified this procedure by clearly establishing a formula to be used in calculating both the needs of the child and each parent's ability to meet those needs. In filling out the Child Support Worksheet (form 13), be sure to convert everything to yearly amounts. The following steps are used in determining the proper amount of support:

1. You and your spouse each provide proof of your *gross* income.

2. Taxes, Social Security, and other deductions are allowed to determine each of your *net* incomes.

3. Your net incomes are added together to arrive at your *combined income*.

4. The combined income and the number of children you have are used to establish the children's needs.

5. The net income of the parent without custody is divided by the combined income. This gives that parent's percentage of the combined income.

6. That percentage is multiplied by the needs of the children, to arrive at the amount of support to be paid by the parent without custody.

CHILD SUPPORT
WORKSHEET
(form 12)

The Child Support Standards Act will be discussed more below, and it can be found in Appendix A (see Domestic Relations Law, Section 240). Now we will begin to fill out the Child Support Worksheet. (see form 13, p.223.) All of the amounts on the worksheet are *yearly* amounts. To complete the Child Support Worksheet:

1. Complete the top portion of the form according to the instructions at the beginning of Chapter 6.

2. By filling in the information in the section marked "Step 1 Mandatory Parental Income," you will determine the gross incomes for you and your spouse. This is the income reported on your latest federal income tax return. If you do not know your spouse's income, make a reasonable guess. You can change it later if you learn his or her income. If your divorce is contested, this information will be disclosed to you when your spouse completes and files his or her Statement of Net Worth. (see form 10, p.195.) Fill in the incomes for each of you in the columns marked "Father" and "Mother." If either you or your spouse receive any of the types of income referred to in items 2 through 14, and it is not included in the amount you filled in for item 1, fill in the amount on the appropriate line. For the Child Support Worksheet form you file with the clerk, you must explain on the lines at the bottom of the first page how you came up with your spouse's income. An example would be "from paystubs and tax returns." Total the columns and fill in the totals on the lines marked "A. Total Mandatory Income" at the bottom of the page.

3. Under the heading marked "Step 2 Non-Mandatory Parental Income," fill in other sources of income, such as meals paid for by employers, company cars, money from relatives, and anything else you or your spouse receive that provides an economic benefit (that is, something you would have to pay for if you had not been given it). This does not include things like holiday and birthday gifts. Total each column and fill in the totals on the lines marked "B. Total Non-Mandatory Income."

4. For each of you, add the totals from "A. Total Mandatory Income" and "B. Total Non-Mandatory Income," and fill in the answers on the lines marked "C. Total Income." These are the total separate gross incomes for you and your spouse.

5. Under the section marked "Step 3 Deductions," you will find items 19 through 27, which are deductions that must be subtracted from the total gross incomes. Item 20 refers to business expenses that are for businesses only and have no personal benefit. For example, a file cabinet for your office is for business only and gives you no benefit in your personal life, but a company VCR you use at home for personal use and take to work occasionally to show a company video gives you a benefit in your personal life and may not be deducted. Item 22 can be filled in only if have already made an agreement about maintenance and the agreement states that when maintenance ends, the amount of child support will increase. Total the deductions for each of you, and fill in the totals on the lines marked "D. Total Deductions."

6. For each parent, subtract the total from line "D. Total Deductions" from the total from line "C. Total Income." Fill in the answer for the father on line "E. Father's Income," and the answer for the mother on line "F. Mother's Income." These are the total separate net incomes for you and your spouse.

7. Add your net income to your spouse's net income (from lines E and F). This will give your combined income, which will be filled in under "Step 4" on the line marked "G. Combined Parental Income." For example: The mother's net income is $17,000 per year. The father's net income is $20,000 per year. The combined income is $37,000 ($17,000 + $20,000).

8. Under the section marked "Step 5," child support calculations are based on the number of children of the marriage as follows:

No. of Children	Percentage	Multiply by:
1 child:	17%	.17
2 children:	25%	.25
3 children	29%	.29
4 children	31%	.31
5 children or more	minimum of 35%	.35

Calculate child support by multiplying your total on line "G. Combined Parental Income," by the percentage from above that applies to you (if your total on line G is over $80,000, use only $80,000 when you calculate the child support). Fill in your answer on the line marked "H. Combined Child Support." This number is the amount of money you and your spouse are theoretically supposed to spend to support you children. Using our example, if the parties have a combined income of $37,000 and have two children, they would multiply $37,000 by .25, and the total combined child support is $9,250.

9. Next, we are going to separate out the amount of child support for the non-custodial parent (the parent with whom the children do not live). Go back to line E or F (E if the father is the non-custodial parent; or F if the mother is the non-custodial parent) and get the total income of the non-custodial parent and place it on the first blank space in item I, under the section marked "Step 6." Next, take the number from line G and place it in the second blank space in item I. Divide the number from E or F by the number from G, then fill in the answer on the third and last blank line under item I (the line with the % symbol after it). Using our example, the father will be the non-custodial parent. The father's income from line E ($20,000) would be divided by the combined income from line G ($37,000), which would give an answer of .54, or 54% (this means that the father's income represents fifty-four percent of the parties' total income).

10. Take the percentage from the last line in item I under "Step 6" and multiply it by the combined child support from line H. Fill in the answer on line J, under the section marked "Step 7." This is the amount of child support to be paid by the non-custodial parent, excluding other expenses that are to be shared. Using our example, the percentage of 54% from line I would be multiplied by the combined child support from line H, to arrive at a child support amount for the father to pay of $4,995 (.54 x $9,259).

11. "Step 8" will apply to you only if the combined parental income from line G is over $80,000. There will be additional child support payable if the total combined income is over $80,000. To calculate this, you can use either of two methods. The first method is to redo steps 5 through 7, using the actual combined parental income number in your calculations, and take the number you get on line J and insert it on line L (skipping line K entirely). The other method is for you and your spouse to agree on the amount of child support that is to come out of the income over $80,000, and insert it on line K. Add K and J, and place this total on line L. To arrive at child support for the income over $80,000, you must consider the factors listed under "Step 11, (c) Additional Factors."

12. "Step 9" deals with additional expenses that parents are to share. For each line, M through Q, determine the total amount of that expense and then multiply it by the percentage on the last line in item I to determine how much the non-custodial parent is to pay. For line Q, courts do not always strictly use the percentages to determine how much a non-custodial parent should contribute for educational expenses. Read the explanation in "Step 11, (b) Educational Expenses," and write in any relevant information to assist the court in deciding how much the non-custodial parent should contribute. Add together lines L, N, P, and Q. This will give you the total amount of child support that must be paid by the non-custodial parent each year.

13. "Step 10. Low Income Exceptions." The legislature has made sure that low income people are protected from having to pay more child support than they are able. At Step 10, place the non-custodial parent's income from E or F on line R. At line S, put the total from lines L, N, P, and Q. Calculate R minus S, and enter the answer on line T, at the top of the fourth page of Form 12. Now you need to determine what the official Federal poverty level is for this year. Look in your phone book under the United States Government listings. Call the U.S. Department of Heath and Human Services, and ask them for this year's Federal poverty level for a single-person household. You may also call the court clerk's office and ask them. You can also go to your local public library and ask the librarian to assist you in locating this information. Now multiply this figure by 135% (1.35). The answer is what is known as the *self-support reserve*. Write this amount on line V. If line T is less than the self-support reserve, then the low income exception applies to your case. If not, continue on to Step 11. If the low income exception applies, then write the non-custodial parent's income (from line E or F) on line U. On line W, write in the answer to U minus V. If W equals $300 or less, the child support owed is $300 per year. If W is greater than $300, then line W is the amount of child support owed. If T is greater than the number you received for the Federal poverty level, but is less than the number on line V, you need to complete lines X, Y, and Z. Line X is the same number you have been using from E or F. Line Y is the same number as V. Subtract Y from X, and write the answer on line Z. If line Z is at $600 or more, then Z is the amount of support owed annually. If Z is less than $600, then child support is $600 per year. Despite all of this, the non-custodial parent may argue to the court that child support should be less than the number determined on this form, and the judge may, in unusual circumstances, set the amount lower.

14. You will sign your name in front of a notary.

CHILD SUPPORT
PAYMENT
PERIODS

Form 13 gives you the amount of child support due yearly, but payments can be paid weekly, bi-weekly, monthly, or any other way you and your spouse agree. If the court determines child support, it will usually be ordered to be paid weekly or monthly. Be aware that child support is not absolutely fixed with your divorce judgment, but can be raised or lowered at a future date by the court, or by your agreement, as incomes and circumstances change. You should review you situation annually. If you need to request a change, you can go to Family Court where the clerks will assist you in filling out the necessary paperwork.

SUPPORT
COLLECTION
UNIT

If you do not trust your spouse to pay the child support regularly, wish to have minimal contact with your spouse, or want a third party to keep records of payments, you can request that child support be paid to the Support Collection Unit (SCU), which is a state agency. Payments are made to SCU, and then forwarded to the custodial parent. A word of caution: SCU has the power to review and adjust child support payments without court intervention. To contest a change, you must go to Family Court. Many people believe it is simpler to handle the exchange of child support without a state agency intervening.

MAINTENANCE (ALIMONY)

Maintenance, which is New York's term for alimony, may be granted to either the husband or the wife. There are two types of maintenance:

TYPES OF
MAINTENANCE

- *Durational.* This is for a limited period of time, and is to enable one of the spouses to get the education or training necessary to find a job or to increase his or her income, to pay debts or expenses or as a sort of division of property. This is often awarded where one of the parties has not been working during the marriage. This is the most common type of maintenance.

- *Permanent.* This continues until the death of one of the parties. This is typically awarded where one of the parties is unable to work due to age, or a physical or mental illness.

MAINTENANCE
FACTORS

If you and your spouse cannot reach an agreement on maintenance (either as to whether it will be paid at all or as to the amount), and the judge must decide the issue, the law requires the judge to consider the following factors:

1. The income and property of the respective parties, including marital property that is divided among the parties.

2. The length of the marriage and age and health of the parties.

3. The present and future earning abilities of both parties.

4. The ability of the person seeking maintenance to become self-supporting and if he or she is not self-supporting, how long it would take to receive the training necessary to be able to be self-supporting.

5. The reduced or lost ability to earn money of the person seeking maintenance because he or she did not pursue or complete education, training or employment during the marriage (usually due to staying home with the children).

6. Whether there are children, and with which parent they reside.

7. The tax consequences of the divorce on each party.

8. Contributions made by the person seeking maintenance as spouse, parent, homemaker and wage earner to the career or career potential of the other party.

9. Wasteful dissipation of marital property by either party (destroying or using up property).

10. Marital assets that have been sold, given away or used as collateral for debts by either party as part of a strategy or plan involving the divorce.

11. Any other factor the court finds to be just and proper.

As a general rule of thumb, you can expect maintenance, if awarded, to last for one-third of the time the marriage lasted, unless there are special circumstances.

As an alternative to maintenance, you may want to try to negotiate to receive a greater percentage of the property instead. This may be less of a hassle in the long run, but it may change the tax consequences of your divorce. (See the section on "Taxes" in Chapter 13.)

WHICH PROCEDURE TO USE

In New York, there are two divorce procedures: (1) uncontested divorce procedure, and (2) contested divorce procedure.

The uncontested and contested procedures use the same basic forms, but the contested procedure will require some additional steps and forms, so it is treated as a separate procedure. Chapter 9 describes the uncontested procedure, and Chapter 10 describes the contested divorce. You should read this entire book once before you begin filling out any court forms.

> **Be sure to review the residency requirements described in Chapter 2 of this book. If you do not fall into one of those categories, you are not eligible for a divorce in New York.**

UNCONTESTED
DIVORCE
PROCEDURE

The uncontested procedure is mainly designed for those who are in agreement (or can reach an agreement). This is also referred to as a *consent* divorce. The uncontested procedure may also be used when your spouse does not respond to your summons, or cannot be located. In other words, the uncontested procedure can be used whenever your spouse will not be fighting you. Chapter 9 will provide more details about the uncontested procedure.

CONTESTED
DIVORCE
PROCEDURE

The contested divorce procedure will be necessary where you and your spouse are arguing over some matter and can't resolve it. This may be the result of disagreement over custody of the children, the payment of child support or maintenance, the division of your property, or any combination of these items. The section of this book dealing with the contested procedure builds on the uncontested procedure section. So, first you will need to read Chapter 9 to get a basic understanding of the forms and procedures, then read Chapter 10 for additional instructions on handling the contested situation. Be sure to read through both chapters before you start filling out any forms. If your case becomes contested, it is also time to seriously consider getting a lawyer. If you do not think you can afford a lawyer, you may be able to require your spouse to pay for your lawyer. Find a lawyer who will give you a free initial consultation. He or she will explain your options regarding the lawyer's fees. See Chapter 3 for more information about lawyers. Chapter 9 and Chapter 10 will provide more information about the contested procedure.

GENERAL PROCEDURES 6

AN INTRODUCTION TO LEGAL FORMS

Most of the forms in this book follow forms recently created by the New York State Unified Court System. Some of these "official" forms were poorly drafted, but they do have one advantage: court clerks and judges are not likely to object to them. The forms in this book are legally correct, however, one occasionally encounters a troublesome clerk or judge who is very particular about how he or she wants the forms. If you encounter any problem with the forms in this book being accepted by the clerk or judge, you can try one or more of the following:

- ☛ Ask the clerk or judge what is wrong with your form, then try to change it to suit the clerk or judge.

- ☛ Ask the clerk or judge if there is a form available in the clerk's office. Then get it and use it. The instructions in this book will still help you to fill it out.

- ☛ Consult a lawyer.

It is best to make photocopies of the forms, and keep the originals blank to use in case you make mistakes, or need additional copies.

Although the instructions in this book tell you to "type in" information, it is not absolutely necessary to use a typewriter. If typing is not possible, print the information required in the forms. Just be sure your handwriting can be easily read or the clerk may not accept your papers.

Each form is referred to by both the title of the form and a form number. Be sure to check the form number because some of the forms have similar titles. The form number is found in the top outside corner of the first page of each form. Also, a list of the forms, by both number and name, is found at the beginning of Appendix B.

You will notice that most of the forms in Appendix B have the same heading. Forms without this heading are not filed with the court. The top portion of these court forms will all be completed in the same manner. The very top of the form tells which court your case is filed in. You will need to type in the county in which the court is located.

Next, you need to type your full name on the line marked "Plaintiff," and your spouse's full name on the line marked "Defendant." Do not use nicknames or shortened versions of names. You should use the names as they appear on your marriage license, if possible. You will not be able to fill in the "index number" designation until after you file your initial papers with the court clerk. The clerk will assign an index number, and will write it on your summons and any other papers you file with it. You must type in the index number on all papers you file later. When completed, the top portion of your forms should look something like the following example:

SUPREME COURT OF THE STATE OF NEW YORK
COUNTY OF _____**Cayuga**_____
-- X

____Jane Doe_____,
                              Plaintiff,
-vs-
                                                          Index No.: __SF 1999/607338__
____John Doe_____,
                              Defendant.
-- X

At the end of most of the forms there will be a place for you to sign your name, and to type in your name, address, and phone number. Your signature must be notarized on certain forms. There should be a notary at your local bank, and there is often no fee if you are an account holder. Do not sign forms that need to be notarized until you are in front of the notary. The notary must see you sign it.

FILING WITH THE COURT CLERK

You will need to file documents with the court clerk several times during the divorce procedure. First, make at least three copies of the form (the original for the clerk, one copy for yourself, one for your spouse or your spouse's attorney, and one for the clerk to stamp "filed" and return to you so you have proof you filed it). You may also want to make an extra copy just in case the clerk asks for an extra or if you later decide to hire an attorney. Never submit any form to the clerk or to the judge without keeping a copy of it. Things get lost!

Filing is actually about as simple as making a bank deposit, although the following information will help things go smoothly. Before filing each document or set of documents, fill them out completely by following the instructions contained in this book. Next, check the section of this book dealing with your form to determine if there is a fee for filing it.

Fees for Divorce Cases	
Index Number	$170
Personal Service (may be more if service is difficult or is out of state)	$ 30
Request for Judicial Intervention	$ 75
Note of Issue	$ 25
Uncontested transcript	$ 30 to $ 60
Certificate of Dissolution	$ 5
Certified copies	$ 4 to $ 8

(Fees are subject to change, so check with your clerk to make sure you pay the correct amount.)

This adds up to a total cost for a divorce of between $339 and $373. If there is a fee for the documents you are filing, bring cash, check, or money order with you (your clerk's office may not accept personal checks; call ahead to make sure). If you do not know where the court clerk's office is located, look in your phone book under county government listings. You may wish to call ahead for their hours or directions. When you arrive at the office, look for the information desk and have them direct you to the appropriate counter or window.

Once you've found the right place, simply hand the papers to the clerk and say, "I'd like to file this." The clerk will examine the papers, and do one of two things: either accept it for filing (and collect the filing fee or direct you to where to pay it), or tell you that something is not correct. If you are told something is wrong, ask the clerk to explain to you what is wrong and how to correct the problem. Although clerks are not permitted to give legal advice, the types of problems they spot are usually very minor things that they can tell you how to correct. Often it is possible to figure out how to correct it from the way they explain what is wrong.

If you live far away from the court clerk's office or for some reason have difficulty getting there, you may mail your forms in to be filed. Write a letter or note asking the clerk to file the enclosed form or forms. Enclose a check or money order in the exact amount of the filing fee. Ask the clerk to keep one form and return the others to you marked "filed." Be sure to enclose a stamped self-addressed envelope for the forms and receipt to be returned to you. If you do file by mail, be aware that the clerk will not be able to help you correct any errors and will simply return it to you unfiled if there are mistakes.

SERVICE OF SUMMONS
The very first documents you must file are the Summons [either the Summons with Notice (form 4) or the Summons (form 5), as described later in this book], and the Request for Index Number (a form you must obtain from the court clerk, which assigns you a case number that will

appear on every document you file). Follow the instructions for completing them as they appear later in this book. Once you have completed them, you must file them. The fee for purchasing the index number is $170. You cannot file the summons without purchasing an index number.

NOTIFYING YOUR SPOUSE

A basic sense of fairness requires that a person be notified of a legal proceeding that involves him or her. You are required to notify your spouse that you have filed for divorce. This gives your spouse a chance to respond to your Summons. If you are unable to find your spouse (and therefore cannot have him or her personally served), you will also need to read Chapter 12. The notice requirements as they relate to your particular situation, will be discussed in later chapters.

The usual way to notify your spouse that you filed for a divorce is called *personal service*, which is where the sheriff, or someone else, personally delivers the papers to your spouse. It is essential that you file the initial papers *before* you have your spouse served.

Call the sheriff's office in the county where your spouse lives, and ask how much it will cost to have your spouse served with divorce papers, and what forms of payment they accept (they may not accept personal checks). It will probably cost about $30.00.

You may also hire a process server to serve the papers (they are listed in the yellow pages and are generally less expensive than the sheriff). You may also have a friend or relative deliver the papers. You are not permitted to do so yourself. The person serving the Summons on your spouse must complete the Affidavit of Service. (see form 6, p.185.) You must then file form 6 with the court clerk. If your spouse tries to avoid being served, you should hire a process server who is an expert at serving people. A professional process server also understands the law about how a person must be served.

OTHER NOTICES

Your spouse has 20 days to respond to the Summons (or 30 days if he or she was served outside New York state). If the 20th or 30th day is a Saturday, Sunday or holiday, the next business day is the deadline for responding. If your spouse does not file a Notice of Appearance (form 37) or a Verified Answer (form 38) within that time period, then your action is uncontested and your spouse has no say in the proceeding. If he or she does file a Notice of Appearance or Verified Answer, then your action is contested and you should think seriously about getting an attorney. The Affidavit of Service must be filed within 120 days after the Summons was filed in the court clerk's office. (see form 6, p.185.) If you fail to do so, your case may be dismissed.

If you and your spouse are in agreement about the divorce and your spouse agrees to sign the Affidavit of Defendant (form 12), then you do not need to have him or her served with a Summons. There is no time limit on when the Affidavit of Defendant must be filed.

Once your spouse has been served with the Summons, you may mail him or her copies of any papers you file later. If your spouse does not file a Notice of Appearance (form 37), or if he or she does file an Affidavit of Defendant (form 12), you are not required to send him or her copies of anything, except for the Judgment of Divorce.

SETTING A COURT HEARING

UNCONTESTED
CASES

If your case is uncontested (if your spouse does not appear by filing a Notice of Appearance or if your spouse signs the Affidavit of Defendant), you need not ever appear in court. You simply complete all of the paperwork described in Chapter 9 including the Affidavit of Plaintiff, and submit it. (see form 11, p.214.) If all of your forms are acceptable, your divorce will be granted without a court appearance.

CONTESTED If your divorce is contested, you will at some point appear in court.
CASES Many contested divorces are settled at a pre-trial conference, where the
parties reach an agreement and it is read into the record. However, you
must still testify about the grounds for the divorce, usually before the
judge's law clerk.

To get a court date, you file two forms. First, file the Request for
Judicial Intervention (known as an "RJI") for which there is a $75 fee.
(see form 35, p.270.) Along with this, file a Note of Issue and
Statement of Readiness, and pay an additional $25 fee. (see form 36,
p.272.) The matrimonial calendar room, or the judge's secretary or
clerk will schedule your case, and you will be notified by mail of the
date and time. They will also notify your spouse. Normally a pre-trial
conference will be your first appearance, unless you are seeking some
immediate, temporary relief (see Chapter 13), in which case you
would appear at what is called a *motion term of the court*, when many
other cases are being heard, and briefly argue your motion. A trial will
be scheduled further down the line.

If a court appearance is scheduled on a day or time when you absolutely
cannot attend, call the judge's secretary in advance and request an
adjournment, which is a postponement. You may be required to get the
permission of your spouse or his or her attorney. You should make every
effort to be at any scheduled appearance. Some judges may be reluctant
to grant your request for an adjournment, so do not ask unless it is very
important. If you fail to appear, your case could be dismissed.

COURTROOM MANNERS

There are certain rules of procedure that are used in a court. These are
really the rules of good conduct, or good manners, and are designed to
keep things orderly. Many of the rules are written down, although some
are unwritten customs that have just developed over many years. They
are not difficult, and most of them do make sense. Following these

suggestions will make the judge respect you for your maturity and professional manner, and possibly even make him forget for a moment that you are not a lawyer. It will also increase the likelihood that you will get the things you request.

SHOW RESPECT
FOR THE JUDGE

Showing respect for the judge basically means do not do anything to make the judge angry at you, such as arguing with him. Be polite, and call the judge "Your Honor" when you speak to him, such as "Yes, Your Honor," or "Your Honor, I brought proof of my income." Although many lawyers address judges as "Judge," this is not proper. Many of the following rules also relate to showing respect for the court. This also means wearing appropriate clothing, such as a coat and tie, or a suit for men; and a dress, suit, or dressy pants for women. This especially means no T-shirts, blue jeans, shorts, sneakers, or "revealing" clothing. Except when you are on the witness stand, stand up each time you speak to the judge.

WHEN THE
JUDGE TALKS;
YOU LISTEN

Think of the judge as the king or queen of the courtroom. If you sit in on some court hearings, you will see that whenever the judge talks everyone else shuts up and listens. Even if the judge interrupts you, stop talking immediately and listen. Judges can become rather upset if you do not allow them to interrupt.

ONLY ONE
PERSON CAN
TALK AT A TIME

Each person is allotted his or her own time to talk in court. The judge can only listen to one person at a time, so do not interrupt your spouse when it is his or her turn. And as difficult as it may be, stop talking if your spouse interrupts you. (Let the judge tell your spouse to keep quiet and let you have your say.)

TALK TO THE
JUDGE; NOT TO
YOUR SPOUSE

Many people get in front of a judge and begin arguing with each other. They actually turn away from the judge, face each other, and begin arguing as if they are in the room alone. This generally has several negative results: The judge can't understand what either one is saying since they both start talking at once, they both look like fools for losing control, and the judge gets angry with both of them. So whenever you speak in a courtroom, look only at the judge. Try to pretend that your spouse is not there. Remember, you are there to convince the judge that you should have certain things. You don't need to convince your spouse.

TALK ONLY WHEN IT'S YOUR TURN

Usually, you present your case first if you are the plaintiff. When you are done saying all you came to say, your spouse will have a chance to say whatever he or she came to say. Let your spouse have his or her say. When he or she is finished, you will get another chance to respond to what has been said.

STICK TO THE SUBJECT

Many people can not resist the temptation to get off the track and start telling the judge all the problems with their marriage over the past twenty years. This just wastes time, and aggravates the judge. So stick to the subject, and answer the judge's questions simply and to the point.

REMAIN CALM

Judges like things to go smoothly in their courtrooms. They don't like shouting, name calling, crying, or other displays of emotion. Generally, judges don't like divorce cases because they get too emotionally charged. So give your judge a pleasant surprise by keeping calm and focusing on the issues.

SHOW RESPECT FOR YOUR SPOUSE

Even if you don't respect your spouse, act like you do. All you have to do is refer to your spouse as "Mr. Smith" or "Ms. Smith" (using his or her correct name, of course). You may also refer to your spouse as "the defendant," if you are the one who filed the divorce. If your spouse filed for divorce, you may refer to him or her as "the plaintiff."

NEGOTIATING

It is beyond the scope of this book to fully present a course in negotiation techniques. However, a few basic rules may be of some help.

ASK FOR MORE THAN YOU WANT

Asking for more than you want always gives you some room to compromise by giving up a few things, and end up with close to what you really want. With property division, this means you will review your Property Inventory (form 1), and decide which items you really want, would like to have, and don't care much about. Also, try to figure out which items your spouse really wants, would like to have, and doesn't care much about. At the beginning you will say that you want certain things. Your list will include: (a) Everything you really want, (b) almost everything you'd like to have, (c) some of the things you don't care about, and (d) some of the things you think your spouse really wants or would like to have. Once you find out what is on your spouse's list, you begin trading items. Generally, you try to give your spouse things that he really wants and that you don't care about, in return for your spouse giving you the items you really care about and would like to have.

Child custody tends to be something that cannot be negotiated. It is often used as a threat by one of the parties in order to get something else, such as more of the property, or lower child support. If the real issue is one of these other matters, don't be concerned by a threatened custody fight, because your spouse probably does not really want custody and won't fight for it. If the real issue is custody, you will not be able to negotiate for it and will end up letting the judge decide anyway.

If child support is involved in your case, you should first work out what you think the judge will order based upon the Child Support Standards Act discussed in Chapter 5. Do this before discussing the matter with your spouse. If you will be receiving child support, you may want to ask for more than the guidelines require, and negotiate down to those requirements. If you will be paying child support, you may want to try for slightly less than the guidelines demand, but keep in mind that the judge will probably look at the schedule and ask questions if you and your spouse are agreeing to less. This does not mean the judge will reject your agreement, but you may need to offer an explanation as to why you are not following the guidelines. You can tell your spouse that there is little room for negotiation on child support as the court will probably require it be set according to the statute. If your spouse won't agree on something very close to the guidelines, give up trying to work it out and let the judge decide.

LET YOUR
SPOUSE START
THE BIDDING

One basic rule of negotiating is: The first person to mention a dollar figure loses. Whether it is a child support figure or the value of a piece of property, try to get your spouse to name the amount he or she thinks it should be first. If your spouse starts with a figure that is almost what you had in mind, it will be much easier to get to your figure. If your spouse begins with a figure far from yours, you know how far in the other direction to begin your bid.

GIVE YOUR
SPOUSE TIME TO
WORRY

Your spouse is probably just as afraid as you about the possibility of losing to the judge's decision and would like to settle. Do not be afraid to state your "final offer" and walk away. Give your spouse a day or two to think it over. Maybe he or she will call back and make a better offer. If not, you can always "reconsider" and make a different offer in a few days, but do not be too willing to do this or your spouse may think you will give in even more.

KNOW YOUR
BOTTOM LINE

Before you begin negotiating you should try to set a point that you will not go beyond. If you have decided that there are four items of property that you absolutely must have, and your spouse is only willing to agree to let you have three, it's time to end the bargaining session and go home.

REMEMBER
WHAT YOU'VE
LEARNED

By the time you have read this far you should be aware of two things:

1. The judge will roughly divide your property equally.

2. The judge will probably come close to the Child Support Standards Act

This awareness should give you an approximate idea of how things will turn out if the judge is asked to decide these issues, which should help you to set your bottom line on them.

SEPARATION 7

WHAT IS A LEGAL SEPARATION?

A legal separation means you and your spouse either have a written Separation Agreement or a Judgment of Separation from Supreme Court. The Separation Agreement or Judgment of Separation divides all of your property and debts, determines custody, child support, and maintenance exactly like a divorce. However, you are not free to marry someone else.

The grounds for divorce based on a separation requires that you live separate and apart "pursuant to a decree or judgment of separation," or "pursuant to a written agreement of separation." If you and your spouse are not ready to undergo all of the legal procedures involved in a legal separation, you can certainly live apart without a Separation Agreement or Judgment of Separation. However, this will not allow you to file for divorce using the grounds of having lived separate and apart for one year. If you do just separate without a Separation Agreement or Judgment of Separation and find you need child support, spousal support, or formal custody, you can go to Family Court and file petitions seeking these things; however, these proceedings are beyond the scope of this book.

Why Get a Separation?

The most common reason to become separated is to eventually get a divorce. If you and your spouse live apart for one year while legally separated, the Separation Agreement or Judgment of Separation can be converted to a Judgment of Divorce with the separation used as the grounds. It is not necessary to give any other reason. Many people feel more comfortable with this situation than they do with having to testify about cruel and inhuman treatment, adultery, or one of the other grounds allowed by law.

The Separation Agreement is more commonly used than the Judgment of Separation because the Separation Agreement can be accomplished without involving the court. It is usually negotiated by the parties' attorneys and signed in an attorney's office. It can also be negotiated with a mediator, or on your own.

How to Become Separated

There are two ways to become legally separated and qualify to use the grounds of separation to obtain a divorce:

1. Commence a court action for separation, and obtain a Judgment of Separation.
2. You and your spouse sign a Separation Agreement.

JUDGMENT OF SEPARATION

To commence a court action for separation, you would follow the procedure for filing for divorce, substituting "separation" for the word "divorce" in all of the papers. However, since this still requires you to prove one of the other grounds, you may as well just file for divorce using the other grounds that applies to your situation. If abandonment is used as a grounds for separation, there is no length of time required as there is when it is used as a grounds for divorce.

SEPARATION AGREEMENT

Instead of filing a lawsuit to get a Judgment of Separation, you may draft a Separation Agreement, sign it with your spouse before a notary, and file either the Separation Agreement (form 44) or a Memorandum of Separation Agreement (form 45) in the county clerk's office. Both of these forms will be explained in more detail later in this chapter.

A Separation Agreement is a document that is signed by you and your spouse, which states your agreement regarding the division of your property and debts, child custody and visitation, child support, and maintenance. A Separation Agreement is usually very long and technical. To be sure of protecting all of your rights, you would be well-advised to retain an attorney to draft it for you or review what you have drafted. Appendix B contains a Separation Agreement. (see form 44, p.283.) However, you must be aware that no form can be designed to cover every possible situation. If anything in your situation seems to vastly differ from the provisions in form 44, and you are not sure of how to modify the form to properly cover your situation, you should contact an attorney. You must be certain that the Separation Agreement you sign completely divides all of your assets and debts, and completely describes all of your agreements on other matters.

CREATING A SEPARATION AGREEMENT

To create your own Separation Agreement, you can begin with the form in Appendix B. (see form 44, p.283.) This form contains most, if not all, of the provisions you will need. If you have agreed to something that does not fit the provision in the form, you may cross it out and insert your own language, but be sure that what you write is accurate. You can always attach additional sheets of paper to form 44 to include agreements on matters not covered elsewhere in the form.

If any of your provisions are too long for the space provided, simply write in "see attached page _____" (filling in whatever page number or letter you choose), and attach an extra sheet with the information that would not fit. This may be likely to occur if you have a very long custody and visitation schedule, or if you have a large number of assets or debts to list. Before you complete a section of form 39, be sure to carefully read the sections in other chapter of this book detailing the law and how to make these decisions.

You and your spouse will have to work very closely to complete your Separation Agreement, and you both must be in total agreement with every provision. Do not expect to negotiate your agreement in one sitting. It will probably take a period of time for you and your spouse to work out these important, and sometimes complicated, issues. You may wish to consult with an attorney for advice before, or during, the drafting of your Separation Agreement. If you prepare your own Separation Agreement, you may want to have an attorney review it before you sign it. Just be aware that it may be in the attorney's interest to find problems with your agreement, and try to charge you a sizeable fee to "correct the problems." You and your spouse may also want to use the services of a mediator to help you work out your agreement.

Your Separation Agreement will eventually become the essence of your Judgment of Divorce. Be sure you read and completely understand the Separation Agreement before signing it. If there is anything that is unclear, incomplete, or incorrect, change it before signing.

You and your spouse will each need to complete a Statement of Net Worth, and exchange them before signing the Separation Agreement. (see form 10, p.195.) You must also share all supporting documents with each other, including tax returns, pay stubs, and all account statements and bills. A Statement of Net Worth for you, and one for your spouse, should be filed with the court at the same time you file your Separation Agreement.

Although most courts will probably accept a Separation Agreement in which the provisions have been handwritten, you would protect your own interests if you type in the provisions. If it is handwritten, it is just too easy for your spouse to write in an extra provision for his or her benefit after you both signed, and submit it to the court that way. If you do type it and need to make any handwritten changes or additions, you will both need to initial anything that is not typed, so the judge knows you both agree to the change or addition, and that it was not written in afterwards by one of you without the other's knowledge. (see form 44, p.283.)

SEPARATION
AGREEMENT
(form 44)

To complete the Separation Agreement:

1. Read through the entire Separation Agreement and cross out the words "Husband" or "Wife," "him" or "her," "he" or "she," etc., as appropriate to describe your agreement.

2. On the cover page, just below the words "By and Between," type your name on the first line, and your spouse's name on the second line.

3. On the second page, in the first paragraph, type in the date of your agreement, and your name and your spouse's name on the appropriate lines.

4. Under the heading "Recitals":

   a. In paragraph A, fill in the date and place of your marriage, and the number of children of your marriage (if any) and their name(s) and birth date(s).

   b. In paragraph D, cross out the first phrase in brackets if you and your spouse have not consulted attorneys regarding your agreement; cross out the second phrase in brackets if you have consulted attorneys.

   c. In paragraph F, cross out the words "Husband" or "Wife" where appropriate to indicate who will eventually be filing for divorce after your one-year period of separation.

   d. In paragraph I, fill in the name of the county where you will be filing your Agreement or memorandum of your Agreement (the county where at least one of you lives).

5. "Article II: Marital Residence" is used to describe what will happen to your marital home.

   a. If you and your spouse own a home together, check the box for paragraph A, which identifies the property and indicates when it was purchased, the purchase price, and the range of the current value. Next, read paragraphs B through E. These are the options most often used by couples getting divorced. You will not check more than one of these paragraphs. If one of you will keep the home, check paragraph B and fill in the name of the mortgage holder and the approximate mortgage balance on the lines (if there is no outstanding mortgage, type in "not applicable" on the first line).

Warning: If your spouse is keeping the home and the existing mortgage, you will still be liable to the mortgage holder if your spouse fails to make the mortgage payments. The only exception is if you can get the mortgage holder to sign a document releasing you from liability — but this is unlikely.

If one of you will buy out the other's interest in the home, check the box for paragraph C and fill in the amount to be paid to the other. If your home is going to be put up for sale, complete paragraph D, choosing either subparagraph 1 or 2, but not both. If you have some other arrangement about how long you will continue to live together in the home, use paragraph E. Paragraphs F, G, and H are common provisions relating to where the home will be sold, and should all be checked unless you and your spouse have agreed otherwise.

b. If you and your spouse already have separate residences, you will use paragraph I. If you and your spouse rent your residence, use paragraph J.

c. Paragraph K can be used if you and your spouse have an agreement about your home that is not stated elsewhere in Article II. If your agreement is more complicated, you can type in: "See attached Marital Residence Addendum for details," and attach a sheet of paper (labeling it "Marital Residence Addendum") containing the details of your agreement.

6. The section titled "Article III: Separate Property" has places to list any property that is, and will remain, your sole property or your spouse's sole property. Be sure to note that the wife's property is listed in the first paragraph and the husband's property is listed in the second paragraph.

7. In "Article IV: Automobiles and Vehicles," list vehicles each of you will keep. To be clear, you should list the year, make, model, and any vehicle identification number. Refer to your Property Inventory (form 1), where this information should be listed.

8. Under "Article V: Bank and Financial Accounts," list the name of the bank, or the name of the stock, mutual fund, or other information to identify the account (include the account number if there is one); the balance; and whether the new owner will be the "Husband" or the "Wife."

9. In Article VI: Interests in Business," list any business interests owned by you or your spouse (or the two of you together). Describe the business, provide an agreed upon value, and indicate how it will be divided. If there are no such business interests, type in "not applicable."

10. List each of your life and disability insurance policies in "Article VII: Life and Disability Insurance." Include the name of the insurance company and the policy number.

11. In "Article IX: Distribution of Personalty and Other Property," check the box for paragraph A if you and your spouse have separate residences and have already divided your personal property. If you have not already divided up and separated your property, check the box for paragraph B, and prepare and attach a separate sheet, labeled "Schedule A," listing all of the property you will keep and all of the property your spouse will keep. Make three columns: description of the item, value of the item, and who is to be the new owner. Describe each item in sufficient detail so it is clear what is going to whom. If you own real estate other than your marital residence (such as a vacation home or an investment lot), check the

box for paragraph C and prepare a separate sheet, labeled "Schedule B," and list the property.

12. In "Article X: Debts," check the box for each paragraph that applies to your situation. If you and your spouse have joint credit cards, list them in paragraph D by the name of the credit card and the bank, financial institution, or company it was issued through (e.g., "BankAmerica Gold Visa"). Since you may be filing the Separation Agreement with the court, where it will become public record, it may not be wise to include the account number.

> *Warning:* Even if you agree that your spouse will be responsible for a particular credit card or account, as long as your name is on it you will still be responsible if your spouse fails to pay. Therefore, you should either close any joint accounts or have your name removed from any account your spouse will keep.

13. Under the heading "Article XI: Maintenance," check either box A, B, or C (do not check more than one box). Box A is if you agree that neither of you will pay maintenance. Box B is for a single, lump sum maintenance payment. Box C if for periodic maintenance payments. If you check box C, you should also check box D and fill in the required information.

14. Complete "Article XII: Health Care Insurance and Expenses" by checking the appropriate boxes to reflect your agreement regarding these matters.

15. Under "Article XIII: Parenting," in paragraph A type in the details of your agreement regarding custody and regular visitation. In paragraph B, type in the details of your agreement regarding visitation for holidays, summer vacation, and other special situations. Paragraphs C through J are other common provisions relating to parenting — check all that reflect your agreement. Paragraph K is to fill in any other provisions that are not found elsewhere in Article XIII.

16. Complete "Article XIV: Child Support" by checking the boxes that apply to your agreement, and filling in any required information.

Use paragraph A if you are following the Child Support Standards Act guidelines. Note that there are separate provisions to complete depending upon whether your income is above or below $80,000 per year. Use paragraph B if you wish to opt-out of the Child Support Standards Act guidelines. Paragraphs C through E are other common matters that arise with respect to child support. Complete any of these paragraphs that reflect your agreement.

17. In "Article XV: Income Tax Returns," check paragraph A if you and your spouse agree to file joint income tax returns for the current year or any other year until you are divorced; and check paragraph B to indicate any year you will file separate returns. If you check paragraph B, then indicate in paragraph C which of you will claim the children as exemptions.

18. Under "Article XVIII: General Provisions," in paragraph L, fill in the number of copies of your Separation Agreement that are being signed as an "original." At least you and your spouse should each have a signed "original."

19. Complete "Article XX: Attorney Fees and Court and Related Costs" if you have any agreement regarding these matters.

20. "Article XXI: Other Agreements" is for you to indicate if there are any additional pages that will be attached to your Separation Agreement. If so, check the box, and fill in the number of additional pages that will be attached.

21. Now go back and read your Separation Agreement over carefully. Be sure that your understand all of it, that you have filled everything out correctly, and that you have crossed out words where necessary. Your spouse should do the same.

22. Now that you are both satisfied that you have a complete and accurate Separation Agreement; you each need to sign it before a notary public on the lines marked "Husband" and "Wife" on the last page. The notary will complete the notary provisions.

FILING YOUR SEPARATION AGREEMENT

For purposes of obtaining a divorce on the grounds of separation, your separation period begins on the date the agreement is signed. You must wait one year from the date of signing, then follow the steps in this book for an uncontested divorce on the grounds of separation. You can also begin an uncontested divorce immediately using one of the other grounds, asking for the relief agreed to in your Separation Agreement. Section 170(6) of the New York Domestic Relations Law says that either your Separation Agreement (form 44) or a Memorandum of Separation Agreement (form 45) must be filed with "the court clerk of the county wherein either party resides."

MEMORANDUM OF SEPARATION AGREEMENT (form 45)

The Memorandum of Separation Agreement simply states that you and your spouse have signed a Separation Agreement. (see form 45, p.299.) If you choose file a Memorandum of Separation Agreement, you will need to show the court clerk your Separation Agreement at the time of filing.

The benefit to filing a Memorandum of Separation Agreement is that all of the details of your Separation Agreement are not open to the public as a matter of public record. The danger in filing a Memorandum of Separation is that you must then hold on to the Separation Agreement yourself for the one year separation period. If you lose the Separation Agreement and cannot locate another original, you are going to have difficulty obtaining a divorce on the grounds of separation. To be safe, it is best to file the Separation Agreement itself, rather than a Memorandum of Separation.

If you decide to file a Memorandum of Separation instead of your Separation Agreement, complete form 45 as follows:

1. At the top, left-hand corner of the form, type in the name of the county where you will file your Memorandum of Separation Agreement (form 45). Just below this, type in the husband's name

on the line before the word "Husband," and the wife's name on the line before the word "Wife."

2. In item A, fill in your names and addresses on the lines indicated.

3. In item B, fill in the date you and your spouse were married.

4. In item C, fill in the date of your Separation Agreement. This should be the date you used in the very first paragraph of your Separation Agreement.

5. In item D, fill in the date, or dates, that each of you signed the Separation Agreement. These will be the dates indicated in each of the notary provisions on the last page of the Separation Agreement.

6. Sign your names on the signature lines before a notary public. The notary will complete the notary provisions. Form 45 is now ready for filing with the court clerk. Take form 45 to the clerk, along with your Separation Agreement. The clerk will examine your Separation Agreement. After accepting form 45 for filing, the clerk will return your Separation Agreement to you. You will need to keep your original Separation Agreement in a safe place, such as a safe deposit box.

PARENTING PLANS 8

If you have children, you are probably very concerned with how you can expect the divorce to affect them. When you divorce, the court uses custody and visitation to determine where the children will spend their time and to make clear how decisions about the children's lives will be made.

Many people, including psychologists and therapists, find the words "custody and visitation" to be disturbing and damaging. Many experts now prefer to use the words "parenting plan", because it is just insulting to expect a parent to "visit" his or her own child. Unfortunately, courts continue to use the words "custody and visitation". However, this does not mean that you cannot think of the entire situation as a parenting plan.

DEVELOPING THE PLAN

As with everything else in divorce, things are ideal when both parties agree on the question of custody of, and visitation with, the children. Generally the judge will accept any agreement you reach, provided it does not appear that your agreement will cause harm to your children.

CUSTODY   Should you and your spouse be unable to agree about custody, a judge will decide. In New York, the law about custody comes from case law. A decision about custody is based on what is in "the best interests of the child." This means the judge is supposed to decide what is best for each child in each case by considering all of the circumstances involved.

There are several different types of custody arrangements that can be agreed to by the parties or ordered by the court.

☛ *Joint custody*. Both parents are to make decisions together about the child. This requires cooperation. Parents who cannot communicate or are extremely hostile towards each other will not be given joint custody by the court. There are two types of joint custody.

   a. *Joint physical custody* (also called *shared custody*). The child spends equal amounts of time with both parents and "resides" with both of them. An example would be if the child spent one week with the mother, one week with the father and so forth. This type of arrangement can be very difficult for children and requires trust and communication between parents. Logistically, it can be very difficult for the entire family and many mental health experts believe this is never in the best interests of the children. Couples often agree to it when they can find no other way to share their children in a way they both believe to be fair.

   b. *Joint custody and a residential parent*. The parties have joint custody and make decisions together, but the child spends most of his or her time at one parent's house (this is where the child "resides") and has visitation with the other parent. This is the most common arrangement.

☛ *Sole custody*. The child spends most of his or her time at the home of one parent (the *residential parent*) and has visitation with the other parent. The residential parent makes all of the decisions about the child's life.

VISITATION   Visitation is the time a child spends with the non-residential parent. It can be any length of time, from a few hours per week to an entire summer. The visitation must be in the child's best interest. The most common visitation schedule is alternate weekends and one weekday each week. You and your spouse should find a schedule that makes your child feel most comfortable and allows both of you the maximum

amount of time with your child. You need to take into ⸺
your child's age and schedule. You will also need to work out a schedule for sharing holidays, school vacations, and birthdays. It is common
to alternate holidays (you have the child for Thanksgiving this year and
your spouse has Thanksgiving next year, etc.). Read the following list of
holidays and mark those that you want to be able to share. Discuss this
list with your spouse and see if you can work out a schedule.

- Child's birthday
- Your birthday
- Your spouse's birthday
- Labor Day
- Rosh Hashanah
- Yom Kippur
- Columbus Day
- Halloween
- Thanksgiving Day
- Thanksgiving school vacation
- Hanukkah
- Christmas Eve
- Christmas Day
- Christmas school vacation
- New Year's Eve
- New Year's Day

- New Year's Day
- Martin Luther King, Jr. Day
- President's Day
- Valentine's Day
- St. Patrick's Day
- Easter
- Easter or spring school vacation
- Passover
- Mother's Day
- Memorial Day
- Father's Day
- Fourth of July
- Other relatives' birthdays
- Other non-school days
- Summer vacation

- Any other holiday or day that is important to you, your spouse, or your child.

If you and your spouse cannot agree on how these matters will be handled, you will be leaving this important decision up to the judge. The
judge cannot possibly know your child as well as you and your spouse,
so doesn't it make sense for you to work this out yourselves? Otherwise,
you are leaving the decision to a stranger.

The most important thing to remember is that no visitation schedule
must be written in stone. You and your spouse will need to work

together and will need to be flexible. You and your spouse can make any adjustments to the schedule as long as you both agree to do so.

For example, you might want to go to a party on your scheduled weekend with the kids; or you might want to take your children to a family reunion on your spouse's scheduled weekend. These same type of things will come up for your spouse too. Plan on being in frequent contact with your spouse about the schedule and make an effort to be flexible and polite. Try to avoid involving your children in any disputes.

How Custody Should Be Decided

Since you and your spouse are the ones who know your children better than anyone in the world, you should really be the ones who decide what your parenting plan will be. It is extremely important that you push aside all of your bad feelings about each other and try to work out a solution that is going to work best for your children. A parenting plan needs to be centered around what is best for your children, not what will make you feel better, or what will vindicate you in the war against your spouse. Parenting plans are about the children, not about the parents.

Think about where both you and your spouse will be living. Where will the child or children be more comfortable? What are your schedules like? Ideally you want to schedule time with each parent when he or she is most available. Think about your child's schedule. Does he or she participate in dance classes, sports or other scheduled activities? You want to make sure that the child will still be able to attend these activities.

If the child is old enough, talk to him or her about the decisions that need to be made. Emphasize that he or she does not have the power to make this decision, but that you both would like to know what he or she thinks and feels and that you want to consider that in making your decision.

Parenting plans or visitation schedules should be custom-designed for your family. If you find that you and your spouse cannot work this out together, try seeing a mediator before heading for a contested divorce proceeding.

How a Judge Decides Custody

If the judge must decide the question of custody, he or she will consider the "totality of the circumstances," which may include:

- ☛ Which parent is most likely to allow the other to visit with the child and to develop and maintain a close and continuing parent-child relationship;

- ☛ The love, affection and other emotional ties existing between the child and each parent;

- ☛ The ability and willingness of each parent to provide the child with food, clothing, medical care, and other material needs;

- ☛ The length of time the child has lived with either parent in a stable environment;

- ☛ The permanence, as a family unit, of the proposed custodial home. (This relates to where one of the parties will be getting remarried immediately after the divorce or, more often, to change of custody petitions at a later date);

- ☛ The moral fitness of each parent;

- ☛ The mental and physical health of each parent;

- ☛ Any special needs the child has;

- ☛ Any domestic violence that has affected the child;

- ☛ The home, school and community record of the child;

- ☛ The preference of the child, providing the child is of sufficient intelligence and understanding; or

- ☛ Any other fact the judge decides is relevant.

LAW GUARDIAN   When the parties are unable to agree on custody, a judge will usually appoint a Law Guardian. A Law Guardian is an attorney who is paid by the state and whose job it is to act as your child's lawyer. The Law Guardian's purpose is to show the court the child's point of view. He or she will meet with you, your spouse and your child and may visit your home and your spouse's home, obtain your child's school and medical records, and interview people such as family, friends, and teachers who may be able to testify at the trial. Be very cooperative with the Law Guardian. He or she will make a recommendation to the judge as to what he or she thinks is the best custody arrangement for your child.

PREPARING FOR A CUSTODY TRIAL

If nothing else works and you are facing a contested custody trial, you need to prepare. Consider hiring an attorney, since there are many judicial decisions about custody that you simply will not have the time to find or become familiar with. If you do decide to go ahead and handle this on your own, you need to be prepared.

 A custody trial is going to require evidence. You need to document your position. If one of your main points is that your spouse skips visits with the child or is constantly late, you should keep a journal and record this every time it happens, so that you can show the judge some proof. If your spouse has ever mistreated or harmed your child, you will want to have doctors, teachers or other witnesses testify. Keep records of everything that happens that has to do with your spouse and your child.

Spend some time outlining your main points and listing the proof you have that will back up your points.

CUSTODY TRIAL   If you and your spouse cannot reach an agreement, a trial will be held where you and your spouse will testify, and you will be permitted to call other witnesses who can help the court decide what is best for your child. If you do not have an attorney, you can simply tell your point of view to the judge. Be sure to give the judge facts, not just opinions. If you are unrepresented, you can call witnesses and you will be responsible for asking them questions. Prepare a list of questions in advance and make sure you only ask about important things that have to do with the child. (How nasty your spouse has been to you is not important, but if your spouse has mistreated your child, that is important!)

Your spouse or your spouse's attorney will cross-examine you and your witnesses (ask questions). The judge may also ask questions. The Law Guardian may also cross-examine any witness and call his or her own witnesses. You will be permitted to cross-examine the witnesses your spouse and the Law Guardian call. It is important to remain calm and not become angry with the person asking you questions.

It is difficult to predict the outcome of a custody battle. There are too many factors and individual circumstances to make such a guess. The only exception is where one parent is clearly unfit and the other can prove it. Drug abuse is one of the most common charges against a spouse, but unless there has been an arrest and conviction it is difficult to prove to a judge. In general, don't charge your spouse with being unfit unless you can prove it. Judges are not impressed with unfounded allegations, and they can do more harm than good.

If your children are older (not infants), it may be a good idea to seriously consider their preference for with whom they would like to live. If you do have a trial, the judge may interview your child in private, with just the Law Guardian and a stenographer in the room. This testimony is sealed and is never available for the parents or their attorneys to read. Your "fairness" and respect for their wishes may benefit you in the long run. If the children choose not to reside with you, be sure that you keep in close contact with them and visit them often.

COPING WITH YOUR PARENTING PLAN

Whatever type of parenting plan or custody and visitation structure you end up with, it is probably not what you would call ideal. After all, in any parenting plan, there are going to be days when do not see your child. There is no denying this is going to be difficult for all of you.

After you spend some time grieving, you are going to need to get up and get on with your life. This means that you need to take your parenting time and make the most of it. You love your child and want the best for him or her. Find a way to deal with the situation. Get counseling or therapy for you and/or your child if it will help. Do not continue to wage war against your ex. This is only going to hurt your child. Accept what has been decided and get on with making it work in your life. No, it may not be perfect, but it is what you have got. Make it work for you and your child.

UNCONTESTED DIVORCE 9

PROCEDURE

There are two ways that a case can be considered *uncontested*. One is where you and your spouse reach an agreement on every issue in the divorce. To be in this situation you must be in agreement on the following points:

1. How your property is to be divided.

2. How your debts are to be divided.

3. Which of you will have custody of the children, and how visitation will work.

4. How much child support is to be paid by the person not having custody.

5. Whether any maintenance is to be paid, and if so, how much and for how long a period of time.

The other type of uncontested case is where your spouse does not respond to your Summons. If your spouse was served (see Chapter 6), and he or she does not respond, you will need to file certain forms. If you cannot find your spouse you will need to file several other forms (see Chapter 12).

Most lawyers have had the following experience: A new client comes in, saying she wants to file for divorce. She has discussed it with her husband, and it will be a "simple, uncontested" divorce. Once the papers are filed, the husband and wife begin arguing over a few items of property. The lawyer then spends a lot of time negotiating with the husband. After much arguing, an agreement is finally reached. The case will proceed in the court as uncontested, but only after a lot of contesting out of court. For purposes of this book, a contested case is one where you and your spouse will be doing your arguing in court, and leaving the decision up to the judge. An uncontested case is one where you will do your arguing and deciding before court, and the judge will only be approving your decision.

You may not know if you are going to have a contested case until you try the uncontested route and fail. Therefore, the following sections are presented mostly to assist you in attempting the uncontested case. Chapter 10 specifically discusses the contested case. To begin your case, follow the instructions below.

CERTIFICATION

This form must be attached to every single form you file with the court, including the child support forms. (see form 3, p.182.) Make lots of copies of this and sign each one and attach them to the forms in this book that are filed with the court. When you sign this form you are swearing that you are not filing a case that is frivolous. A frivolous case is one that has no legal basis, is brought just as an annoyance or harassment or one that makes statements that are false. Be sure that you follow this promise as you fill out the rest of the forms.

REQUEST FOR INDEX NUMBER

The Request for Index Number is the first form that must be filed and is the one that officially opens your case. An example of a Request for Index Number is shown on page 118. However, the Request for Index Number form must be obtained from the clerk's office because it is a special color, is on legal-sized paper, and is perforated. If the form you obtain from your clerk's office appears different from our example and you do not understand how to complete it, ask the clerk for assistance. ***Warning:* Do not use the Request for Index Number form on page 118 of this book!** Once you have obtained the form from the clerk, the following instructions will help you to complete it:

1. On the top line just below the words "Title of Action or Proceeding," write in the word "Supreme." If the name of the county is blank, fill that it.

2. Fill in the date you are filing the form and the case heading.

3. Fill in your name and address on the line for name and address of attorney for plaintiff, and fill in the name and address of your spouse or his or her attorney (if one has been retained) on the line for defendant's attorney.

4. Fill in the case heading on both of the detachable portions at the bottom of the page.

There is a $170 fee for filing this form. After you file it, the bottom portions will be returned to you and will give you the index number that has been assigned to your case. Remember to fill this number in on every form you file. After you have an index number, you will complete, file and serve the Summons.

SUMMONS

The Summons is a document that will be served on (delivered to) your spouse to notify him or her that you are seeking a divorce and that he of she has a certain number of days in which to respond. There are two Summons forms: the Summons with Notice (form 4), and the Summons, which does not contain a notice provision. (see form 5, p.184.) In general, these forms are used in the following circumstances:

☞ The Summons (form 5) is used if you are filing and serving it with the Verified Complaint. (see form 7, p.187.) If you and your spouse are in agreement about the divorce, it is more simple to file the Summons and Verified Complaint together.

☞ The Summons with Notice (form 4) is used if you do not want to serve your spouse with a copy of the Verified Complaint. (see form 7, p.187.) If your spouse is not in agreement or is unaware that you are filing for divorce, you should use the Summons with Notice. The Verified Complaint contains statements about why you are seeking a divorce which can anger your spouse and make the entire process more difficult.

You need to determine which Summons form you want to use. In this book, unless accompanied by the designation "(form 5)," the word "Summons" will be used generally to refer to whichever type of Summons you have chosen to use. We will now provide some instructions to help you in filling in whichever type of Summons you are using.

SUMMONS WITH
NOTICE
(form 4)

To complete the Summons with Notice (see form 4, p.183):

1. Fill in your case heading according to the instructions at the beginning of Chapter 6.

2. In the upper, right-hand corner, fill in the index number, the date you are filing the Summons, and the name of the county on the lines indicated. For "basis of venue," fill in either "Plaintiff resides in this county," or "Defendant resides in this county." Beneath the words "Summons with Notice," fill in the address of the person (plaintiff or defendant) used as the basis of venue.

3. In the second line of the first paragraph, cross out "Plaintiff's Attorney(s)," as you are representing yourself. (If you have an attorney, your attorney should be completing this form for you.)

4. Fill in the date underneath the first paragraph. To the right of that, cross out "Attorney(s) for," as you are representing yourself, and fill in your address and phone number.

5. Next, complete the "Notice" portion. Look at the very bottom of the form and find the grounds you are using. Fill in its section number and name on the blank lines after the designation "**DRL §170 Subd." You can't change the grounds you are using easily, so be sure about which one is correct in your situation.

6. The blank lines in the last paragraph of the form must be filled in with everything you are asking the court to do for you. Choose any of the following:

☞ custody and visitation (you will need to specify what type of custody and who it will be granted to, as well as the details about visitation);

☞ child support (including health insurance, child care and educational expenses, and medical expenses that are not covered by insurance);

☞ equitable distribution of property (including real estate and personal property) and debts;

☞ a declaration that all property in your possession be declared your sole and separate property, and a declaration that all debts in your spouse's name be declared his or her sole responsibility;

☞ maintenance;

☞ an incorporation but not a merger of a stipulation or Separation Agreement or Judgment of Separation (this is the language to use to ask a court to turn a Separation Agreement or Judgment or Separation into a divorce);

☞ costs and fees of the action (this means you are asking the court to have your spouse reimburse you for all of the court costs and your attorney's fees if any); or

☞ the right for you or your spouse to resume the use of a pre-marriage name (also known as a maiden name).

You can also ask to have a current Family Court Order (of support or custody and visitation) continued. You must list the docket number and name of the court that ordered it. If you have a prior order of support either from Family Court or an interim order from Supreme Court, and your spouse has missed three or more payments or has not made any payments for one month, you can ask that payments for the ordered amount and the *arrears* (the amount overdue) be deducted from your spouse's paycheck and sent to you directly.

If you fail to ask for something here, you will not be able to change your mind and ask for it later without refiling and re-serving your spouse. However, you can ask for something on this form, then change your mind and not ask for it later. If you are not sure about something, you should request it just to be safe. You need to consider your strategy at this point. If, for example, you ask for a large amount of maintenance, sole custody with no visitation for your spouse, child support over and above the CSSA amount, and all the marital property, it is much more likely that your spouse will contest the things for which you are asking. It is also more likely your spouse will hire an attorney. Ask for those things you want, but don't ask for a lot of things you really do not want if you want your divorce to be uncontested.

You must first file the Summons with Notice, then have it served upon your spouse. (see form 4, p.183.) If you have it served before you file it, it will not be valid. Your spouse then has twenty days (if served in New York State) or thirty days (if served outside of New York State) to respond. If he or she does not respond, your case is uncontested. If you are in agreement, your spouse will fill out an Affidavit of Defendant and will not need to respond to the Summons with Notice. (see form 12, p.220.)

SUMMONS
(form 5)

Remember that if you are going to use the Summons (form 5), you must file and serve it with the Verified Complaint. (see form 7, p.187.) Form 5 is completed in the same manner as the Summons with Notice (form 4), except that there are not sections in which to state the grounds or describe the relief you are requesting. No grounds or relief sections are needed because they are already stated in the Verified Complaint that accompanies the Summons.

AFFIDAVIT OF SERVICE

(form 6)   The Affidavit of Service must be completed by the person who serves the Summons with Notice (form 4), or the Summons (form 5) and Verified Complaint (form 7) on your spouse. The Affidavit of Service must be filed within 120 days of when the Summons was filed. (see form 6, p.185.) If it is not, you will have to start your case all over again.

If you are using a professional process server or the sheriff, they will have, and complete, this form. If someone else, such as a friend or relative, serves the Summons, that person will complete the form and should read these instructions. To complete the Affidavit of Service:

1. Fill in your case heading and index number according to the instructions at the beginning of Chapter 6.

2. Fill in your county underneath the case heading.

3. The person serving the Summons fills in his or her name and address in paragraph 1.

4. Paragraph 2: Fill in the date, time, and place of service. In three places in this paragraph you will need to cross out either "summon with notice" or "summons with verified complaint," whichever type of Summons was **not** served on your spouse. Fill in your spouse's name on the last line in this paragraph.

5. For paragraph 4, the server (the person who served the papers on your spouse) must indicate how he or she knew your spouse was the person served. Select one of the four options by checking the appropriate box. If identification was made by a photograph, that photograph must be attached to the Affidavit of Service when it is filed.

6. A description of the defendant must be given in paragraph 5 by checking the appropriate boxes which match your spouse. Other identifying features would include prominent moles, tattoos, markings, scars, etc.

7. The server must ask the defendant if he or she is in the military, as indicated in paragraph 6.

8. The server must sign and date this before a notary.

Forms 7 through 13 and 18 through 20 must be filed together, any time *after* the Affidavit of Service (form 6) is filed. Be sure to pay the fees indicated at the time you file.

VERIFIED COMPLAINT

(form 7)   The Verified Complaint details the reasons why a divorce is being sought and the relief you are seeking. (see form 7, p.187.) If your spouse has not responded to the Summons within the time allowed, then your case is uncontested and he or she will never see this form. The same is true if your spouse has completed an Affidavit of Defendant. (see form 12, p.220.) However, if your spouse has responded to your Summons, he or she will see this Verified Complaint. If that is the case, you should try to tone down your descriptions of the grounds for divorce so that you do not unnecessarily enrage your spouse. Many times people feel they should unload in the Verified Complaint and describe everything their spouse has done that is wrong, but this serves no purpose and may make your spouse so upset that a settlement becomes difficult to achieve. To complete the Verified Complaint:

1. Fill in the heading and index number according to the instructions at the beginning of Chapter 6. If you are not using an attorney, on the first line cross out "/ by _____." If you do have an attorney, your attorney should prepare this form for you and will cross out "herein" and fill in your attorney's name.

2. In the section marked "Second," you must check the box or boxes that indicate how you or your spouse fulfill the residency requirement. At least one box must be checked.

3. In the section marked "Third," fill in your date of marriage and place of marriage. You may wish to consult your marriage license to be sure you are accurate about the city, town, or village.

4. The section marked "Fourth" must be completed with the number of children, and the names, social security numbers, dates of birth, and addresses of any children of the marriage. Do not include children that are not the biological or adopted children of both you and your spouse. If there are no children, fill in "0" and leave the rest blank.

5. In the section marked "Fifth," choose the grounds for divorce you are using. Fill in the details of your situation. If you are using cruel and inhuman treatment, try to list at least three separate incidents.

6. As indicated in the section marked "Sixth," you cannot file for divorce if you or your spouse already have a case pending.

7. In the section beginning with the word "Wherefore," you must list all the relief you are seeking, as you did in the "Notice" part of the Summons with Notice (form 4). You must be more specific here than you were in the Summons with Notice (form 4). You must list how you want the debts and property to be divided, including real estate. For debts, list the name of the creditor and the amount owed. For property, describe the property and give its value. You also need to state the amount of maintenance you are seeking, if any; and the amount of child support you are seeking. State whether the child support amount is in accordance with the CSSA, or if it is outside the CSSA. If you are seeking to convert a Separation Agreement to a divorce, or if you have a stipulation, attach a copy of the document to the Verified Complaint. If you used a plain Summons (form 5), read the directions for the Summons with Notice (form 4) to understand how to complete this section. Attach an extra sheet of paper if necessary.

8. Sign and date this form before a notary.

SWORN STATEMENT OF REMOVAL OF BARRIERS TO REMARRIAGE

(form 8)   You must complete the Sworn Statement of Removal of Barriers to Remarriage only if you were married in a religious ceremony. (see form 8, p.192.) If you were not, do not complete it. To complete the Sworn Statement of Removal of Barriers to Remarriage:

1. Fill in the case heading and index number according to the instructions at the beginning of Chapter 6.

2. In the main body of the text, cross out one of the italicized sentences, whichever does not apply.

3. Sign before a notary.

4. This is the only document [other than the Summons with Notice (form 4) and the Judgment of Divorce (form 23)] that must be served on your spouse if your divorce is uncontested. You may have someone serve it personally or you may have someone mail it to your spouse. The "Affidavit of Service" on the second page of form 8 must be completed by the person who serves the form, and it must be notarized.

AFFIRMATION (AFFIDAVIT) OF REGULARITY

(form 9)   The Affirmation (Affidavit) of Regularity is a form you file to verify to the court that your spouse has been properly notified of the divorce case, and how your spouse responded (if at all). (see form 9, p.194.) To complete the Affirmation (Affidavit) of Regularity:

1. Fill in the case heading and index number according to the instructions at the beginning of Chapter 6.

2. After the case heading, fill in the name of the county.

3. If you do not have an attorney, cross out the first italicized paragraph and cross out the italicized words "the attorney for" in the

third paragraph. If you do have an attorney, your attorney will be completing and filing this form for you.

4. In the fourth paragraph that begins with "The Summons," cross out either "with Notice was" or "and verified complaint were," depending on which type of Summons you did ***not*** use. Also in that paragraph, cross out either "within" or "outside," depending on where your spouse was served.

5. If your spouse has not responded to your Summons or has not filled out an Affidavit of Defendant (form 12), then cross out the sixth paragraph and leave the seventh paragraph, which indicates that your spouse is in default. If your spouse has completed an Affidavit of Defendant (form 12), cross out the seventh paragraph and leave the sixth paragraph. If your spouse does not have an attorney, cross out "by the firm of_____." If your spouse does have an attorney, cross out "on his or her own behalf" and insert the name of the attorney on the blank line.

6. Sign this before a notary.

STATEMENT OF NET WORTH

(form 10)   The Statement of Net Worth gives the court all of your financial information. (see form 10, p.195.) This information provides the basis used to determine how your property and debts should be divided, as well as whether maintenance should be awarded. Consult your Property Inventory (form 1) and Debt Inventory (form 2) to help you complete this form. It is important to be as accurate as possible in completing this; however, if there is information you do not have and cannot get, you may provide an estimate. Do not expect to be able to complete this form in one sitting as it is extremely comprehensive. To complete the Statement of Net Worth:

1. Fill in the case heading and index number according to the instructions at the beginning of Chapter 6.

2. For the "Action Commencement date," fill in the date you filed the Summons.

3. Fill in the county underneath the case heading.

4. In the first, unnumbered paragraph, fill in your name in the first blank, and fill in the date you are completing the form in the blank after the words "an accurate statement as of."

5. The section marked "I. Family Data" is mostly self-explanatory. "Date of Separation" in item (d) means the date you and your spouse stopped living together. If you are still living together, write in "N/A." In item (g), "H/W/J" means husband/wife/joint. Circle whichever applies, and do so wherever this abbreviation appears in the form.

6. The section marked "II. Expenses" uses monthly figures. Note that each subsection has questions on the left and right side of the page. Fill in only those expenses you have. If an expense is listed that does not apply to you, leave it blank. Use estimates if you do not have an exact number. For example, few people know how much it costs them per month to do laundry at home [subsection (e)1], so just enter a reasonable estimate. Total each category at its end in the right column. At the end of the section, total all of the categories to get your total monthly expenses. Multiply that number by 12 to get your total annual expenses.

7. In the section marked "III. Gross Income," list your income and all of the deductions that are taken from your paychecks. Remember to use monthly amounts. There are other subsections dealing with specific types of income that may not apply to you. Read them over to be sure they do not apply. Leave them blank if they do not apply. Item (o) applies if you live with someone other than your spouse who has an income. This does not apply if you have a roommate, but if you and the person you live with share expenses and support each other, you will need to include his or her income. You do not need to include any income your child has in this column. To reach your monthly total, use a calculator and go down the col-

umn adding or subtracting depending on whether there is a plus or minus sign in front of each number. Multiply the monthly amount by twelve to get your annual total. Do not panic if your total income is less than your total expenses. It is quite common to have this happen.

8. In the section marked "IV. Assets," the total for each identified type of asset should be written on the line at the far right. Many of the items ask for the "title holder" or "title owner." This is the person whose name appears on the account or paperwork. It is acceptable to give just a year for "date opened." If you do not have the information requested, you can obtain it from your bank, broker, insurance agent, etc. The questions about vehicles ask for the amount of lien unpaid. This means the amount still owed on a loan on the vehicle.

9. In the section marked "V. Liabilities," list your debts. "Accounts Payable" refers to things like credit cards or medical bills. "Notes Payable" refers to any loans you may have taken out. The "note holder" is the bank, person, or institution from which you borrowed the money.

10. Under the heading "Net worth," subtract your total debts from total assets and you have your net worth. Again, do not be concerned if this is a negative number.

11. If you have given away an asset within the past three years you must explain in the section marked "VI. Assets Transferred." If you sold something and were paid a fair price, you do not need to list that. For example, if you sold your car and got a reasonable price for it, do not include it. However, if you transferred all of your stocks to your sister and she did not pay you for them, you must list this.

12. If you are not seeking child support or maintenance, skip the section marked "VII. Support Requirements." If you are seeking one or both, you must complete this section. Check the first box if you are not paying or receiving child support or spousal support. If you are paying or receiving support, circle paying or receiving and fill in the amounts and how often it is paid or received. If you received or

paid support prior to separating, fill in that section. Indicate if payment is being made due to a court order or voluntarily. If there are arrears (missed payments), indicate the amount. If not, check the box for no arrears outstanding. If you are seeking child support, check the box for the third paragraph. If you are seeking maintenance, check the box for the fourth paragraph and indicate how much you are seeking and whether you want to be paid weekly or monthly. The last paragraph is where you indicate when you want payments to be due.

13. The section marked "VIII. Counsel Fee Requirements" is where you can request that your spouse pay for your attorney fees and costs. If you are not asking for either, check the first box. If you want one or both, check the second box and indicate the amount you are seeking. If you do not have an attorney, you can only receive the amounts you have paid to the court, process server, or court stenographer. The amount you can request will vary depending on how much you paid for process service and for the transcript (if you never appear in court, there will be no fee for this). The third box should be checked if you have agreed to pay your spouse's attorney fees. The fourth box applies only if you have an attorney; plus, you must attach a copy of the retainer agreement.

14. The section marked "IX. Account and Appraisal Fee Requirements" refers to amounts you paid to have any property appraised or valued. This often occurs if either spouse owns a business or a very valuable item, such as an antique or a very expensive piece of jewelry. If you have not used such an expert, or if you have but are not seeking to be reimbursed for the expert's fee, check the first box. If you want to be reimbursed for accountant's fees, check the second box and indicate the amount and if the expert was paid by the hour or by a flat fee. Check the third box if you want reimbursement for an appraiser and indicate the fee information. The fourth and fifth boxes are where you must explain why an expert was needed.

15. Use the section marked "X. Other Data" if there is other important financial information the court should be aware of that has no other place on the form. The last paragraph in this section is for you to indicate whether you have attached any extra pages, and if so, how many. If there are no extra pages, do nothing with this paragraph. If there are extra pages, place a checkmark in the brackets [ ], and fill in the number of extra pages in the blank.

16. On the last page of form 10 are three paragraphs with the heading "Client Certification." Fill in your name in the blank in the first paragraph.

17. Sign your name before a notary on the lines designated "Plaintiff" on each of the last two pages of form 10.

AFFIDAVIT OF PLAINTIFF

(form 11)   The Affidavit of Plaintiff is a substitute for you giving oral testimony before the court. (see form 11, p.214.) If you are using adultery for your grounds, you will have to have a hearing and will need witnesses. Do not complete this form if you are using adultery as the grounds for divorce. To complete the Affidavit of Plaintiff:

1. Fill in the case heading and index number according to the instructions at the beginning of Chapter 6.

2. Fill in the county underneath the heading.

3. Fill in your name on the line beneath that, and your address on the long line directly above paragraph 1. On the line in paragraph 1, fill in your spouse's address, and check any of the boxes below it that are true. This is the residency requirement again. Check the boxes indicating the residency requirement you have met.

4. In paragraph 3, fill in the details about when and where you were married. Delete the italicized word "not" if you were married in a religious ceremony, and on the second page select one of the three options and cross out the remaining two.

5. Paragraph 4 is to be filled in with information regarding children of the marriage. At the end of this section are three "yes or no" questions. The first one should be marked "yes" if there has been any case in which custody of your children was at issue. In New York, this would have occurred in Family Court. The second question pertains to a custody case in any other state. The third question would be marked "yes" if someone other than you or your spouse has custody of or visitation with your children, such as the children's grandparents or the Department of Social Services.

6. In paragraph number 5, fill in the relief you are asking for. Copy this from your complaint.

7. In paragraph number 6 fill in the same information you used in your complaint.

8. Complete paragraph number 7.

9. Complete paragraph number 8 about Public Assistance.

10. Complete paragraph number 10 only if a photograph is attached to the summons.

11. Select the appropriate choice in paragraph number 11. Attach a separate sheet of paper if you choose 11B 1-4 with the information requested.

AFFIDAVIT OF DEFENDANT

(form 12)   The Affidavit of Defendant is the form your spouse must complete if he or she is going to consent to the divorce. (see form 12, p.220.) To complete the Affidavit of Defendant:

1. Fill in the case heading and index number according to the instructions at the beginning of Chapter 6.

2. Fill in the county underneath the heading.

3. Fill in your spouse's name on the line before the words "being duly sworn, says:", and your spouse's address on the line in the next unnumbered paragraph.

4. In paragraph 1, circle which type of Summons you used and write in the date it was served and the name and section number of the grounds listed in the Summons with Notice (form 4) or Verified Complaint (form 7). Write in the grounds you used.

   Allow your spouse to choose 4A or 4b. Cross out the italicized part of paragraph number 5 if you do not have a written stipulation.

5. If your spouse is in the military, cross out the word "not" in paragraph 3. If you and your spouse do not have a written stipulation or Separation Agreement, cross out the words "other than what was already agreed to in a written stipulation."

6. Cross out paragraph 6 if you were not married in a religious ceremony. Select the appropriate choice for your spouse for number 7 and attach additional information if needed.

7. Have your spouse sign and date this form before a notary.

CHILD SUPPORT FORMS

CHILD SUPPORT WORKSHEET (form 13)

The instructions for the Child Support Worksheet were given in Chapter 5. Obtain and prepare a good copy, with the most current information available, to file with the court and sign it before a notary. Attach a signed copy of Certification when you submit it to court. (see form 3, p.182.)

SUPPORT COLLECTION UNIT INFORMATION SHEET (form 14)

This form must be filed when child support is going to be paid to the Support Collection Unit. (see form 14, p.227.) Use this form only if child support payments are going to be made to the Unit. Complete the information as follows:

1. Fill in the heading.

2. Fill in the address, date of birth and social security information.

3. Complete date and place of marriage.

4. Check and circle who has custody and whether public assistance is being received.

5. List the names and dates of the children that support is being sought for.

6. Leave the amount of support blank for the court to complete.

7. Indicate who will be receiving the support and fill in the name of the non-custodial parent's employer.

8. Submit this form to the court with a child support worksheet.

QUALIFIED
MEDICAL CHILD
SUPPORT ORDER
(form 21)

Use this form if there are children and they will be covered by your spouse's medical insurance. (see form 21, p.234.) This form will be filed with the court and once it is signed by the judge, it must be given to the employer of the parent who will be providing health insurance for the children.

1. Fill in the heading and then list the names of the children, their dates of birth, social security numbers and addresses.

2. Fill in for "participant" the name of your spouse and his or her information.

3. If you are going to have custody, fill in your name and information under the paragraph beginning "the Dependents' Custodial Parent."

4. Fill in the name of the health plan and the information about it.

5. Fill in the name of the administrator of the health plan. This is the person at your spouse's place of employment who is in charge of the health insurance. If you don't know who this is, call and ask.

6. Fill in the type of coverage, such as medical, medical and dental, medical and drugs, etc.

7. Leave the rest of the form blank and submit with a child support worksheet.

Note on Procedure

If you will give oral testimony at a hearing, file the above forms and stop here. Include a self-addressed, stamped envelope with your case name and index number on it. The court will contact you with your hearing date. You will fill out the rest of the forms after your hearing. You will be contacted when your transcript has been prepared. Send the correct amount in a check or money order, and the transcript will be sent to you. At the end of the hearing, the referee will state what he or she is recommending. Use the referee's wording, copied from the transcript, to complete the Findings of Fact and Conclusions of Law (form 22) and the Judgment of Divorce (form 23).

If you will not be giving oral testimony, complete the forms described below at the same time you complete the forms noted above. Take the entire packet to the clerk's office. When you file the papers, you must include a self-addressed, stamped postcard with the name of your case and index number written on it. The clerk will use this to notify you if there are any problems with your documents. Remember to include payment for the fees.

INCOME DEDUCTION ORDER (form 16)

This form must be completed if child support or maintenance payments are going to be automatically deducted from the paying parents' pay. (see form 16, p.229.) The form is self-explanatory, except for the choice of direct payment or forwarded payment. Choose *direct payment* if the money is being deducted for child support. Choose *forwarded payment* if the money is for maintenance. Fill in your information for the creditor and the spouse's information for the debtor and the amount of payments as well as the date payments will end. If the money is being paid for maintenance or for child support and maintenance combined, you must fill in the following name and address under creditor instead of your own:

Office of Temporary and Disability Assistance
P.O. Box 15365
Albany, NY 12212-5365

NEW YORK STATE
CASE REGISTRY
FILING FORM
(form 17)

Fill out this form if child support is NOT going to be paid through Child Support Collection and will be paid directly to you. (see form 17, p.230.) When you fill the form out, remember that "payor" is the person paying support and "payee" is the person receiving the support payments.

1. Complete the name of court, county name and index number of your case.

2. Fill in your spouse's information on the line for payor and your information on the line for payee.

3. Complete the information needed for each child that child support will be paid for. Answer the questions on the bottom of the form.

NOTE OF ISSUE

(form 18)

There is a $25 fee to file the Note of Issue. (see form 18, p.231.) To complete the Note of Issue:

1. Fill in the case heading and index number according to the instructions at the beginning of Chapter 6. Leave the "Calendar Number" blank.

2. After "Filed By," circle the word "Plaintiff" (if you have an attorney, he or she will be preparing this form).

3. Fill in the date the Summons was filed and the date it was served.

4. After "Date Issue Joined," circle the word "waiver" if your spouse completed the Affidavit of Defendant (form 12). Circle the word "Default" if your spouse never responded to your Summons and did not complete an Affidavit of Defendant. Circle stipulation or separation agreement if that is what you are using.

5. Fill in your name and address, and your spouse's name and address.

6. If you will have a hearing instead of submitting an Affidavit of Plaintiff (form 11), cross out "No Trial" near the top of the form.

REQUEST FOR JUDICIAL INTERVENTION

(form 19)   There is a $75 fee to file the Request for Judicial Intervention. (see form 19, p.232.) This form is not required in New York City. To complete the Request for Judicial Intervention:

1. Fill in the case heading, index number, and the date you purchased the index number (this will be the date you filed your Request for Index Number and paid the fee).

2. In the section titled "Attorney(s) for Plaintiff," cross out the words "Attorney(s) for," and fill in your name, address, and phone number.

3. In the section titled "Attorney(s) for Defendant," if your spouse does not have an attorney, cross out the words "Attorney(s) for," and fill in your spouse's name, address, and phone number. If you spouse has an attorney, fill in the attorney's name, address, and phone number, instead of your spouse's.

4. In the section designated "Related Cases," if you have a Family Court order you wish to have continued, fill in the name of the case, the docket number (under "index #"), the name of the Court, and what type of case it was.

5. Sign the form, and print or type your name on the lines indicated.

AFFIDAVIT PURSUANT TO DOMESTIC RELATIONS LAW 75-J

(form 20)   The Affidavit Pursuant to Domestic Relations Law 75-j must be filed if there are children of the marriage and there has never been any judgment or court order directing custody of the children. (see form 20, p.233.) If there is such a judgment or order, do not complete this form. Instead, you must indicate on other forms that this is the case, and attach the judgment or order. To complete the Affidavit Pursuant to Domestic Relations Law 75-j:

1. Fill in the case heading and index number according to the instructions at the beginning of Chapter 6.

2. Fill in your name on the line before the words "being duly sworn deposes and states:"

3. In paragraph 2, list the number of children in the first blank, and their names and dates of birth in the following blanks.

4. In paragraph 3, list the children's current address.

5. In paragraph 4, list any other residences the children have had.

6. In paragraph 5, indicate the length of time the children lived with both you and your spouse together.

7. Sign the form before a notary.

All of the above forms should be filed together.

NOTICE OF SETTLEMENT

(form 15) This form must be served, if the judge or your spouse requests, on the other party if you are seeking to have a Judgment, Qualified Medical Child Support Order, or any other order signed by the judge. (see form 15, p.228.) If you ever need to use it:

1. Fill in the heading on the form.

2. Check and circle what it is the judge will be signing and the date it will be presented to the court.

The form must be personally served with a copy of the Judgment or Order you are seeking to have signed at least five days before the papers are presented to the court, or mailed to the other person at least ten days before the papers are presented to the judge.

FINDINGS OF FACT AND CONCLUSIONS OF LAW (REFEREE'S REPORT)

(form 22)

After you fill out the Referee's Report, the matrimonial referee assigned to your case will review and sign it. (see form 22, p.236.) The point at which you fill out this form will depend upon whether you submit an Affidavit of Plaintiff (form 11) or appear at a hearing to give testimony.

If you submit an Affidavit of Plaintiff (form 11) and do not give oral testimony, you should fill in the items on form 22 according to what you asked for in your Verified Complaint (form 7). Form 22 will then be submitted along with your other court papers.

If you give testimony, you will not be able to fill in form 22 until after the hearing. At the end of the hearing the referee will tell you what he or she is awarding. Do not try to write it all down. Instead, request a transcript from the court stenographer. He or she will call you when it is ready and after you send a check for the proper amount, he or she will mail it you. Copy what the referee awarded you from the transcript, using the exact language used by the referee. Depending upon the referee's wording, you may need to make changes to form 22. If you need help, call the referee's office. Do the best you can. Your referee may write in changes before signing it.

To complete the Findings of Fact and Conclusions of Law (Referee's Report) (see form 22, p.236):

1. Fill in the case heading and index number according to the instructions at the beginning of Chapter 6.

2. Check and circle whether the case has been submitted or heard orally.

3. In "Second" indicate the residency requirement.

4. In "Third" fill in the date and place of marriage.

5. In "Fifth" check and circle the type of summons you used and the date filed. Check and circle how it was served and the date served. Indicate the action the defendant has taken.

6. In "Sixth" indicate the military status of your spouse.

7. In "Seventh: complete information about the children/

8. In "Eighth" indicate the grounds and description, the same as in the complaint.

9. Choose the appropriate statement in "Ninth".

10. In "Tenth" circle that the parties have agreed if there is an agreement and indicate the amount, otherwise leave this blank to completed by the court.

11. In "Eleventh" indicate where the children live and leave the rest for the court to complete.

12. Allow the court to complete this.

13. In "Thirteenth" indicate if there are emancipated (children who are underage but who live on their own) or not. Fill in names and dates of birth of children.

14. In part B of Thirteenth, check one of 1-3. Allow the court to complete this section.

15. In "Fourteenth" fill in addresses and social security numbers. Also indicate health care information. Check "the parties have agreed or stipulated" if that is the case, otherwise allow the court to complete the rest.

16. In "Fifteenth" complete this section if the court has issued orders in your case up to this point.

17. In "Sixteenth" check and circle plaintiff if you will using a pre-martial name and indicate what it is.

18. Under "Conclusions of Law" indicate the section number for the grounds you chose.

JUDGMENT OF DIVORCE

(form 23)

The Judgment of Divorce is the document that makes your divorce final and official. (see form 23, p.244.) Once the Judgment of Divorce is signed by a judge, you will be divorced and free to remarry whenever you wish. It also means that you and your spouse are officially bound by the terms of the Judgment of Divorce. To complete the Judgment of Divorce:

1. Leave the lines in the top, right-hand corner blank.

2. Fill in the case heading and index number according to the instructions at the beginning of Chapter 6 leaving the "calendar number" blank. Do not make any changes in the first paragraph.

3. Complete the rest of the form in accordance with the way you completed the Findings of Fact and Conclusions of Law (Referee's Report).

UCS 113

(form 24)

The UCS 113 must be completed for court recordkeeping purposes. (see form 24, p.253.) The information to be filled in is straightforward. Fill in your name at the bottom as the person who prepared it.

CERTIFICATE OF DISSOLUTION

(form 25)

The Certificate of Dissolution must be filed with the clerk, along with a $5.00 filing fee. (see form 25, p.254.) To complete form 25:

1. Fill in your index number at the top left corner.

2. Fill in the section labeled "husband" with the husband's information, and do the same for the wife.

3. Next is an area to fill in information about where and when you were married, and the children of the marriage. Leave the "Decree" section blank.

4. Fill in the "Confidential Information" section for both husband and wife.

5. In number 23, fill in who was the plaintiff (husband or wife). For number 24, fill in the same name as in number 23. Fill in the grounds for divorce in number 25.

6. Sign the certificate and cross out "Attorney at Law."

Note on Procedure

If you had a hearing, submit the Findings of Fact and Conclusions of Law (Referee's Report) (form 22), Judgment of Divorce (form 23), transcript prepared by the court stenographer, and UCS 113 (form 24) together. If you submitted an Affidavit of Plaintiff (form 11), submit the Referee's Report, Judgment of Divorce, and UCS 113 with all of your other forms.

Once the Referee's Report and Judgment of Divorce are signed, they will be returned to you. Now your divorce is final, but there are a few more steps that need to completed. Bring the original Judgment of Divorce, original Referee's Report, original transcript (if any), original Verified Complaint, Affirmation (Affidavit) of Regularity, Statement of Net Worth, Certificate of Dissolution (instructions below), and any exhibits that were used at the hearing to the clerk's office for filing. The clerk will stamp the Judgment of Divorce with an official stamp. You will need to purchase at least two certified copies of the Judgment of Divorce. Next, you must complete a few more forms.

NOTICE OF ENTRY

(form 26)

After the Judgment of Divorce (form 23) has been signed by the judge and entered in the court clerk's office, you must mail a certified copy to your spouse. The Notice of Entry must be attached to the copy of the certified Judgment of Divorce you mail to your spouse. (see form 26, p.255.) To complete the Notice of Entry:

1. Fill in the case heading and index number according to the instructions at the beginning of Chapter 6.

2. Fill in the name of the county after the words "County of."

3. In the main paragraph, fill in the county where the court is located, and the date the Judgment of Divorce was *filed* in the clerk's office (*not* the date it was signed by the judge, but the date you filed it with the clerk).

4. Fill in the date, your name and address, and your spouse's name and address on the lines indicated.

5. Mail this form to your spouse, along with a certified copy of the Judgment of Divorce. You may obtain a certified copy of the Judgment of Divorce from the court clerk—for a fee. Also mail a copies of the Judgment of Divorce to the Family Court in your county and to the Support Collection Unit in your county if their services will be utilized.

Example of a Request for Index Number form:

81-1401.01 (Rev. 4/92)

Erie County Clerk
Buffalo, New York

Application for INDEX NUMBER
Pursuant to Section 8018 C.P.L.R.

APPLICANT MUST PRINT OR
TYPE ALL THREE SECTIONS

Index Number

Do not write in this space

TITLE OF ACTION OR PROCEEDING

FEE $170.00

_____ Supreme _____ Court, Erie County

MARY LOUISE SMITH

v.

JOHN DAVID SMITH

}

Date __July 7, 1999__

Type of Action

MATRIMONIAL

__Mary L. Smith, 123 Niagara St., Buffalo, NY 14240__
Name and Address of
Attorney for Plaintiff
or Petitioner

__John D. Smith, 28 Erie Dr., Buffalo, NY 14240__
Name and Address of
Attorney for Defendant
or Respondent

Checked by _____ Indexed by _____
Do not write on above line
DO NOT DETACH

These Two Sections will be Returned to Attorney filing Application

ERIE COUNTY CLERK
TITLE OF ACTION OR PROCEEDING

Complete

This Copy

MARY LOUISE SMITH

v.

JOHN DAVID SMITH

Endorse this INDEX
NUMBER on All Papers
Pertaining to this action
- FEE $170.00

Do not write in this space

RETAIN THIS COPY FOR YOUR RECORDS

ERIE COUNTY CLERK
TITLE OF ACTION OR PROCEEDING

Complete

This Copy

MARY LOUISE SMITH

v.

JOHN DAVID SMITH

Forward This Form or
Advise Adversary of
INDEX NUMBER Assigned

Do not write in this space

FORWARD THIS COPY OR INFORMATION TO ADVERSARY

Contested Divorce 10

Procedure Differences from Uncontested Divorce

This book cannot turn you into a trial lawyer. Although it has been done, it can be very risky to try to handle a contested case yourself. There are several differences between a contested and an uncontested case. First, in an uncontested case the judge will usually go along with whatever you and your spouse have worked out or whatever you are asking for (as long as it is not unreasonable) if your spouse does not appear. In a contested case, you need to prove that you are entitled to that for which you are asking. This means you will need a longer time for the hearing. You will also need to present papers as evidence, and you may even need to have witnesses testify for you.

Second, you may have to do some extra work to get the evidence you need, such as by sending out subpoenas (which are discussed in the next section of this chapter), or even hiring a private investigator. Also, you will need to pay extra attention to assure that your spouse is properly notified of any court hearings, and that he or she is sent copies of any papers you file with the court clerk.

When it becomes apparent that you have a contested divorce, it is probably time to consider hiring an attorney, especially if the issue of child custody is involved. If you are truly ready to go to war over custody, it shows that this is an extremely important matter for you, and you may want to get professional assistance. You can predict a contested case when your spouse is seriously threatening to fight you every inch of the way, or when he or she hires an attorney.

On the other hand, you should not assume that you need an attorney just because your spouse has hired one. Sometimes it will be easier to deal with the attorney than with your spouse. The attorney is not as emotionally involved and may see your settlement proposal as reasonable. So discuss things with your spouse's attorney first and see if things can be worked out. You can always hire your own lawyer if your spouse's is not reasonable. Just be very cautious about signing any papers until you are certain you understand what they mean. You may want to have an attorney review any papers prepared by your spouse's lawyer before you sign them.

Aside from deciding if you want a lawyer, there are two main procedure differences between the uncontested and the contested divorce. First, you will need to be more prepared for the hearing. Second, you will not prepare the Judgment of Divorce (form 23) until after the hearing with the judge, and you will not prepare the Findings of Fact and Conclusions of Law (form 22) at all. This is because you won't know what to put in the Judgment of Divorce until the judge decides the various matters in dispute.

The next chapter will discuss how to prepare for the issues to be argued at the hearing, and provide more information about how to prepare the Judgment of Divorce.

When your divorce is contested, some of the forms you file will be different. Instead of the Request for Judicial Intervention (form 19) and Note of Issue (form 18), that are used for uncontested divorces, you must use the contested type of these forms.

REQUEST FOR JUDICIAL INTERVENTION

(form 35)

The contested Request for Judicial Intervention must be completed and filed whenever you need a judge assigned to your case for the first time. (see form 35, p.270.) If you are filing a Notice of Motion or an Order to Show Cause (see Chapter 13), you need a judge to be assigned, and must file form 35. If not already filed, form 35 must be filed when you are ready for a pre-trial conference or trial. You will have to pay a filing fee with this form. To complete the contested Request for Judicial Intervention:

1. In the heading section, fill in the county at the top, and your index number and the date you bought it. Fill in your name on the "Plaintiff(s)" line, and your spouse's name on the "Defendant(s)" line. Mark whether a Bill of Particulars was served by you or your spouse.

2. Under "Nature of Judicial Intervention," check request for "Request for preliminary conference" if you are ready to go ahead to a pre-trial and then a trial. Check "Notice of motion" if that is what you are filing. Check "Order to show cause" if that is what you are filing.

3. Under "Nature of Action or Proceeding," check the box for "Contested" under "Matrimonial."

4. For the "yes or no" questions on the second page of the form, check "no" for all but the question "Does this action/proceeding seek equitable relief?" If you are seeking to have property distributed, check "yes" for this question.

5. Fill in the names and addresses of the attorneys, if there are any. If not, use your name and your spouse's.

6. Leave the section marked "Insurance Carriers" blank.

7. Sign and date it at the bottom, filling your address. Remember to pay the fee when you file it.

NOTE OF ISSUE AND CERTIFICATE OF READINESS

(form 36) The Note of Issue and Certificate of Readiness must be filed when you are ready for trial. (see form 36, p.272.) You are not ready for trial if discovery is still being completed or if you are scheduled for a pre-trial conference. To complete the Note of Issue and Certificate of Readiness:

1. Fill in your index number, case heading, and name of the judge.

2. Under "Notice for Trial," check the box for "Trial without jury." (Although you have the right to a jury trial, a jury trial is beyond the scope of this book. If you want a jury—get a lawyer!)

3. After "Filed by," fill in your name. On the lines below that, fill in the date the Summons was served, and the date service was completed.

4. Under "Nature of Action or Special Proceeding," check "Contested Matrimonial."

5. At the lower, left-hand side of the first page, fill in your and your spouse's names and addresses (or those of any attorneys involved).

6. On the second page in the left column, you must indicate how this was served on your spouse. You should try to get him or her to admit service (bottom left). If he or she won't, then it must be personally delivered, and the top part must be completed by the server.

7. In the right column, for items 1 through 7, check whether each item is complete, waived, or not required. Check "Completed" for numbers 1, 6, and 7. For the other numbers, check "Completed" if it was done, and "Not Required" if it was not done.

8. For numbers 8 through 10, check "Yes." Leave item 11 blank and check "Yes" for item 12.

9. Sign and date it, and fill in your address. Ask your spouse to sign at the bottom right. You must sign here as well. If your spouse will not sign, leave that part blank.

> **Note on Procedure**
>
> Another difference in a contested case is that once a judge is assigned to your case, you file all papers (except the Note of Issue and all the papers filed after the Judgment of Divorce is signed) with the judge's office, not the clerk's office.
>
> If a Law Guardian is assigned to your case, you must send him or her copies of all the things you send to your spouse.

MOTIONS

In this chapter and the following chapters, there are instructions about how to complete motion papers. A *motion* is the way you ask the court to do something for you, like sign a subpoena, allow you to use an alternate form of service, or give you temporary child support.

For any type of motion you will need to prepare and file a *notice of motion*, as well as the motion itself and any supporting papers such as affidavits. The court will notify you of the date and time your motion will be heard, which will be filled in on the notice of motion. You will then send these papers to your spouse or his or her attorney.

When you appear in court at the designated time, there will most likely be many other cases on the calendar that day. Check in with the courtroom clerk or bailiff and wait for your case to be called. When it is called, stand at one of the empty tables before the bench. If there are no tables, or if they are occupied, stand before the bench. Explain to the judge why you need what you are requesting. Your spouse, or his or her attorney, will have a chance to respond to what you say.

Collecting Information and Obtaining Subpoenas

The court rules require each party to file a Statement of Net Worth. (see form 10, p.195.) If your spouse has indicated that he or she will not cooperate, and will not provide a Statement of Net Worth, you may have to try to get the information yourself. You can go to the hearing and tell the judge that your spouse will not cooperate, but the judge may just issue an order requiring your spouse to provide information (or be held in contempt of court), and continue the hearing to another date. It may help to speed things up if you are able to get the information yourself and have it available at the hearing. This will require you to get a Subpoena Duces Tecum issued. (see form 40, p.278.)

If you were able to do a good job of making copies of important papers while preparing to file for divorce, you should have the information you need to figure out where you need to send subpoenas. Your spouse's income information can be obtained from his or her employer. Stock and bond information can be obtained from his or her stock broker; bank account balances from the bank; auto loan balances from the lender; etc. You can have subpoenas issued to any or all of these places, but do not overdo it. Concentrate on income information (especially if you are asking for, or expect to pay, child support or maintenance), and information about major property items. It may not be necessary to send out subpoenas if you already have recent copies of the papers relating to these items. At the hearing, you can always show the judge the copies of your spouse's paystubs, W-2 tax statements, or other papers.

Before you send a Subpoena Duces Tecum to your spouse's employer, bank, or accountant, you need to let your spouse know what you are about to do. The thought that you are about to get these other people involved in your divorce may be enough to get your spouse to cooperate. If your spouse calls and says "I'll give you the information," give him or her a few days to follow through. Ask when you can expect to receive his or her completed Statement of Net Worth, and offer to send your spouse another blank copy if he or she needs one. If your spouse sends a completed Statement of Net Worth as promised, don't send the Subpoena Duces Tecum. If your spouse doesn't follow through, go ahead with the Subpoena Duces Tecum. You can send out subpoenas to as many people or organizations as you need, but you will need to use the following procedure for each subpoena.

NOTICE OF MOTION FOR SUBPOENA DUCES TECUM (form 39)

Only an attorney or a judge has the power to issue a subpoena. Therefore, you must ask the court to sign your subpoena. First, fill out the Notice of Motion for Subpoena Duces Tecum. (see form 39, p.276.) Fill in the heading and fill in your name and address at the bottom. Fill in your spouse's name or that of his or her attorney after "To:" The Court will fill in the date your motion will be heard.

SUBPOENA DUCES TECUM (form 40)

Next, fill out the affidavit attached to the motion. Complete the heading and index number and fill in your name on the first line. In number 1, fill in the names of all people or businesses, and what information you need from them. Sign before a notary and attach it to the Notice of Motion for Subpoena Duces Tecum (form 39).

To complete the Subpoena Duces Tecum (see form 40, p.278):

1. Fill in the case heading and index number according to the instructions at the beginning of Chapter 6.

2. After "To:" fill in one name or business.

3. Attach a separate sheet of paper and list on it everything you want that person or business to provide. Remember, you will need to prepare a separate subpoena for each person or business.

4. The second paragraph says that the person may just provide the documents and need not appear in court. If you want the person to appear to testify as well as to produce the documents, cross out this paragraph. If you want the person to appear and testify as to matters not contained in the documents, you will need to prepare

the Notice of Motion for Subpoena for Appearance (form 41) and Subpoena for Appearance (form 42), described below.

SERVING THE
SUBPOENA
DUCES TECUM

File the papers with the court. When you receive the papers back with the motion hearing date filled in on the Notice of Motion for Subpoena Duces Tecum (form 39), send them to your spouse (or his or her attorney). Appear at the court date and explain to the judge why you need these records. Once the judge signs the Subpoena Duces Tecum (form 40), have it served on the person or business.

Next, have the sheriff personally serve the Subpoena to the person or place named in the Subpoena. The sheriff will need at least one extra copy of the Subpoena, and a check for the service fee. The employer, bank, etc., should send the requested information to you, or to the court where you will be able to access it. If the employer, bank, etc., calls you and says you must pay for copies, ask how much they will cost and send a check or money order (if the amount is not too high and you do not already have some fairly recent income information).

If the employer, bank, etc., does not provide the information, you can try sending a letter to the employer, bank, etc., saying: "unless you provide the information requested in the Subpoena Duces Tecum within seven days, a motion for contempt will be filed with the Supreme Court." This may scare the employer, bank, etc., into sending you the information. The sheriff will have also filed an affidavit verifying when the Subpoena Duces Tecum was served. There are more procedures you could go through to force the employer, bank, etc., to give the information. Still, it probably is not worth the hassle and you would more than likely need an attorney to help you with it. At the final hearing, you can tell the judge that your spouse refused to provide information, and that the Subpoena was not honored by the employer, bank, etc. The judge may do something to help you out, or may advise you to see a lawyer to pursue it further.

There are other ways to get documents and information from your spouse or his or her attorney, but you should really retain an attorney if you get to that point. If you wish to do this on your own, your options include notices for discovery, inspections, and depositions. You can also issue demands for witness lists and demands for statements. Go to your local law library to get forms for these and to read the law about what procedure to follow.

WITNESS
SUBPOENAS

If you need to compel witnesses to appear and testify for you in court, you will need to use the Notice of Motion for Subpoena for Appearance (form 41) and the Subpoena for Appearance (form 42). For example, if your spouse is always late picking up your child from daycare, you may want to have the daycare provider testify as to this; or if your spouse came to the marital residence and removed all of the expensive items and now denies it, you can have your neighbor testify if she saw it occur.

> ***Important Note:*** In selecting your witnesses, it is important to have a basic understanding of what is commonly called the hearsay rule. Basically, this rule says that a person can only testify about something he or she knows about firsthand. This applies to you and any of your witnesses. For example, you can testify that you saw your spouse hit your child, but you cannot testify that your mother told you she saw your spouse hit your child. In this example, you would need to have your mother testify as to what she saw. If you (or your witness) didn't see or hear it happening, you (or your witness) can't tell the court about it. You must have the person who saw or heard it firsthand testify about it.

Complete the Notice of Motion for Subpoena for Appearance in the same way as the Notice of Motion for Subpoena Duces Tecum. (see form 39, p.276.) Explain who you need to testify and why. Complete the Subpoena for Appearance — one for each witness — and file the papers with the court. (see form 42, p.281.)

Once you receive them back with the date filled in on form 41, mail them to your spouse. Appear before the court and explain why you need the subpoena or subpoenas signed. Once the court signs the Subpoena for Appearance (form 42), have it served on the person you want to testify. You would be wise to speak to that person before the trial to get an idea as to his or her testimony. You need not subpoena people, like your mother, who you are sure will come. Only have those witnesses who can tell the court something important about your children or assets, income or debts. Do not waste the court's time with witnesses who will testify about what a bad person your spouse is or what a great person you are. Be aware that you must pay each witness a witness fee of $15 plus twenty-three cents per mile that he or she traveled to get to court. Check with the judge's law clerk to be sure this is the current figure.

PROPERTY AND DEBTS

Generally, the judge will look at your property and debts, and will try to divide them up "fairly." This does not necessarily mean they will be divided 50-50. What you want to do is offer the judge a reasonable solution that looks fair.

Now review the Property Inventory (form 1) and the Debt Inventory (form 2) you prepared earlier. For each item or property note which of the following categories it fits into (it may fit into more than one):

1. You really want.

2. You'd like to have.

3. You don't care either way.

4. Your spouse really wants.

5. Your spouse would like to have.

6. Your spouse doesn't care either way.

Now start a list of what each of you should end up with, using the categories listed above. You will eventually end up with a list of things you can probably get with little difficulty (you really want and your spouse doesn't care), those which you'll fight over (you both really want), and those which need to be divided but can probably be easily divided equally (you both don't really care).

At the hearing the judge will probably try to get you to work out your disagreements, but he won't put up with arguing for very long. In the end he will arbitrarily divide up the items you can't agree upon, or he may order you to sell those items and divide the money you get equally.

On the few items that are really important to you, it may be necessary for you to try to prove why you should get them. It will help if you can convince the judge of one or more of the following:

1. You paid for the item out of your own earnings or funds.

2. You are the one who primarily uses that item.

3. You use the item in your employment, business, or hobby.

4. You are willing to give up something else you really want in exchange for that item. (Of course you will try to give up something from your "don't care" or your "like to have" list.)

5. The item is needed for your children (assuming you'll have custody).

Next, make up a list of how you think the property should be divided. Make it a reasonably fair and equal list, regardless of how angry you are at your spouse. Even if the judge changes some of it to appear fair to your spouse, you will most likely get more of what you want than if you don't offer a suggestion. (No, this is not an exception to the negotiating rule of letting your spouse make the first offer because at this point you are no longer just negotiating with your spouse. You are now negotiating with the judge. At this point you are trying to impress the judge with your fairness; not trying to convince your spouse.)

Special problems arise if a claim of separate property becomes an issue. This may be in terms of your spouse trying to get your separate property, or in terms of you trying to get property you feel your spouse is wrongly claiming to be separate. Basically, separate property is property either of you had before you were married, and kept separate or any property you received by gift or inheritance. (Refer to Chapter 5.)

It is also a good idea to have any papers that prove that the property you claim to be separate property is actually separate property. These would be papers showing that:

☞ You bought the item before you were married (such as dated sales receipts).

☞ You inherited the item as your own property (such as certified copies of wills and probate court papers).

☞ You got the property by exchanging it for property you had before you got married, or for property you received as a gift or through an inheritance (such as a statement from the person you made the exchange with, or some kind of receipt showing what was exchanged).

If you want to get at assets your spouse is claiming are separate assets, you will need to collect the following types of evidence:

☞ Papers showing that you helped pay for the asset (such as a check that you wrote, or bank statements showing that your money went into the same account that was used to make payments on the asset). For example, suppose your spouse purchased a house before you got married. During your marriage you made some of the mortgage payments with your own checking account. (You will have cancelled checks, hopefully, with the mortgage account number on them to prove this.) At other times, you deposited some of your paychecks into your spouse's checking account, and your spouse wrote checks from that account to pay the mortgage. (Again, there should be some bank records and cancelled checks can show that this was done.) Since you contributed to the purchase of the house, you can claim some of the value of the house as a marital asset.

☞ Papers showing that you paid for repairs of the asset. If you paid for repairs on the home, or a car your spouse had before you were married, you can claim part of the value.

☞ Papers showing that the asset was improved, or increased in value during your marriage. Example 1: Your spouse owned the house before you were married. During your marriage, you and your spouse added a family room to the house. This will enable you to make a claim for some of the value of the house. Example 2: Your spouse owned the house before you were married. The day before you got married, the house was worth $85,000: now the house is appraised at $115,000. You can claim part of the $30,000 of increased value.

If you want to make a claim on what would otherwise appear to be your spouse's separate property, list what you want in your summons. Also list it in your complaint and give an explanation as to why you are entitled to it or a part of it. At the trial you will need to testify and provide evidence proving why you are entitled to it. The judge will consider this and listen to any witnesses you call and make a decision.

The judge will either announce at the hearing who gets which items, or notify you in writing by preparing the Judgment of Divorce. If the judge announces his or her decision at the hearing, make a list of this as the judge tells you, then complete the Judgment of Divorce accordingly. (see form 23, p.244.)

Once you have completed the Judgment of Divorce, mail or deliver it to the judge along with a cover letter stating: "Enclosed is my proposed Judgment of Divorce, which is being submitted to you for approval and signature. Thank you." At the bottom of the cover letter put "cc:" followed by the name of your spouse (or his or her attorney). Mail or deliver the original letter and original Judgment of Divorce to the judge, and mail copies of the letter and Judgment of Divorce to your spouse (or his or her attorney). If your spouse (or his or her attorney) does not object, the judge will sign the Judgment of Divorce and return a copy to you and your spouse. Follow the instructions in Chapter 9 for how to file the Judgment of Divorce with the court clerk.

CHILD CUSTODY AND VISITATION

Start out by reviewing the guidelines the judge will use to decide the custody question. These can be found in Chapter 5. For each item listed in that section, write down an explanation of how that item applies to you. This will be your argument when you have your hearing with the judge.

Many custody battles revolve around the moral fitness of one or both of the parents. If you become involved in this type of a custody fight, you should consult a lawyer. Charges of moral unfitness (such as illegal drug use, child abuse, immoral sexual conduct) can require long court hearings involving the testimony of many witnesses, as well as possibly the employment of private investigators. For such a hearing, you will require the help of an attorney who knows the law, what questions to ask witnesses, and the rules of evidence.

However, if the only question is whether you or your spouse have been the main caretaker of the child, you can always have friends, neighbors and relatives come into the hearing (if they are willing to help you out) to testify on your behalf. And it may not be necessary for you to have an attorney. But, if you need to subpoena unwilling witnesses to testify, you should have an attorney.

The judge's decision regarding custody will have to be put into the Judgment of Divorce. Read Chapter 9 for instructions on preparing the Judgment of Divorce.

CHILD SUPPORT

In New York, as in most states, the question of child support is mostly a matter of a mathematical calculation. Getting a fair child support amount depends upon the accuracy of the income information presented to the judge. If you feel fairly sure that the information your spouse presents is accurate, or that you have obtained accurate information about his or her income, there isn't much about which to argue. The judge will simply take the income information provided, use the formula to calculate the amount to be paid, and order that amount to be paid.

In most cases, there will not be much room to dispute the amount of child support, so there usually is not a need to get an attorney. If you claim your spouse has not provided accurate income information, it will be up to you to prove this to the judge by showing the income information you have obtained from your spouse's employer or other source of income.

The judge's decision regarding child support will have to be put into the Judgment of Divorce. Read Chapter 9 for instructions on preparing the Judgment of Divorce.

MAINTENANCE (ALIMONY)

A dispute over maintenance may require a lawyer, especially if there is a request for permanent maintenance because of a disability. Such a claim may require the testimony of expert witnesses (such as doctors, accountants, and actuaries), which requires the special knowledge of an attorney.

If maintenance has been requested, take a look at the section of the Verified Complaint (form 7) asking for maintenance, and review the reasons maintenance was requested. These reasons will be the subject of the court hearing on this question. You should determine what information (including papers and the testimony of witnesses) you will need to present to the judge to either support or refute the reasons maintenance was requested.

For temporary maintenance, the most common reason is that the person needs help until he or she can get training to enter the work force. The questions that will need to be answered are:

1. What has the person been trained for in the past?

2. What type of training is needed before the person can again be employable in that field?

3. How long will this training take?

4. What amount of income can be expected upon employment?

5. How much money is required for the training?

Questions that may be asked in either a temporary or a permanent maintenance situation include: an examination of the situation of the parties during their marriage that led to the person not working or not fully pursuing his or her career, and what contribution to the marriage that person made. You should be prepared to present evidence regarding these questions.

PROVING GROUNDS

UNCONTESTED
GROUNDS

In most contested cases, the parties agree that they want to be divorced, but disagree as to custody or property matters. If this is true in your case, your spouse will agree not to contest the grounds in your divorce. When you have your hearing, or even if you reach a settlement before a trial, you will still need to testify as to grounds. Your spouse will leave the room and you will give your testimony about the grounds. Simply explain which grounds you are using, and give the details as they were described in Chapter 9 in the instructions for the Verified Compliant (form 7). There will then be a regular hearing regarding the matter upon which you and your spouse disagree.

CONTESTED
GROUNDS

Should your spouse decide that he or she does not want to be divorced, you will have what is called a *grounds trial*. You would be well-advised to have an attorney in such a case. Should you decide not to hire one, you will need to provide very specific details about specific incidents to support your grounds. For example, you may need to testify about arguments you and your spouse had, any violence that occurred, what your spouse said to you, as well as the exact dates of such incidents. You may need to have witnesses who were present at such incidents testify as to what they saw and heard. Your spouse or his or her attorney will attempt to prove either that these things never happened at all, or that you are the one who caused or provoked the arguments and behaved violently.

APPEALS

NOTICE OF
APPEAL
(form 43)

After the judge decides your case, if you feel he or she did not decide fairly about anything, you have the right to appeal the judge's decision. To do this, you must file a Notice of Appeal. (see form 43, p.282.) Do this within thirty days of the day you receive the signed Judgment of Divorce. You will definitely need an attorney to handle the appeal.

The appeal will be heard by the next highest level of New York courts, the Appellate Division. In an appeal, the appellate court reviews the papers and transcript from your case and decides if the trial judge made any mistakes. The only thing considered is whether the judge followed the law. There is no opportunity to present more evidence, give more testimony or change the way you did things during the case.

If you do not file the Notice of Appeal within the time limit, you will not be allowed to appeal. You can however file it and withdraw it at any point. So, to be safe, if you are not sure if you want to appeal, file the form and you can always withdraw it later.

To complete the Notice of Appeal (see form 43, p.282):

1. Fill in the case heading and index number according to the instructions at the beginning of Chapter 6.

2. After "Please take notice that," fill in your name.

3. Call the clerk's office and ask them what Judicial Department you are in; the first, second, third, or fourth; and fill that in before "Department."

4. Fill in the county where your case was filed after "county of," and fill in the judge's name after "Hon. J.." Fill in the county again before "county."

5. Date it and fill in your name and address at the bottom right.

6. After "To:" fill in your spouse's name and address or that of his or her attorney, the court clerk and address, and that of your Law Guardian if you have one. Mail it to all of these people.

THE COURT HEARING 11

REASONS FOR A HEARING

UNCONTESTED
CASES

There are several ways you could end up having a hearing, even in an uncontested case. The first is if your divorce is uncontested, but you did not complete the Affidavit of Plaintiff. (see form 11, p.214.) If this happens, you will need to appear before a matrimonial referee and testify as to all of the information that would have been included in your Affidavit of Plaintiff had you filed one.

A second way you may have a hearing is if your divorce is uncontested and you did complete the Affidavit of Plaintiff (form 11), but the matrimonial referee thinks that the information in it is incomplete, or if he or she has questions to ask you. You will need to appear and testify as to whatever information the referee asks you.

CONTESTED
CASES

A third way you could be scheduled for a hearing is if your divorce is contested. Unless you and your spouse reach a settlement, you will definitely have a pre-trial conference before the judge's law clerk. The purposes of a pre-trial conference are to identify what issues are in dispute, and to try to get you and your spouse to reach a settlement. If you do not reach a settlement at that point, you will have a trial before the judge.

PREPARATION

WHAT PAPERS
TO BRING

You should bring copies of all papers to the hearing, including the following documents:

☞ All documents filed in your case (these should also be in the court clerk's file);

☞ Your most recent paystub, Federal income tax return, and W-2 forms, and any other papers showing your or your spouse's financial situation;

☞ Any papers showing your spouse's income or property;

☞ Any Family Court orders;

☞ Deeds to any real estate and titles to any vehicles;

☞ Any papers showing marital debt; and

☞ Any items you want to use as evidence, such as proof of child abuse, proof your spouse has been convicted of a crime, experts' reports, etc.

THE HEARING

If you testify before a referee, your hearing will be in a small courtroom or conference room. If you have a trial before the judge, you will appear in a regular courtroom.

When you arrive, go into the assigned room. There will usually be either a court clerk or a bailiff who will take your name. If there is not, have a seat and wait until your case is called.

OPENING
STATEMENTS

When your case is called, you will be told where to sit. If this is a contested case, you will first have a chance to give an opening statement. Simply describe what you are asking the judge to do and very briefly explain how you will prove you are right. Your spouse will also have an opportunity to give an opening statement.

TESTIMONY

Next, you will swear to tell the truth, sit on the witness stand and give formal testimony. Before you go, try to have an outline of the things you need to say. If you do not have an attorney, you will simply talk and tell the judge everything you have to say. If you have an attorney, he or she will ask you questions and you will answer them. When you are done, if your divorce is uncontested, the referee may ask you some questions. Answer them carefully and if you do not understand, tell the referee.

If you have any information which is different and more current than what is in the Statement of Net Worth (form 10), you should mention to the judge that you have more current information. You will then give a copy of whatever papers you have to show the changed situation (such as current paystub showing an increase in pay, or a current bank statement showing a new balance). The judge may ask to see any papers you have to prove what you have put in your Statement of Net Worth. Your basic job at the hearing is to answer the judge's questions, and give the judge the information he or she needs to give you a divorce.

If there are any items upon which you and your spouse have not yet agreed, tell the judge what these items are. Refer to Chapter 10, relating to the contested divorce, for more information about how to handle these unresolved issues. Be prepared to make a suggestion as to how these matters should be settled, and to explain to the judge why your suggestion is the best solution. If the judge asks for any information that you have not brought with you, tell the judge that you do not have it with you but you will be happy to provide him or her with the information by the end of the following day. Just be sure you get the papers to the judge as you promised.

If your divorce is contested, after you are done with your outline, your spouse or his or her attorney will ask you questions. If there is a Law Guardian, he or she may also ask you questions. If you have any witnesses, you would call them next and ask them questions. Then your spouse will testify, as well as any witnesses he or she may have. You may ask your spouse and the witnesses questions. After all the testimony is taken, the judge may ask you to give a final argument. Just simply say what it is you want the court to do for you and why.

If at any point you feel you are lost or confused, if your spouse's attorney makes technical objections, if you are not managing to say what you need to say, tell the judge you would now like an attorney and are requesting an adjournment to retain one. The judge will stop the hearing and schedule a new date. You have the right to do this at any point in any court appearance, so do not be afraid to ask for it.

If your divorce is contested, do not be surprised if it takes several court appearances to complete your case. There will be other cases on the calendar and you will not have the whole day or whole half day for which you are scheduled. However, you must come prepared to do the whole trial because you cannot guess how much time you will have.

When You Can't Find Your Spouse

12

What do you do if your spouse has run off or has moved and you do not know where to tell the sheriff or process server to go? What if you know where your spouse works, but not where he or she is living? What if you know where he or she lives, but the process server cannot ever seem to catch up with him or her?

Types of Alternative Service

There are several other methods of service that can be used; however, you must first get a court order allowing you to do so. First read about the types of service available.

SERVICE UPON A "PERSON OF SUITABLE AGE AND DISCRETION"

If you know where your spouse lives or works, but the server can never catch up with him or her, the Summons can be given to someone else at your spouse's residence or to someone else who works at your spouse's place of employment. The person it is served upon must be "of suitable age and discretion." Basically, this means that it should not be served on anyone under the age of eighteen or anyone who is clearly mentally disabled. In addition to such delivery, the Summons must also be mailed by first class mail to your spouse. The envelope must say "personal and confidential" and must not indicate on the outside what it is regarding. The delivery and mailing must happen within twenty days of each other and the Affidavit of Service must be filed within twenty days of mailing or service, whichever happens last.

AFFIXING TO A DOOR

If you know where your spouse lives or works, but cannot find him or her to serve and cannot find a person of suitable age and discretion at either location, the Summons can be affixed (usually by tape or a thumbtack) to the door of your spouse's residence. One copy must also be mailed by first class mail. This method is commonly known as "nail and mail." The copy affixed to the door and the mailed copy must each be in an envelope addressed to your spouse, must be marked "personal and confidential," and must not indicate what it is regarding. Both types of service must happen within twenty days of each other and the Affidavit of Service must be filed within twenty days of whichever type happens last. This method can only be used if *due diligence* has been used to locate your spouse and a person of suitable age and discretion. (Due diligence is explained in the next section of this chapter.) This means the server must have tried numerous times to serve the Summons, but was unable.

SERVICE BY PUBLICATION

If you do not have an address where your spouse might be found, or if neither of the other methods of service were successful, you can use *service by publication*. This is where either the Summons with Notice (form 4), or the Summons (form 5) and the Verified Complaint (form 7), are published in the English language in one newspaper that is most likely to be seen by your spouse. You will want to use a Summons with Notice (form 4), as there is no need to print the details of your life in a newspaper (as would be done if you published the entire Verified Complaint). It must be published at least once a week for three successive weeks. The Summons, including the Notice of Publication (this is the actual item that appears in the newspaper), must also be mailed to your spouse on or before the first day of publication unless you cannot with due diligence find out where to send mail so that your spouse will receive it. The first publication must be made within thirty days after the court order is granted. The Affidavit of Service must be filed within twenty days after the last publication. (see form 29, p.259.)

SEARCHING FOR YOUR SPOUSE

All of these types of service require the use of due diligence to locate your spouse. Due diligence can include:

- ☛ checking the phone book and directory assistance in the area where your spouse was last known to live;

- ☛ asking friends and relatives if they know where your spouse might be;

- ☛ checking with the post office where your spouse last lived for a forwarding address;

- ☛ checking with the Department of Motor Vehicles to see if your spouse has any car registrations; or

- ☛ checking with anyone else who may know where to find your spouse such as landlords or former employers.

If you are able to find a current address or current place of employment for your spouse, go back to using personal service. If not, you will have to list any of these steps that you have taken when you ask the court for permission to use one of these methods.

FORMS AND PROCEDURES FOR ALTERNATE SERVICE

If you wish to have your spouse served using one of the methods described above, you must file a Notice of Motion for Alternate Service. (see form 27, p.256.) You must file it along with the Request for Judicial Intervention. (see form 19, p.232.) You will have already filed your Request for Index Number and Summons. A judge will be assigned to hear your motion. You will receive form 27 back from the court with the time and date it will be heard filled in by the court. You do not need to send a copy to your spouse or his or her attorney. (After all, if you knew where to send it, you would not need alternative service). When you appear in court, explain why you need to be able to serve your spouse this way.

NOTICE OF MOTION FOR ALTERNATE SERVICE

To complete the Notice of Motion for Alternate Service (see form 27, p.256):

1. Fill in the case name and index number according to the instructions at the beginning of Chapter 6.

2. In the first sentence, leave the time and date blank for the court to complete.

3. Next there are three lines that begin with the words "Allowing Plaintiff." Cross out all but the type of service you are requesting, and check the box for your request. If you choose service by publication, fill in the name of the newspaper you would like to use.

4. Fill in your name and address on the three blank lines at the bottom of the page and fill in your spouse's name after "To" at the bottom left-hand corner.

5. The next page is your affidavit, which must be attached to the Notice of Motion for Alternative Service. Fill in the heading and index number and put your name on the first blank line. Fill in the information in number 1 and the type of service you are seeking in number 2. In number 3, fill in where your spouse is living. If you don't know, fill in "unknown." Do the same for his or her place of business. Fill in the number of attempts that have been made to serve your spouse. If none have been made, cross out this sentence. If you do not know where your spouse is, fill in the paragraph describing the steps you have taken to locate him or her. If you have any other information about where your spouse can be found, fill it in in the last paragraph.

6. Date the form and sign it before a notary, filling in your address under your name.

If attempts at service have been made, have the server complete the affidavit on the next page of the form. The server should fill in the dates, times. and places of attempts in number 1. In number 2, it should be explained why service was unsuccessful; for example: "Defendant was not home or did not answer the door," "Defendant had moved out," "Defendant no longer was employed there," etc. This must be signed before a notary and attached to the Notice of Motion for Alternative Service.

ORDER DIRECTING SERVICE (form 28)

Next, fill out the Order Directing Service. (see form 28, p.258.) This is what the judge signs which allows you to have your spouse served in the manner you are requesting. To complete the Order Directing Service:

1. Fill in the heading and index number.

2. Fill in your name in the first blank in the first line and the date you signed the affidavit.

3. Fill in the name of the server in the second long blank and the date that affidavit was signed. If service has not been attempted, cross out the part of the sentence about the server. If your spouse cannot be located, cross out "Appearing that __ attempts have been made to serve Defendant personally." If your spouse can be located, cross out "Appearing that the present whereabouts of the Defendant cannot be ascertained" and fill in how many attempts at service have been made.

4. You will cross out two of the three paragraphs beginning with the word "ORDERED," leaving the one that you want checked. If you are seeking service by publication, fill in the name of the newspaper you want to use and where it is published. Leave the date and signature blank for the judge to complete. The judge may sign this at the time you appear for the motion or may mail it to you.

PUBLICATION AND AFFIDAVIT OF SERVICE (form 29)

Once you have the signed order, you may have your spouse served. If you are going to use publication, the newspaper will provide you with an affidavit of service and proof of publication for you to file. If you are using one of the other two methods, your server must complete an Affidavit of Service. (see form 29, p.259.) Fill out form 29 as follows:

1. Fill in the case heading and index number, as well as information about the process server.

2. Check the appropriate box to indicate what was served.

3. Check the box for "suitable age person" if that was how it was served. Mark where it was served and the name of the person served. If service was by affixing to a door, check that box and check where it was affixed and how many times prior to this personal service was attempted.

4. Check the box for "mailing use with" and fill in with the address of where it was mailed. If service was made on a person of suitable age, the "description of recipient" portion must be completed and a description must be given of the person with whom the Summons was left. The box for military service should not be completed.

5. The process server must sign this before a notary.

SPECIAL CIRCUMSTANCES 13

WHEN YOU CAN'T AFFORD COURT COSTS

If you can't afford to pay the filing fee and other costs associated with the divorce, you will need to file a Notice of Motion for Permission to Proceed as a Poor Person. (see form 30, p.260.) In order to qualify for a waiver of the filing fee, you must be "indigent." If you are indigent, your income is probably low enough for you to qualify for public assistance (welfare).

> *Caution:* If you decide to use this form, you will probably be asked for more information to prove that you meet the requirements for being declared indigent, and are eligible to have the filing and service fees waived. Before you file this form, you may want to see if the court clerk will give you any information on what is required to be declared indigent. You should also be aware that you can be held in contempt of court for giving false information on this form.

Form 30 should be filed at the time you file your Summons. Go to the clerk's office with this form and your Summons. Do not purchase an index number. Hand the papers to the clerk and explain that you want to file a Summons but that you need permission to do so as a poor person. Should you become indigent at some point during a case that has already begun, you may file this form at that time and not have to pay any further fees.

NOTICE OF
MOTION FOR
PERMISSION TO
PROCEED AS A
POOR PERSON
(form 30)

To complete the Notice of Motion for Permission to Proceed as a Poor Person (see form 30, p.260):

1. Fill in your case name. Leave the index number blank.

2. Fill in your name and address at the bottom right.

3. Fill in your spouse's name after "To." However, you do not need to send this to your spouse.

4. Now you need to complete the portion of form 30 titled "Affidavit in Support of Application to Proceed as a Poor Person." First, fill in your case heading. Leave the index number blank. Then fill in the county and place your name on the first long blank.

5. Fill in your address and how long you have lived there in number 1.

6. In number 2, fill in "divorce" for the first sentence and the grounds for the second sentence.

7. Complete the information about your income in number 3.

8. In number 4, fill in information about your property and its value.

9. Complete number 7 only if you have previously made this request in this same case.

10. Sign the form before a notary.

POOR PERSON
ORDER
(form 31)

You must also complete the Poor Person Order. (see form 31, p.263.). To complete the Poor Person Order:

1. Leave the section at the top right-hand corner blank. Fill in your case heading, leaving the index number blank.

2. In the first paragraph, fill in your name in the first blank and the date you signed the affidavit. If you have an attorney, he or she must file a certificate stating your case has merit. Fill in this information after "the certificate of." If you do not have an attorney, leave this blank.

3. In the second paragraph, after the words "claim based upon," fill in the name and section number of your grounds and describe the incidents that you described in your Verified Complaint.

4. In the fourth paragraph, after the words "Now on motion c., ..." in your name.

5. In the fifth paragraph, fill in your name in the blank after "ORDERED that" and your spouse's name in the second blank.

You may have to appear before a judge who may ask you questions to make sure you qualify for having your fees waived. If your fees are waived, you will receive a signed copy of the Poor Person Order. This will need to be filed in the clerk's office and you will also need to provide a copy to the sheriff to have the fee for process service waived. Be aware that the Poor Person Order only applies to certain government agencies and fees (e.g., court fees and the sheriff's process serving fees). A private process server is not required to waive the fee for service. If you have to publish the Summons in a newspaper, you will still have to pay the newspaper's fee.

PROTECTING YOURSELF, YOUR CHILDREN, AND YOUR PROPERTY

Some people have special concerns when getting prepared to file for a divorce: Fear of physical attack by their spouse, fear that their spouse will take the children and run away or hide, and fear that their spouse will try to take the marital property and hide it. There are additional legal papers you can file if you are in either of these situations.

Of course, if your spouse is determined and resourceful, there is no guaranteed way to prevent the things discussed in this section from happening. All you can do is put as many obstacles in his or her way as possible, and prepare your spouse to suffer legal consequences for acting improperly.

PROTECTING YOURSELF

If your spouse has ever physically harmed you or threatened to harm you, go to Family Court and ask the clerk to help you file a petition to obtain an Order of Protection. This will order your spouse to stay away from you and/or not harm you. You may have an Order of Protection continued in your Judgment of Divorce. Ask for it in your Summons, Verified Complaint and Affidavit of Plaintiff.

PROTECTING YOUR CHILDREN

If you fear physical violence directed at your children, you can use the same procedures you would use for protecting yourself from violence. If you are worried that your spouse may try to kidnap your children, you should make sure that the day care center, baby-sitter, relative, or whomever you leave the children with at any time is aware that you are in the process of a divorce and that the children are only to be released to you personally (not to your spouse or to any other relative, friend, etc.). To prevent your spouse from taking the children out of the United States, you can apply for a passport for each child. Once a passport is issued, the government will not issue another. So get their passport and lock it up in a safe deposit box. (This will not prevent them from being taken to Canada or Mexico, where passports are not required, but will prevent them from being taken overseas.) You can also file a motion to prevent the removal of the children from the state and to deny passport services. You should be able to obtain forms for this motion from the court clerk of your local law library.

PROTECTING YOUR PROPERTY

If you genuinely fear that your spouse will try to remove money from bank accounts and try to hide important papers showing what property you own, you may want to take this same action before your spouse can. However, you can make a great deal of trouble for yourself with the judge if you do this to try to get these assets for yourself. So make a complete list of any property you do take, and be sure to include these items in your Statement of Net Worth. (see form 10, p.195.) You may need to convince the judge that you only took these items temporarily, in order to preserve them until a Judgment of Divorce is entered. Also, do not spend any cash you take from a bank account, or sell or give away any items of property you take. Any cash should be placed in a separate bank account, without your spouse's name on it, and kept separate from any other cash you have. Any papers, such as deeds, car titles, stock or bond certificates, etc., should be placed in a safe deposit box, without your spouse's name on it. The idea is not to take these things for yourself, but to get them in a safe place so your spouse can not hide them and deny they ever existed.

If your spouse moves out of the home, you can change the locks immediately.

AUTOMATIC TEMPORARY ORDERS

Some judges in New York are issuing automatic orders when divorce papers are filed. This order is supposed to protect both the spouses and the children by freezing everything in place the way it is at the time of filing. If your court issues such an order it will probably say that neither one of you can sell or get rid of any assets, rack up a lot of debts, remove children from health insurance policies, change the beneficiaries of any life insurance policy, cancel any type of insurance policy, remove the children from the state, prevent contact between the children and the other parent, or force one another to move out.

These kinds of orders are issued automatically, without regard to your particular circumstances. If you are given this kind of order, you can ask that the court change all or parts of it to reflect on your situation.

TEMPORARY SUPPORT AND CUSTODY

If your spouse has left you with the children, the mortgage, monthly bills, and is not helping you out financially, you may want to consider asking the court to order the payment of support for you and the children during the divorce procedure. Of course, if you were the only person bringing in income and have been paying all the bills, do not expect to get any temporary support.

The simplest way to obtain a temporary order of custody or child or spousal support is to file papers in Family Court. The clerks will help you fill out the papers. However, if you have already started your divorce case, Family Court is not allowed to handle these matters while a divorce case is pending. If this is the case, then you will need to file a motion in Supreme Court. You can also get a temporary order for things like exclusive occupancy of the marital residence, exclusive use of a car, payment of the mortgage and household bills by your spouse as well as an injunction directing your spouse not to sell or dispose of marital assets.

First decide how urgent your need for these things are. If it is extremely urgent, then file an Order to Show Cause (form 34) along with the Affidavit in Support of Request for Temporary Relief. (see form 33, p.266.) Usually this is filed at the same time the Summons is filed and they are served together on your spouse. Your request will go before a judge in two to three days. If you are not in a hurry and there is no urgency, use the Notice of Motion for Temporary Relief. (see form 32, p.264.) In addition, use the Affidavit in Support of Motion for Temporary Relief. (see form 33, p.266.) This can be mailed to your spouse or his or her attorney. After you complete the forms, go to the clerk's office and ask them to help you file them. You will need to file the contested Request for Judicial Intervention (see form 35, p.270) and a contested Note of Issue and Certificate of Readiness (see form 36, p.272) with the documents (see Chapter 10).

Affidavit in
Support of
Motion for
Temporary
Relief
(form 33)

To complete the Affidavit in Support of Motion for Temporary Relief (see form 33, p.266):

1. In number 1, fill in all the things for which you are asking.

2. Fill in information about your marriage in number 3.

3. Read numbers 4 through 11 and cross out the ones you are not seeking. For the things you are seeking, write in your reasons.

4. Use number 12 if there is anything else you are seeking, like an order restraining your spouse from selling or disposing of marital assets.

5. Sign this before a notary.

ORDER TO
SHOW CAUSE
(form 34)

To complete the Order to Show Cause (see form 34, p.268):

1. Fill in the case heading, your name, and the date you signed the Affidavit in Support of Motion for Temporary Relief (form 33). Leave the date and time blank as to when the Court will hear it.

2. After the word "Granting," write in everything you asked for in your affidavit. If you are not seeking a restraining order, cross out the paragraph beginning with the word "ORDERED." Leave everything else blank.

File this form with the affidavit when you file your summons. The Judge will sign it and you will appear in court when directed to, and explain why you need the things you requested.

NOTICE OF
MOTION FOR
TEMPORARY
RELIEF
(form 32)

To complete the Notice of Motion for Temporary Relief (see form 32, p.264):

1. Leave the date and time blank, and cross out any relief you do not want.

2. Fill in number 8 for anything else you want.

3. Fill in your name and address at the end and write in your spouse's name, or his or her attorney's, after "To."

File this with the Affidavit in Support of Motion for Temporary Relief (form 33). Once the court fills in the date and time, send it to your spouse or his or her attorney. Appear in court when directed and explain to the court what you are seeking and why.

TAXES

As you are no doubt aware, the United States' income tax code is complicated and ever-changing. For this reason it is impossible to give detailed legal advice with respect to taxes in a book such as this. Any such information could easily be out of date by the time of publication. Therefore, it is strongly recommended that you consult your accountant, lawyer, or whomever prepares your tax return, about the tax consequences of a divorce. A few general concerns are discussed in this chapter, to give you an idea of some of the tax questions that can arise.

TAXES AND
PROPERTY
DIVISION

You and your spouse may be exchanging title to property as a result of your divorce. Generally, there will not be any tax to pay as the result of such a transfer. However, whomever gets a piece of property will be responsible to pay any tax which may become due upon sale.

The Internal Revenue Service (I.R.S.) has issued numerous rulings about how property is to be treated in divorce situations. You need to be especially careful if you are transferring any tax shelters or other complicated financial arrangements.

Be sure to read the following section on alimony, because fancy property settlements are asking for tax problems.

TAXES AND
MAINTENANCE
(ALIMONY)

Maintenance can cause the most tax problems of any aspect of divorce. The I.R.S. is always making new rulings on whether an agreement is really alimony or is really property division. The basic rule is that alimony is treated as income to the person receiving it, and as a deduction for the person paying it. Therefore, in order to manipulate the tax consequences, many couples try to show something as part of the property settlement, instead of as alimony, or the reverse. As the I.R.S. becomes aware of these "tax games" it issues rulings on how it will view a certain arrangement. If you are simply talking about the regular, periodic payment of cash, the I.R.S. will probably not question that it is alimony. If you try to call it property settlement you may run into problems. The important thing is to consult a tax expert if you are considering any unusual or creative property settlement or alimony arrangements.

TAXES AND
CHILD SUPPORT

There are simple tax rules regarding child support:

1. Whoever has custody gets to claim the children on his or her tax return (unless both parents file a special I.R.S. form agreeing to a different arrangement each year).

2. The parent receiving child support does not need to report it as income.

3. The parent paying child support cannot deduct it.

If you are sharing physical custody, the parent with whom the child lives for the most time during the year is entitled to claim the child as a dependent.

The I.R.S. form to reverse this must be filed each year. Therefore, if you and your spouse have agreed that you will get to claim the children (even though you don't have custody), you should get your spouse to sign an open-ended form that you can file each year, so that you do not have to worry about it each year. A phone call to the I.R.S. can help you get answers to questions on this point.

PENSION PLANS

Pension plans, or retirement plans, belonging to you and your spouse are marital assets. They may be very valuable assets. If you and your spouse are young, and have not been working very long, your pension plans may not be worth the worry. Also, if you have both worked, and have pensions plans of similar value, you may as well each keep your own plan. In such cases it may be best just to include a provision in your Separation Agreement that "each party shall keep his or her own pension plan." However, if you have been married a long time and your spouse worked while you stayed home to raise the children; your spouse's pension plan may be worth a lot of money, and may be necessary to see you through retirement. If you and your spouse cannot agree on how to divide a pension plan, you should see an attorney. The valuation of pension plans, and how they are to be divided, is a complicated matter which you should not attempt.

IF YOUR SPOUSE FILED FOR DIVORCE

If your spouse filed for divorce before you did, you have twenty days (or thirty days if you were served outside of New York State) to respond to the Summons in writing. How you respond will depend upon the type of documents that were served on you.

NOTICE OF
APPEARANCE
(form 37)

If you were served with a Summons with Notice (form 4), you must respond with a Notice of Appearance. (see form 37, p.274.) To complete the Notice of Appearance:

1. Fill in the case heading and index number, and place your name in the first blank after "Defendant."

2. Place your name and address on the bottom lines and fill in your spouse's name after "To:."

You must file your Notice of Appearance with the court clerk, and then you may mail it to your spouse (or to your spouse's attorney if he or she has one). Once you receive the Verified Complaint (form 7), complete the Verified Answer described below. (see form 38, p.275.)

VERIFIED
ANSWER
(form 38)

If you were served with a Summons (form 5) and Verified Complaint (form 7), you must file a Verified Answer , and send a copy to your spouse or his or her attorney. To complete the Verified Answer:

1. If you are not contesting what your spouse is asking for, fill in the case heading and index number, and cross out paragraphs designated "First," "Second," and "Third."

2. If you are contesting the divorce, you should probably get an attorney before completing this form. If you choose not to hire a lawyer, read your spouse's complaint carefully. For each numbered paragraph, decide if it is something that is a fact that there is no need to contest, such as the date of your marriage, your addresses, or the names and birthdates of your children. Write in the numbers of those paragraphs that you agree with in the paragraph labeled "Third." You will want to deny paragraphs that state things such as

that you have abused your children or that all of the marital property should be granted to your spouse, or anything else that you know is not true or definitely should not be granted by the court. Write in the numbers of the paragraphs that you do not agree with in the paragraph labeled "First." You should write in the numbers of any remaining paragraphs in the paragraph labeled "Second." If you are not sure how to complete this form, consult an attorney.

3. After you have completed the paragraphs section, fill in your name and address on the three blank lines, and your spouse's name or that of his or her attorney after "To:."

4. Sign at the bottom in front of a notary.

You can also file *counterclaims* in your answer, which are things you are asking the court to do that are either not asked for by your spouse, or are opposite or different from the way your spouse is asking the court to handle them, such as granting you custody of the children or granting you a portion of your spouse's pension plan. If you wish to do this, see an attorney or go to your local law library for forms.

If you filed for divorce, your spouse may make counterclaims against you. In this event, you will need to file an Answer to Counterclaims. See an attorney or go to your local law library for assistance.

AFTER THE DIVORCE 14

WAITING FOR IT TO BE FINAL

Once you have filed all the papers and appeared in court if necessary, you may be exhausted and tired, but you are not divorced yet. You need to wait to get your Judgment of Divorce in the mail with the judge's signature. Once you receive that, you are officially divorced. Expect to wait two to four weeks for this paperwork. If you feel you should have had it by now, call the judge's office and politely ask about the status of it.

CHANGING YOUR NAME

If you used a different name before your marriage and requested that the court allow you to begin using it again, you can do so legally once your Judgment is signed. You do not need to do anything else to get legal permission to change your name after a divorce. Contact your bank, creditors, employer, insurance company, etc. If proof is required by any agency (such as the Department of Motor Vehicles), show them your Judgment of Divorce.

Expect it to take several months before you can get everything changed over. Expect it to take even longer for acquaintances to remember.

ADJUSTING TO BEING SINGLE

When you hold the signed divorce papers in your hand it might not feel as if your life is any different. You and your spouse probably physically separated before this and if you have children, you have been dealing with visitation schedules throughout the separation. It is going to take some time to really feel as if you are single. If you have children, you will never be completely free of your ex. You will continue to be parents together the rest of your lives, so in that sense you will always have a connection.

Give yourself some time to adjust to your new status as single. Expect to feel sadness, even if you are truly happy to be divorced. Expect to have feelings of failure and blame. These too are normal. Think about how you want to live the rest of your life. What goals do you have? How can you go about achieving them? When it is time to pursue them, you will know.

If you find you are having a very hard time being single and handling the divorce, consider seeing a therapist or counselor. It is very common to need a professional to help you through this process, and you should not feel embarrassed or ashamed.

There are many local and national organizations that can provide you with support and encouragement as you explore your new role as a divorced person. The American Association for Single People is committed to assisting single people and advocating for them. They can be reached at 323-258-8955, or at **http://www.singlepeople.org**. Parents Without Partners is an international organization that is devoted to supporting single parents. They can be reached at 561-391-8833, or at **http://www.parentswithoutpartners.org**. Find out information about your local chapter. In addition, there are many other local community and church organizations that can you become involved with.

Helping Your Children Adjust

As hard as adjusting to the divorce is for you, it is probably ten times harder for your children. Make time in your life for your kids. Make time in your kids' lives for them to see the other parent. Never argue or fight with your ex in front of your children if you can help it. Expect your children to run the gamut with their emotions - angry, sad, depressed, withdrawn, expressive, etc.

It is so important to talk to your children about their feelings. Listen to what they say and do not try to censor them. Make them feel accepted and loved. Tell them you love them and that you will never ever leave them. Assure them they will always have two parents.

Helping your children through the adjustment process after the divorce is going to be difficult. Do not hesitate to take them to a counselor or therapist if you find you don't know what to do or how to handle things.

Dealing with Your Ex

So here you are, divorced, but in many ways you still feel like you are still married to your ex. Mental health experts often explain that there are really three divorces: the legal divorce (which happens in court), the physical divorce (which happens when you separate) and the emotional divorce (which takes the longest). You got through the first two, now you have to deal with the third. Different people develop different kinds of relationships with their ex-spouses. Some people never see or speak to each other again, some people develop friendships and some people find something in between. Only you are going to know what you are comfortable with and only you can signal this to your ex.

If you have children, let them be your guiding factor in this situation. Make sure they will not be in the middle of an unpleasant relationship. If you do not have children, you will find your own way through this.

CHANGING THINGS AFTER THE DIVORCE

What happens if you get your Judgment of Divorce and it is wrong? It depends on what is wrong with it. If you and your spouse reached an agreement and somehow it was not fully included or changed in the Judgment, you need to let the court know there was an error. If you have an attorney, call him or her and explain the problem. If you do not, call the judge's secretary and explain the problem.

If you get your Judgment of Divorce and it contains the agreement you made or the things the court decided correctly, but you think that it should now be different, you need to think carefully about the specific items. In general, you just can't change your mind after the divorce, although many people have second thoughts. Whatever you agreed to or whatever the judge decided is now written in stone. If you want to try to change something that has to do with money, debts, or property, you are going to need a lawyer. You are going to have to prove that your spouse lied and hid assets, or that the situation was far different than you and the court were led to believe. If you want to change something about custody, you are going to need to show that there has been a significant change in circumstances. Some judges in New York now require that the family return to Supreme Court if there is any problem with custody or visitation within 18 months of the divorce. Other judges allow you to go to Family Court to have custody or visitation changed after a divorce.

APPENDIX A
NEW YORK DOMESTIC RELATIONS LAW

This appendix contains portions of the New York Domestic Relations Law. You will note that the legislature has not been consistent in its designation of subsections. For example, in Section 170 the subsections are designated 1), 2), 3), etc.; whereas in Section 200 the subsections are designated 1., 2., 3., etc. If you need more information, go to a public library or law library and look up the other divorce-related statutes in the volumes marked "Domestic Relations Law," as well as the volumes marked "Civil Practice Law and Rules."

DOMESTIC RELATIONS LAW

Sec. 170. Action for divorce. An action for divorce may be maintained by a husband or wife to procure a judgment divorcing the parties and dissolving the marriage on any of the following grounds:

1) The cruel and inhuman treatment of the plaintiff by the defendant such that the conduct of the defendant so endangers the physical or mental well being of the plaintiff as renders it unsafe or improper for the plaintiff to cohabit with the defendant.

2) The abandonment of the plaintiff by the defendant for a period of one or more years.

3) The confinement of the defendant in prison for a period of three or more consecutive years after the marriage of plaintiff and defendant.

4) The commission of an act of adultery, provided that adultery for the purposes of articles ten, eleven, and eleven-A of this chapter, is hereby defined as the commission of an act of sexual or deviate sexual intercourse, voluntarily performed by the defendant, with a person other than the plaintiff after the marriage of plaintiff and defendant.

Deviate sexual intercourse includes, but not limited to, sexual conduct as defined in subdivision two of Section 130.00 and subdivision three of Section 130.20 of the penal law.

5) The husband and wife have lived apart pursuant to a decree or judgment of separation for a period of one or more years after the granting of such decree or judgment, and satisfactory proof has been submitted by the plaintiff that he or she has substantially performed all the terms and conditions of such decree or judgment.

6) The husband and wife have lived separate and apart pursuant to a written agreement of separation, subscribed by the parties thereto and acknowledged or proved in the form required to entitle a deed to be recorded, for a period of one or more years after the execution of such agreement and satisfactory proof has been submitted by the plaintiff that he or she has substantially performed all the terms and conditions of such agreement. Such agreement shall be filed in the office of the clerk of the county wherein either party resides. In lieu of filing such agreement, either party to such agreement may file a memorandum of such agreement, which memorandum shall be similarly subscribed

and acknowledged or proved as was the agreement of separation and shall contain the following information: (a) the names and addresses of each of the parties, (b) the date of marriage of the parties, (c) the date of the agreement of separation and (d) the date of this subscription and acknowledgment or proof of such agreement of separation.

Sec. 200. Action for separation. An action may be maintained by a husband or wife against the other party to the marriage to procure a judgment separating the parties from bed and board, forever, or for a limited time, for any of the following causes:

1. The cruel and inhuman treatment of the plaintiff by the defendant such that the conduct of the defendant so endangers the physical or mental well being of the plaintiff as renders it unsafe or improper for the plaintiff to cohabit with the defendant.

2. The abandonment of the plaintiff by the defendant.

3. The neglect or refusal of the defendant-spouse to provide for the support of the plaintiff-spouse where the defendant-spouse is chargeable with such support under the provisions of section thirty-two of this chapter or of section four hundred twelve of the family court act.

4. The commission of an act of adultery by the defendant; except where such offense is committed by the procurement or with the connivance of the plaintiff or where there is voluntary cohabitation of the parties with the knowledge of the offense or where action was not commenced within five years after the discovery by the plaintiff of the offense charged or where the plaintiff has also been guilty of adultery under such circumstances that the defendant would have been entitled, if innocent, to a divorce, provided that adultery for the purposes of this subdivision is hereby defined as the commission of an act of sexual or deviate sexual intercourse, voluntarily performed by the defendant, with a person other than the plaintiff after the marriage of plaintiff and defendant. Deviate sexual intercourse includes, but not limited to, sexual conduct as defined in subdivision two of Section 130.00 and subdivision three of Section 130.20 of the penal law.

5. The confinement of the defendant in prison for a period of three or more consecutive years after the marriage of plaintiff and defendant.

Sec. 230. Required residence of parties. An action to annul a marriage, or to declare the nullity of a void marriage, or for divorce or separation may be maintained only when:

1. The parties were married in the state and either party is a resident thereof when the action is commenced and has been a resident for a continuous period of one year immediately preceding, or

2. The parties have resided in this state as husband and wife and either party is a resident thereof when the

action is commenced and has been a resident for a continuous period of one year immediately preceding, or

3. The cause occurred in the state and either party has been a resident thereof for a continuous period of at least one year immediately preceding the commencement of the action, or

4. The cause occurred in the state and both parties are residents thereof at the time of the commencement of the action, or

5. Either party has been a resident of the state for a continuous period of at least two years immediately preceding the commencement of the action.

Sec. 236. Special controlling provisions; prior actions or proceedings; new actions or proceedings. Except as otherwise expressly provided in this section, the provisions of part A shall be controlling with respect to any action or proceeding commenced prior to the date on which the provisions of this section as amended become effective and the provisions of part B shall be controlling with respect to any action or proceeding commenced on or after such effective date. Any reference to this section or the provisions hereof in any action, proceeding, judgment, order, rule or agreement shall be deemed and construed to refer to either the provisions of part A or part B respectively and exclusively, determined as provided in this paragraph any inconsistent provision of law notwithstanding.

Part A

Prior Actions or Proceedings

Alimony, temporary and permanent.

1. Alimony. In any action or proceeding brought (1) during the lifetime of both parties to the marriage to annul a marriage or declare the nullity of a void marriage, or (2) for a separation, or (3) for a divorce, the court may direct either spouse to provide suitably for the support of the other as, in the court's discretion, justice requires, having regard to the length of time of the marriage, the ability of each spouse to be self supporting, the circumstances of the case and of the respective parties. Such direction may require the payment of a sum or sums of money either directly to either spouse or to third persons for real and personal property and services furnished to either spouse, or for the rental of or mortgage amortization or interest payments, insurance, taxes, repairs or other carrying charges on premises occupied by either spouse, or for both payments to either spouse and to such third persons. Such direction shall be effective as of the date of the application therefore, and any retroactive amount of alimony due shall be paid in one sum or periodic sums, as the court shall direct, taking into account any amount of temporary alimony which has been paid. Such direction may be made in the final judgment in such action or proceeding, or by one or more orders from time to time before or subsequent to final judgment, or by both such order or orders and the

final judgment. Such direction may be made notwithstanding that the parties continue to reside in the same abode and notwithstanding that the court refuses to grant the relief requested by either spouse (1) by reason of a finding by the court that a divorce, annulment or judgment declaring the marriage a nullity had previously been granted to either spouse in an action in which jurisdiction over the person of the other spouse was not obtained, or (2) by reason of the misconduct of the other spouse, unless such misconduct would itself constitute grounds for separation or divorce, or (3) by reason of a failure of proof of the grounds of either spouse's action or counterclaim. Any order or judgment made as in this section provided may combine in one lump sum any amount payable to either spouse under this section with any amount payable to either spouse under section two hundred forty of this chapter. Upon the application of either spouse, upon such notice to the other party and given in such manner as the court shall direct, the court may annul or modify any such direction, whether made by order or by final judgment, or in case no such direction shall have been made in the final judgment may, with respect to any judgment of annulment or declaring the nullity of a void marriage rendered on or after September first, nineteen hundred forty or any judgment of separation or divorce whenever rendered, amend the judgment by inserting such direction. Subject to the provisions of section two hundred forty-four of this chapter, no such modification or annulment shall reduce or annul arrears accrued prior to the making of such application unless the defaulting party shows good cause for failure to make application for relief from the judgment or order directing such payment prior to the accrual of such arrears. Such modification may increase such support nunc pro tunc based on newly discovered evidence.

2. Compulsory financial disclosure. In all matrimonial actions and proceedings commenced on or after September first, nineteen hundred seventy-five in supreme court in which alimony, maintenance or support is in issue and all support proceedings in family court, there shall be compulsory disclosure by both parties of their respective financial states. No showing of special circumstances shall be required before such disclosure is ordered. A sworn statement of net worth shall be provided upon receipt of a notice in writing demanding the same, within twenty days after the receipt thereof. In the event said statement is not demanded, it shall be filed by each party, within ten days after joinder of issue, in the court in which the procedure is pending. As used in this section, the term net worth shall mean the amount by which total assets including income exceed total liabilities including fixed financial obligations. It shall include all income and assets of whatsoever kind and nature and wherever situated and shall include a list of all assets transferred in any manner during the preceding three years, or the length of the marriage, whichever is shorter; provided, however that transfers in the routine course of business which resulted in an exchange of assets of substantially equivalent value need not be specifically disclosed where such assets are otherwise identified in the statement of net worth. Noncompliance shall be punishable by any or all of the penalties prescribed in section thirty-one hundred twenty-six of the civil practice law and rules, in examination before or during trial.

Part B

New Actions or Proceedings

Maintenance and distributive award.

1. Definitions. Whenever used in this part, the following terms shall have the respective meanings hereinafter set forth or indicated:

a. The term "maintenance" shall mean payments provided for in a valid agreement between the parties or awarded by the court in accordance with the provisions of subdivision six of this part, to be paid at fixed intervals for a definite or indefinite period of time, but an award of maintenance shall terminate upon the death of either party or upon the recipient's valid or invalid marriage, or upon modification pursuant to paragraph (b) of subdivision nine of section two hundred thirty-six of this part or section two hundred forty-eight of this chapter.

b. The term "distributive award" shall mean payments provided for in a valid agreement between the parties or awarded by the court, in lieu of or to supplement, facilitate or effectuate the division or distribution of property where authorized in a matrimonial action, and payable either in a lump sum or over a period of time in fixed amounts. Distributive awards shall not include payments which are treated as ordinary income to the recipient under the provisions of the United States Internal Revenue Code.

c. The term "marital property" shall mean all property acquired by either or both spouses during the marriage and before the execution of a separation agreement or the commencement of a matrimonial action, regardless of the form in which title is held, except as otherwise provided in agreement pursuant to subdivision three of this part. Marital property shall not include separate property as hereinafter defined.

d. The term separate property shall mean:

1) property acquired before marriage or property acquired by bequest, devise, or descent, or gift from a party other than the spouse;

2) compensation for personal injuries;

3) property acquired in exchange for or the increase in value of separate property, except to the extent that such appreciation is due in

part to the contributions or efforts of the other spouse;

4) property described as separate property by written agreement of the parties pursuant to subdivision three of this part.

e. The term "custodial parent" shall mean a parent to whom custody of a child or children is granted by a valid agreement between the parties or by an order or decree of a court.

f. The term "child support" shall mean a sum paid pursuant to court order or decree by either or both parents or pursuant to a valid agreement between the parties for care, maintenance and education of any unemancipated child under the age of twenty-one years.

2. Matrimonial actions. Except as provided in subdivision five of this part, the provisions of this part shall be applicable to actions for an annulment or dissolution of a marriage, for a divorce, for a separation, for a declaration of the nullity of a void marriage, for a declaration of the validity or nullity of a foreign judgment of divorce, for a declaration of the validity or nullity of a marriage, and to proceedings to obtain maintenance or a distribution of marital property following a foreign judgment of divorce, commenced on and after the effective date of this part. Any application which seeks a modification of a judgment, order or decree made in an action commenced prior to the effective date of this part shall be heard and determined in accordance with the provisions of part A of this section.

3. Agreement of the parties. An agreement by the parties, made before or during the marriage, shall be valid and enforceable in a matrimonial action if such agreement is in writing, subscribed by the parties, and acknowledged or proven in the manner required to entitle a deed to be recorded. Such an agreement may include (1) a contract to make a testamentary provision of any kind, or a waiver of any right to elect against the provisions of a will; (2) provision for the ownership, division or distribution of separate and marital property; (3) provision for the amount and duration of maintenance or other terms and conditions of the marriage relationship, subject to the provisions of section 5-311 of the general obligations law, and provided that such terms were fair and reasonable at the time of the making of the agreement and are not unconscionable at the time of entry of final judgment; and (4) provision for the custody, care, education and maintenance of any child of the parties, subject to the provisions of section two hundred forty of this chapter. Nothing in this subdivision shall be deemed to affect the validity of any agreement made prior to the effective date of this subdivision.

4. Compulsory financial disclosure.

a. In all matrimonial actions and proceedings in which alimony, maintenance or support is in issue, there shall be compulsory disclosure by both parties of their respective financial states. No showing of special circumstances shall be required before such disclosure is ordered. A sworn statement of net worth shall be provided upon receipt of a notice in writing demanding the same, within twenty days after the receipt thereof. In the event said statement is not demanded, it shall be filed with the clerk of the court by each party, within ten days after joinder of issue, in the court in which the proceeding is pending. As used in this part, the term "net worth" shall mean the amount by which total assets including income exceed total liabilities including fixed financial obligations. It shall include all income and assets of whatsoever kind and nature and wherever situated and shall include a list of all assets transferred in any manner during the preceding three years, or the length of the marriage, whichever is shorter; provided, however that transfers in the routine course of business which resulted in an exchange of assets of substantially equivalent value need not be specifically disclosed where such assets are otherwise identified in the statement of net worth. All such sworn statements of net worth shall be accompanied by a current and representative paycheck stub and the most recently filed state and federal income tax returns including a copy of the W-2(s) wage and tax statement(s) submitted with the returns. In addition, both parties shall provide information relating to any and all group health plans available to them for the provision of care or other medical benefits by insurance or otherwise for the benefit of the child or children for whom support is sought, including all such information as may be required to be included in a qualified medical child support order as defined in section six hundred nine of the employee retirement income security act of 1974 (29 USC 1169) including, but not limited to: (i) the name and last known mailing address of each party and of each dependent to be covered by the order; (ii) the identification and a description of each group health plan available for the benefit or coverage of the disclosing party and the child or children for whom support is sought; (iii) a detailed description of the type of coverage available from each group health plan for the potential benefit of each such dependent; (iv) the identification of the plan administrator for each such group health plan and the address of such administrator; (v) the identification numbers for each such group health plan; and (vi) such other information as may be required by the court to ensure that an order for medical support is qualified in the manner required. Noncompliance shall be punishable by any or all of the penalties prescribed in section thirty-one hundred twenty-six of the civil practice law and rules, in examination before or during trial.

b. As soon as practicable after a matrimonial action has been commenced, the court shall set the date or dates the parties shall use for the valuation of each asset. The valuation date or dates may be anytime from the date of commencement of the action to the date of trial.

5. Disposition of property in certain matrimonial actions.

a. Except where the parties have provided in an agreement for the disposition of their property pursuant to subdivision three of this part, the court, in an action wherein all or part of the relief granted is divorce, or the dissolution, annulment or declaration of the nullity of a marriage, and in proceedings to obtain a distribution of marital property following a foreign judgment of divorce, shall determine the respective rights of the parties in their separate or marital property, and shall provide for the disposition thereof in the final judgment.

b. Separate property shall remain such.

c. Marital property shall be distributed equitably between the parties, considering the circumstances of the case and of the respective parties.

d. In determining an equitable disposition of property under paragraph c, the court shall consider:

1) the income and property of each party at the time of marriage, and at the time of the commencement of the action;

2) the duration of the marriage and the age and health of both parties;

3) the need of a custodial parent to occupy or own the marital residence and to use or own its household effects;

4) the loss of inheritance and pension rights upon dissolution of the marriage as of the date of dissolution;

5) any award of maintenance under subdivision six of this part;

6) any equitable claim to, interest in, or direct or indirect contribution made to the acquisition of such marital property by the party not having title, including joint efforts or expenditures and contributions and services as a spouse, parent, wage earner and homemaker, and to the career or career potential of the other party;

7) the liquid or non-liquid character of all marital property;

8) the probable future financial circumstances of each party;

9) the impossibility or difficulty of evaluating any component asset or any interest in a business, corporation or profession, and the economic desirability of retaining such asset or interest intact and free from any claim or interference by the other party;

10) the tax consequences to each party;

11) the wasteful dissipation of assets by either spouse;

12) any transfer or encumbrance made in contemplation of a matrimonial action without fair consideration;

13) any other factor which the court shall expressly find to be just and proper.

e. In any action in which the court shall determine that an equitable distribution is appropriate but would be impractical or burdensome or where the distribution of an interest in a business, corporation or profession would be contrary to law, the court in lieu of such equitable distribution shall make a distributive award in order to achieve equity between the parties. The court in its discretion, also may make a distributive award to supplement, facilitate or effectuate a distribution of marital property.

f. In addition to the disposition of property as set forth above, the court may make such order regarding the use and occupancy of the marital home and its household effects as provided in section two hundred thirty-four of this chapter, without regard to the form of ownership of such property.

g. In any decision made pursuant to this subdivision, the court shall set forth the factors it considered and the reasons for its decision and such may not be waived by either party or counsel.

h. In any decision made pursuant to this subdivision the court shall, where appropriate, consider the effect of a barrier to remarriage, as defined in subdivision six of section two hundred fifty-three of this article, on the factors enumerated in paragraph d of this subdivision.

6. Maintenance.

a. Except where the parties have entered into an agreement pursuant to subdivision three of this part providing for maintenance, in any matrimonial action the court may order temporary maintenance or maintenance in such amount as justice requires, having regard for the standard of living of the parties established during the marriage, whether the party in whose favor maintenance is granted lacks sufficient property and income to provide for his or her reasonable needs and whether the other party has sufficient property or income to provide for the reasonable needs of the other and the circumstances of the case and of the respective parties. Such order shall be effective as of the date of the application therefor, and any retroactive amount of maintenance due shall be paid in one sum or periodic sums, as the court shall direct, taking into account any amount of temporary maintenance which has been paid. In determining the amount and duration of maintenance the court shall consider:

1) the income and property of the respective parties including marital property distributed pursuant to subdivision five of this part;

2) the duration of the marriage and the age and health of both parties;

3) the present and future earning capacity of both parties;

4) the ability of the party seeking maintenance to become self-supporting and, if applicable, the period of time and training necessary therefor;

5) reduced or lost lifetime earning capacity of the party seeking maintenance as a result of having foregone or delayed education, training, employment, or career opportunities during the marriage;

6) the presence of children of the marriage in the respective homes of the parties;

7) the tax consequences to each party;

8) contributions and services of the party seeking maintenance as a spouse, parent, wage earner and homemaker, and to the career or career potential of the other party;

9) the wasteful dissipation of marital property by either spouse;

10) any transfer or encumbrance made in contemplation of a matrimonial action without fair consideration; and

11) any other factor which the court shall expressly find to be just and proper.

b. In any decision made pursuant to this subdivision, the court shall set forth the factors it considered and the reasons for its decision and such may not be waived by either party or counsel.

c. The court may award permanent maintenance, but an award of maintenance shall terminate upon the death of either party or upon the recipient's valid or invalid marriage, or upon modification pursuant to paragraph (b) of subdivision nine of section two hundred thirty-six of this part or section two hundred forty-eight of this chapter.

d. In any decision made pursuant to this subdivision the court shall, where appropriate, consider the effect of a barrier to remarriage, as defined in sub-

division six of section two hundred fifty-three of this article, on the factors enumerated in paragraph a of this subdivision.

7. Child support.

a. In any matrimonial action, or in an independent action for child support, the court as provided in section two hundred forty of this chapter shall order either or both parents to pay temporary child support or child support without requiring a showing of immediate or emergency need. The court shall make an order for temporary child support notwithstanding that information with respect to income and assets of either or both parents may be unavailable. Where such information is available, the court may make an order for temporary child support pursuant to section two hundred forty of this article. Such order shall, except as provided for herein, be effective as of the date of the application therefor, and any retroactive amount of child support due shall be support arrears/past due support and shall be paid in one sum or periodic sums, as the court shall direct, taking into account any amount of temporary child support which has been paid. In addition, such retroactive child support shall be enforceable in any manner provided by law including, but not limited to, an execution for support enforcement pursuant to subdivision (b) of section fifty-two hundred forty-one of the civil practice law and rules. When a child receiving support is a public assistance recipient, or the order of support is being enforced or is to be enforced pursuant to section one hundred eleven-g of the social services law, the court shall establish the amount of retroactive child support and notify the parties that such amount shall be enforced by the support collection unit pursuant to an execution for support enforcement as provided for in subdivision (b) of section fifty-two hundred forty-one of the civil practice law and rules, or in such periodic payments as would have been authorized had such an execution been issued. In such case, the court shall not direct the schedule of repayment of retroactive support. The court shall not consider the misconduct of either party but shall make its award for child support pursuant to section two hundred forty of this article.

b. Notwithstanding any other provision of law, any written application or motion to the court for the establishment of a child support obligation for persons not in receipt of family assistance must contain either a request for child support enforcement services which would authorize the collection of the support obligation by the immediate issuance of an income execution for support enforcement as provided for by this chapter, completed in the manner specified in section one hundred eleven-g of the social services law; or a statement that the applicant has applied for or is in receipt of such services; or a statement that the applicant knows of the availability of such services, has declined them at this time and where support enforcement services pursuant to section one hundred eleven-g of the social services law have been declined that the applicant understands that an income deduction order may be issued pursuant to subdivision (c) of section five thousand two hundred forty-two of the civil practice law and rules without other child support enforcement services and that payment of an administrative fee may be required. The court shall provide a copy of any such request for child support enforcement services to the support collection unit of the appropriate social services district any time it directs payments to be made to such support collection unit. Additionally, the copy of any such request shall be accompanied by the name, address and social security number of the parties; the date and place of the parties' marriage; the name and date of birth of the child or children; and the name and address of the employers and income payors of the party from whom child support is sought. Unless the party receiving child support has applied for or is receiving such services, the court shall not direct such payments to be made to the support collection unit, as established in section one hundred eleven-h of the social services law.

c. The court shall direct that a copy of any child support or combined child and spousal support order issued by the court on or after the first day of October, nineteen hundred ninety-eight, in any proceeding under this section be provided promptly to the state case registry established pursuant to subdivision four-a of section one hundred eleven-b of the social services law.

8. Special relief in matrimonial actions.

a. In any matrimonial action the court may order a party to purchase, maintain or assign a policy of insurance providing benefits for health and hospital care and related services for either spouse or children of the marriage not to exceed such period of time as such party shall be obligated to provide maintenance, child support or make payments of a distributive award. The court may also order a party to purchase, maintain or assign a policy of insurance on the life of either spouse, and to designate either spouse or children of the marriage as irrevocable beneficiaries during a period of time fixed by the court. The interest of the beneficiary shall cease upon the termination of such party's obligation to provide maintenance, child support or a distributive

award, or when the beneficiary remarries or predeceases the insured.

b. In any action where the court has ordered temporary maintenance, maintenance, distributive award or child support, the court may direct that a payment be made directly to the other spouse or a third person for real and personal property and services furnished to the other spouse, or for the rental or mortgage amortization or interest payments, insurances, taxes, repairs or other carrying charges on premises occupied by the other spouse, or for both payments to the other spouse and to such third persons. Such direction may be made notwithstanding that the parties continue to reside in the same abode and notwithstanding that the court refuses to grant the relief requested by the other spouse.

c. Any order or judgment made as in this section provided may combine any amount payable to either spouse under this section with any amount payable to such spouse as child support or under section two hundred forty of this chapter.

9. Enforcement and modification of orders and judgments in matrimonial actions.

a. All orders or judgments entered in matrimonial actions shall be enforceable pursuant to section fifty-two hundred forty-one or fifty-two hundred forty-two of the civil practice law and rules, or in any other manner provided by law. Orders or judgments for child support, alimony and maintenance shall also be enforceable pursuant to article fifty-two of the civil practice law and rules upon a debtor's default as such term is defined in paragraph seven of subdivision (a) of section fifty-two hundred forty-one of the civil practice law and rules. The establishment of a default shall be subject to the procedures established for the determination of a mistake of fact for income executions pursuant to subdivision (e) of section fifty-two hundred forty-one of the civil practice law and rules. For the purposes of enforcement of child support orders or combined spousal and child support orders pursuant to section five thousand two hundred forty-one of the civil practice law and rules, a "default" shall be deemed to include amounts arising from retroactive support. The court may, and if a party shall fail or refuse to pay maintenance, distributive award or child support the court shall, upon notice and an opportunity to the defaulting party to be heard, require the party to furnish a surety, or the sequestering and sale of assets for the purpose of enforcing any award for maintenance, distributive award or child support and for the payment of reasonable and necessary attorney's fees and disbursements.

b. Upon application by either party, the court may annul or modify any prior order or judgment as to maintenance or child support, upon a showing of the recipient's inability to be self-supporting or a substantial change in circumstance or termination of child support awarded pursuant to section two hundred forty of this article, including financial hardship. Where, after the effective date of this part, a separation agreement remains in force no modification of a prior order or judgment incorporating the terms of said agreement shall be made as to maintenance without a showing of extreme hardship on either party, in which event the judgment or order as modified shall supersede the terms of the prior agreement and judgment for such period of time and under such circumstances as the court determines. Provided, however, that no modification or annulment shall reduce or annul any arrears of child support which have accrued prior to the date of application to annul or modify any prior order or judgment as to child support. The court shall not reduce or annul any arrears of maintenance which have been reduced to final judgment pursuant to section two hundred forty-four of this chapter. No other arrears of maintenance which have accrued prior to the making of such application shall be subject to modification or annulment unless the defaulting party shows good cause for failure to make application for relief from the judgment or order directing such payment prior to the accrual of such arrears and the facts and circumstances constituting good cause are set forth in a written memorandum of decision. Such modification may increase maintenance or child support nunc pro tunc as of the date of application based on newly discovered evidence. Any retroactive amount of maintenance, or child support due shall, except as provided for herein, be paid in one sum or periodic sums, as the court directs, taking into account any temporary or partial payments which have been made. Any retroactive amount of child support due shall be support arrears/past due support. In addition, such retroactive child support shall be enforceable in any manner provided by law including, but not limited to, an execution for support enforcement pursuant to subdivision (b) of section fifty-two hundred forty-one of the civil practice law and rules. When a child receiving support is a public assistance recipient, or the order of support is being enforced or is to be enforced pursuant to section one hundred eleven-g of the social services law, the court shall establish the amount of retroactive child support and notify the parties that such

amount shall be enforced by the support collection unit pursuant to an execution for support enforcement as provided for in subdivision (b) of section fifty-two hundred forty-one of the civil practice law and rules, or in such periodic payments as would have been authorized had such an execution been issued. In such case, the court shall not direct the schedule of repayment of retroactive support. The provisions of this subdivision shall not apply to a separation agreement made prior to the effective date of this part.

c. Notwithstanding any other provision of law, any written application or motion to the court for the modification or enforcement of a child support or combined maintenance and child support order for persons not in receipt of family assistance must contain either a request for child support enforcement services which would authorize the collection of the support obligation by the immediate issuance of an income execution for support enforcement as provided for by this chapter, completed in the manner specified in section one hundred eleven-g of the social services law; or a statement that the applicant has applied for or is in receipt of such services; or a statement that the applicant knows of the availability of such services, has declined them at this time and where support enforcement services pursuant to section one hundred eleven-g of the social services law have been declined that the applicant understands that an income deduction order may be issued pursuant to subdivision (c) of section five thousand two hundred forty-two of the civil practice law and rules without other child support enforcement services and that payment of an administrative fee may be required. The court shall provide a copy of any such request for child support enforcement services to the support collection unit of the appropriate social services district any time it directs payments to be made to such support collection unit. Additionally, the copy of such request shall be accompanied by the name, address and social security number of the parties; the date and place of the parties' marriage; the name and date of birth of the child or children; and the name and address of the employers and income payors of the party ordered to pay child support to the other party. Unless the party receiving child support or combined maintenance and child support has applied for or is receiving such services, the court shall not direct such payments to be made to the support collection unit, as established in section one hundred eleven-h of the social services law.

d. The court shall direct that a copy of any child support or combined child and spousal support order issued by the court on or after the first day of October, nineteen hundred ninety-eight, in any proceeding under this section be provided promptly to the state case registry established pursuant to subdivision four-a of section one hundred eleven-b of the social services law.

Sec. 240. Custody and child support; orders of protection.

1. In any action or proceeding brought (1) to annul a marriage or to declare the nullity of a void marriage, or (2) for a separation, or (3) for a divorce, or (4) to obtain, by a writ of habeas corpus or by petition and order to show cause, the custody of or right to visitation with any child of a marriage, the court shall require verification of the status of any child of the marriage with respect to such child's custody and support, including any prior orders, and shall enter orders for custody and support as, in the court's discretion, justice requires, having regard to the circumstances of the case and of the respective parties and to the best interests of the child. Where either party to an action concerning custody of or a right to visitation with a child alleges in a sworn petition or complaint or sworn answer, cross-petition, counterclaim or other sworn responsive pleading that the other party has committed an act of domestic violence against the party making the allegation or a family or household member of either party, as such family or household member is defined in article eight of the family court act, and such allegations are proven by a preponderance of the evidence, the court must consider the effect of such domestic violence upon the best interests of the child, together with such other facts and circumstances as the court deems relevant in making a direction pursuant to this section. An order directing the payment of child support shall contain the social security numbers of the named parties. In all cases there shall be no prima facie right to the custody of the child in either parent. Such direction shall make provision for child support out of the property of either or both parents. The court shall make its award for child support pursuant to subdivision one-b of this section. Such direction may provide for reasonable visitation rights to the maternal and/or paternal grandparents of any child of the parties. Such direction as it applies to rights of visitation with a child remanded or placed in the care of a person, official, agency or institution pursuant to article ten of the family court act, or pursuant to an instrument approved under section three hundred fifty-eight-a of the social services law, shall be enforceable pursuant to part eight of article ten of the family court act and sections three hundred fifty-eight-a and three hundred eighty-four-a of the social services law and other applicable provisions of law against any person having care and custody, or temporary care and custody, of the child. Notwithstanding any other provision of law, any written application or motion to the court for the establishment, modification or enforcement of a child support obligation for persons not in receipt of family assistance must contain either a request for child support enforcement services which would authorize the collection of the support obligation by the immediate issuance of an income execution for support enforcement as provided for by this chapter, completed in the manner specified in section one hundred eleven-g of the social services law; or a statement that the applicant has applied for or is in receipt of such services; or a statement that the applicant knows of the availability of such services, has declined them at this time and where support enforcement services pursuant to section one hundred eleven-g of the social services law have been declined that the applicant understands that an income deduction order may be issued pursuant to subdivision (c) of section five thousand two hundred forty-two of the civil practice law and rules without other child support enforcement services and that payment of an administrative fee may be required. The court shall provide a copy of any such request for child support enforcement services to the support collection unit of the appropriate social services district any time it directs payments to be made to such support collection unit. Additionally, the copy of any such request shall be accompanied by the name, address and social security number of the parties; the date and place of the parties' marriage; the name and date of birth of the child or children; and the name and address of the employers and income payors of the party from whom child support is sought or from the party ordered to pay child support to the other party. Such direction may require the payment of a sum or sums of money either directly to the custodial parent or to third persons for goods or services furnished for such child, or for both payments to the custodial parent and to such third persons; provided, however, that unless the party seeking or receiving child support has applied for or is receiving such services, the court shall not direct such payments to be made to the support collection unit, as established in section one hundred eleven-h of the social services law. Such direction shall require that if either parent currently, or at any time in the future, has health insurance available through an employer or organization that may be extended to cover the child, such parent is required to exercise the option of additional coverage in favor of such child and execute and deliver any forms, notices, documents or instruments necessary to assure timely payment of any health insurance claims for such child. Where employer or organization health insurance coverage is available, the court shall order the legally responsible relative immediately to enroll the eligible dependents named in the order who are otherwise eligible for such coverage without regard to any seasonal enrollment restrictions. Such order shall further direct the legally responsible relative to maintain such coverage as long as it remains available to such relative. Upon a finding that a responsible relative willfully failed to obtain such health insurance in violation of a court order, such relative will be presumptively liable for all medical expenses incurred on behalf of such dependents

from the first date such dependent was eligible to be enrolled in medical insurance coverage after the issuance of the order of support directing the acquisition of such coverage. In making an order for employer or organization provided health insurance pursuant to this section the court shall consider the availability of such insurance to all parties to the order and direct that either or both parties obtain such insurance and allocate the costs therefor consistent with obtaining comprehensive medical insurance for the child at reasonable cost to the parties. In making such direction, the court shall determine the identity and nature of any and all group health plans available to each party for the provision of care or other medical benefits by insurance or otherwise for the benefit of the child or children for whom support is sought, and shall identify and include all information necessary to ensure the order's characterization as a qualified medical child support order as defined by section six hundred nine of the employee retirement income security act of 1974 (29 USC 1169). Such order shall: (i) clearly state that it creates or recognizes the existence of the right of the named dependent to be enrolled and to receive benefits for which the legally responsible relative is eligible under the available group health plans, and shall clearly specify the name, social security number and mailing address of the legally responsible relative, the alternate recipient and of each dependent to be covered by the order; (ii) provide a clear description of the type of coverage to be provided by the group health plan to each such dependent or the manner in which the type of coverage is to be determined; and (iii) specify the period of time to which the qualified order applies and the identity of each group health plan to which the qualified order applies. The court shall not require the group health plan to provide any type or form of benefit or option not otherwise provided under the group health plan except to the extent necessary to meet the requirements of a law relating to medical child support described in section one thousand three hundred and ninety-six g of title forty-two of the United States code. The court's issuance of a qualified medical child support order shall be made separately from the order of support. The order shall be effective as of the date of the application therefor, and any retroactive amount of child support due shall be support arrears/past due support and shall, except as provided for herein, be paid in one lump sum or periodic sums, as the court shall direct, taking into account any amount of temporary support which has been paid. In addition, such retroactive child support shall be enforceable in any manner provided by law including, but not limited to, an execution for support enforcement pursuant to subdivision (b) of section fifty-two hundred forty-one of the civil practice law and rules. When a child receiving support is a public assistance recipient, or the order of support is being enforced or is to be enforced pursuant to section one hundred eleven-g of the social services law, the court shall establish the amount of retroactive child support and notify

the parties that such amount shall be enforced by the support collection unit pursuant to an execution for support enforcement as provided for in subdivision (b) of section fifty-two hundred forty-one of the civil practice law and rules, or in such periodic payments as would have been authorized had such an execution been issued. In such case, the courts shall not direct the schedule of repayment of retroactive support. Where such direction is for child support and paternity has been established by a voluntary acknowledgment of paternity as defined in section forty-one hundred thirty-five-b of the public health law, the court shall inquire of the parties whether the acknowledgment has been duly filed, and unless satisfied that it has been so filed shall require the clerk of the court to file such acknowledgment with the appropriate registrar within five business days. Such direction may be made in the final judgment in such action or proceeding, or by one or more orders from time to time before or subsequent to final judgment, or by both such order or orders and the final judgment. Such direction may be made notwithstanding that the court for any reason whatsoever, other than lack of jurisdiction, refuses to grant the relief requested in the action or proceeding. Any order or judgment made as in this section provided may combine in one lump sum any amount payable to the custodial parent under this section with any amount payable to such parent under section two hundred thirty-six of this chapter. Upon the application of either parent, or of any other person or party having the care, custody and control of such child pursuant to such judgment or order, after such notice to the other party, parties or persons having such care, custody and control and given in such manner as the court shall direct, the court may annul or modify any such direction, whether made by order or final judgment, or in case no such direction shall have been made in the final judgment may, with respect to any judgment of annulment or declaring the nullity of a void marriage rendered on or after September first, nineteen hundred forty, or any judgment of separation or divorce whenever rendered, amend the judgment by inserting such direction. Subject to the provisions of section two hundred forty-four of this article, no such modification or annulment shall reduce or annul arrears accrued prior to the making of such application unless the defaulting party shows good cause for failure to make application for relief from the judgment or order directing such payment prior to the accrual of such arrears. Such modification may increase such child support nunc pro tunc as of the date of application based on newly discovered evidence. Any retroactive amount of child support due shall be support arrears/past due support and shall be paid in one lump sum or periodic sums, as the court shall direct, taking into account any amount of temporary child support which has been paid. In addition, such retroactive child support shall be enforceable in any manner provided by law including, but not limited to, an execution for support enforcement pursuant to subdivision (b) of section fifty-two hundred forty-one of the civil practice law and rules.

1-a. In any proceeding brought pursuant to this section to determine the custody or visitation of minors, a report made to the statewide central register of child abuse and maltreatment, pursuant to title six of article six of the social services law, or a portion thereof, which is otherwise admissible as a business record pursuant to rule forty-five hundred eighteen of the civil practice law and rules shall not be admissible in evidence, notwithstanding such rule, unless an investigation of such report conducted pursuant to title six of article six of the social services law has determined that there is some credible evidence of the alleged abuse or maltreatment and that the subject of the report has been notified that the report is indicated. In addition, if such report has been reviewed by the state commissioner of social services or his designee and has been determined to be unfounded, it shall not be admissible in evidence. If such report has been so reviewed and has been amended to delete any finding, each such deleted finding shall not be admissible. If the state commissioner of social services or his designee has amended the report to add any new finding, each such new finding, together with any portion of the original report not deleted by the commissioner or his designee, shall be admissible if it meets the other requirements of this subdivision and is otherwise admissible as a business record. If such a report, or portion thereof, is admissible in evidence but is uncorroborated, it shall not be sufficient to make a fact finding of abuse or maltreatment in such proceeding. Any other evidence tending to support the reliability of such report shall be sufficient corroboration.

1-b. (a) The court shall make its award for child support pursuant to the provisions of this subdivision. The court may vary from the amount of the basic child support obligation determined pursuant to paragraph (c) of this subdivision only in accordance with paragraph (f) of this subdivision.

b) For purposes of this subdivision, the following definitions shall be used:

1) "Basic child support obligation" shall mean the sum derived by adding the amounts determined by the application of subparagraphs two and three of paragraph (c) of this subdivision except as increased pursuant to subparagraphs four, five, six and seven of such paragraph.

2) "Child support" shall mean a sum to be paid pursuant to court order or decree by either or both parents or pursuant to a valid agreement between the parties for care, maintenance and education of any unemancipated child under the age of twenty-one years.

3) "Child support percentage" shall mean:

i) seventeen percent of the combined parental income for one child;

ii) twenty-five percent of the combined parental income for two children;

iii) twenty-nine percent of the combined parental income for three children;

iv) thirty-one percent of the combined parental income for four children; and

v) no less than thirty-five percent of the combined parental income for five or more children.

4) "Combined parental income" shall mean the sum of the income of both parents.

5) "Income" shall mean, but shall not be limited to, the sum of the amounts determined by the application of clauses (i), (ii), (iii), (iv), (v) and (vi) of this subparagraph reduced by the amount determined by the application of clause (vii) of this subparagraph:

i) gross (total) income as should have been or should be reported in the most recent federal income tax return. If an individual files his/her federal income tax return as a married person filing jointly, such person shall be required to prepare a form, sworn to under penalty of law, disclosing his/her gross income individually;

ii) to the extent not already included in gross income in clause (i) of this subparagraph, investment income reduced by sums expended in connection with such investment;

iii) to the extent not already included in gross income in clauses (i) and (ii) of this subparagraph, the amount of income or compensation voluntarily deferred and income received, if any, from the following sources:

A) workers' compensation,

B) disability benefits,

C) unemployment insurance benefits,

D) social security benefits,

E) veterans benefits,

F) pensions and retirement benefits,

G) fellowships and stipends, and

H) annuity payments;

iv) at the discretion of the court, the court may attribute or impute income from, such other resources as may be available to the parent, including, but not limited to:

A) non-income producing assets,

B) meals, lodging, memberships, automobiles or other perquisites that are provided as part of compensation for employment to the extent that such perquisites constitute expenditures for personal use, or which expenditures directly or indirectly confer personal economic benefits,

C) fringe benefits provided as part of compensation for employment, and

D) money, goods, or services provided by relatives and friends;

v) an amount imputed as income based upon the parent's former resources or income, if the court determines that a parent has reduced resources or income in order to reduce or avoid the parent's obligation for child support;

vi) to the extent not already included in gross income in clauses (i) and (ii) of this subparagraph, the following self-employment deductions attributable to self-employment carried on by the taxpayer:

A) any depreciation deduction greater than depreciation calculated on a straight-line basis for the purpose of determining business income or investment credits, and

B) entertainment and travel allowances deducted from business income to the extent said allowances reduce personal expenditures;

vii) the following shall be deducted from income prior to applying the provisions of paragraph (c) of this subdivision:

A) unreimbursed employee business expenses except to the extent said expenses reduce personal expenditures,

B) alimony or maintenance actually paid to a spouse not a party to the instant action pursuant to court order or validly executed written agreement,

C) alimony or maintenance actually paid or to be paid to a spouse that is a party to the instant action pursuant to an existing court order or contained in the order to be entered by the court, or pursuant to a validly executed written agreement, provided the order or agreement provides for a specific adjustment, in accordance with this subdivision, in the amount of child support payable upon the termination of alimony or maintenance to such spouse,

D) child support actually paid pursuant to court order or written agreement on behalf of any child for whom the parent has a legal duty of support and who is not subject to the instant action,

E) public assistance,

F) supplemental security income,

G) New York city or Yonkers income or earnings taxes actually paid, and

H) federal insurance contributions act (FICA) taxes actually paid.

6) "Self-support reserve" shall mean one hundred thirty-five percent of the poverty income guidelines amount for a single person as reported by the federal department of health and human services. For the calendar year nineteen hundred eighty-nine, the self-support reserve shall be eight thousand sixty-five dollars. On March first of each year, the self-support reserve shall be revised to reflect the annual updating of the poverty income guidelines as reported by the federal department of health and human services for a single person household.

c) The amount of the basic child support obligation shall be determined in accordance with the provision of this paragraph:

1) The court shall determine the combined parental income.

2) The court shall multiply the combined parental income up to eighty thousand dollars by the appropriate child support percentage and such amount shall be prorated in the same proportion as each parent's income is to the combined parental income.

3) Where the combined parental income exceeds the dollar amount set forth in subparagraph two of this paragraph, the court shall determine the amount of child support for the amount of the combined parental income in excess of such dollar amount through consideration of the factors set forth in paragraph (f) of this subdivision and/or the child support percentage.

4) Where the custodial parent is working, or receiving elementary or secondary education, or higher education or vocational training which the court determines will lead to employment, and incurs child care expenses as a result thereof, the court shall determine reasonable child care expenses and such child care expenses, where incurred, shall be prorated in the same proportion as each parent's income is to the combined parental income. Each parent's pro rata share of the child care expenses shall be separately stated and added to the sum of subparagraphs two and three of this paragraph.

5) The court shall prorate each parent's share of future reasonable health care expenses of the child not covered by insurance in the same proportion as each parent's income is to the combined parental income. The non-custodial parent's pro rata share of such health care expenses shall be paid in a manner

determined by the court, including direct payment to the health care provider.

6) Where the court determines that the custodial parent is seeking work and incurs child care expenses as a result thereof, the court may determine reasonable child care expenses and may apportion the same between the custodial and non-custodial parent. The non-custodial parent's share of such expenses shall be separately stated and paid in a manner determined by the court.

7) Where the court determines, having regard for the circumstances of the case and of the respective parties and in the best interests of the child, and as justice requires, that the present or future provision of post-secondary, private, special, or enriched education for the child is appropriate, the court may award educational expenses. The non-custodial parent shall pay educational expenses, as awarded, in a manner determined by the court, including direct payment to the educational provider.

d) Notwithstanding the provisions of paragraph (c) of this subdivision, where the annual amount of the basic child support obligation would reduce the non-custodial parent's income below the poverty income guidelines amount for a single person as reported by the federal department of health and human services, the basic child support obligation shall be twenty-five dollars per month or the difference between the non-custodial parent's income and the self-support reserve, whichever is greater. Notwithstanding the provisions of paragraph (c) of this subdivision, where the annual amount of the basic child support obligation would reduce the non-custodial parent's income below the self-support reserve but not below the poverty income guidelines amount for a single person as reported by the federal department of health and human services, the basic child support obligation shall be fifty dollars per month or the difference between the non-custodial parent's income and the self-support reserve, whichever is greater.

(e) Where a parent is or may be entitled to receive non-recurring payments from extraordinary sources not otherwise considered as income pursuant to this section, including but not limited to:

1) Life insurance policies;

2) Discharges of indebtedness;

3) Recovery of bad debts and delinquency amounts;

4) Gifts and inheritances; and

5) Lottery winnings, the court, in accordance with paragraphs (c), (d) and (f) of this subdivision may allocate a proportion of the same to child support, and such amount shall be paid in a manner determined by the court.

f) The court shall calculate the basic child support obligation, and the non-custodial parent's pro rata share of the basic child support obligation. Unless the court finds that the non-custodial parent's pro-rata share of the basic child support obligation is unjust or inappropriate, which finding shall be based upon consideration of the following factors:

1) The financial resources of the custodial and non-custodial parent, and those of the child;

2) The physical and emotional health of the child and his/her special needs and aptitudes;

3) The standard of living the child would have enjoyed had the marriage or household not been dissolved;

4) The tax consequences to the parties;

5) The non-monetary contributions that the parents will make toward the care and well-being of the child;

6) The educational needs of either parent;

7) A determination that the gross income of one parent is substantially less than the other parent's gross income;

8) The needs of the children of the non-custodial parent for whom the non-custodial parent is providing support who are not subject to the instant action and whose support has not been deducted from income pursuant to subclause (D) of clause (vii) of subparagraph five of paragraph (b) of this subdivision, and the financial resources of any person obligated to support such children, provided, however, that this factor may apply only if the resources available to support such children are less than the resources available to support the children who are subject to the instant action;

9) Provided that the child is not on public assistance (i) extraordinary expenses incurred by the non-custodial parent in exercising visitation, or (ii) expenses incurred by the non-custodial parent in extended visitation provided that the custodial parent's expenses are substantially reduced as a result thereof; and

10) Any other factors the court determines are relevant in each case, the court shall order the non-custodial parent to pay his or her pro rata share of the basic child support obligation, and may order the non-custodial parent to pay an amount pursuant to paragraph (e) of this subdivision.

g) Where the court finds that the non-custodial parent's pro rata share of the basic child support obligation is unjust or inappropriate, the court shall order the non-custodial parent to pay such amount of child support as the court finds just and appropriate, and the court shall set forth, in a written order, the factors it considered; the amount of each party's pro rata share of the basic child support obligation; and the reasons that the court did not order the basic child support obligation. Such written order may not be waived by either party or counsel; provided, however, and notwithstanding any other provision of law, the court shall not find that the non-custodial parent's pro rata share of such obligation is unjust or inappropriate on the basis that such share exceeds the portion of a public assistance grant which is attributable to a child or children. In no instance shall the court order child support below twenty-five dollars per month. Where the non-custodial parent's income is less than or equal to the poverty income guidelines amount for a single person as reported by the federal department of health and human services, unpaid child support arrears in excess of five hundred dollars shall not accrue.

h)   A validly executed agreement or stipulation voluntarily entered into between the parties after the effective date of this subdivision presented to the court for incorporation in an order or judgment shall include a provision stating that the parties have been advised of the provisions of this subdivision, and that the basic child support obligation provided for therein would presumptively result in the correct amount of child support to be awarded. In the event that such agreement or stipulation deviates from the basic child support obligation, the agreement or stipulation must specify the amount that such basic child support obligation would have been and the reason or reasons that such agreement or stipulation does not provide for payment of that amount. Such provision may not be waived by either party or counsel. Nothing contained in this subdivision shall be construed to alter the rights of the parties to voluntarily enter into validly executed agreements or stipulations which deviate from the basic child support obligation provided such agreements or stipulations comply with the provisions of this paragraph. The court shall, however, retain discretion with respect to child support pursuant to this section. Any court order or judgment incorporating a validly executed agreement or stipulation which deviates from the basic child support obligation shall set forth the court's reasons for such deviation.

i)   Where either or both parties are unrepresented, the court shall not enter an order or judgment other than a temporary order pursuant to section two hundred thirty-seven of this article, that includes a provision for child support unless the unrepresented party or parties have received a copy of the child support standards chart promulgated by the commissioner of social services pursuant to subdivision two of section one hundred eleven-i of the social services law. Where either party is in receipt of child support enforcement services through the local social services district, the local social services district child support enforcement unit shall advise such party of the amount derived from application of the child support percentage and that such amount serves as a starting point for the determination of the child support award, and shall provide such party with a copy of the child support standards chart. In no instance shall the court approve any voluntary support agreement or compromise that includes an amount for child support less than twenty-five dollars per month.

j)   In addition to financial disclosure required in section two hundred thirty-six of this article, the court may require that the income and/or expenses of either party be verified with documentation including, but not limited to, past and present income tax returns, employer statements, pay stubs, corporate, business, or partnership books and records, corporate and business tax returns, and receipts for expenses or such other means of verification as the court determines appropriate. Nothing herein shall affect any party's right to pursue discovery pursuant to this chapter, the civil practice law and rules, or the family court act.

k)   When a party has defaulted and/or the court is otherwise presented with insufficient evidence to determine gross income, the court shall order child support based upon the needs or standard of living of the child, whichever is greater. Such order may be retroactively modified upward, without a showing of change in circumstances.

Appendix B
Forms

Be sure to read the section "An Introduction to Legal Forms" in Chapter 6 before you begin using the forms in this appendix. The instructions for a particular form may be found by looking in the index. With the exception of form 13, make photocopies of the forms, and use the copies for both practice worksheets and the forms you will file with the court. The blank forms can then be used to make more copies in the event you make mistakes or need additional copies.

Table of Forms

The following forms are included in this appendix:

form 1

PROPERTY INVENTORY

(1) S	(2) DESCRIPTION	(3) ID#	(4) VALUE	(5) BALANCE OWED	(6) EQUITY	(7) OWNER H-W-J	(8) H	(9) W

DEBT INVENTORY

(1) S	(2) CREDITOR	(3) ACCOUNT NO.	(4) NOTES	(5) MONTHLY	(6) BALANCE OWED	(7) DATE	(8) OWNER H-W-J	(9) H	(10) W

SUPREME COURT OF THE STATE OF NEW YORK
COUNTY OF _____
\--x

Plaintiff,	**Index No.** _____
-against-	
	PART 130
	CERTIFICATION
Defendant.	

\--x

CERTIFICATION: I hereby certify that all of the papers that I have served, filed or submitted to the court in this divorce action are not frivolous as defined in subsection (c) of Section 130-1.1 of the Rules of the Chief Administrator of the Courts.

Dated: _____   _____
                                                 SIGNATURE
                                                 Print or type name below signature

SUPREME COURT OF THE STATE OF NEW YORK

COUNTY OF _____

--X

Plaintiff

    -against-

Defendant

--X

Index No:_____

Date Summons filed:_____

Plaintiff designates _____
County as the place of trial
The basis of venue is:

_____
_____

SUMMONS WITH NOTICE
Plaintiff/Defendant resides at:

_____
_____
_____

ACTION FOR A DIVORCE

To the above named Defendant:

YOU ARE HEREBY SUMMONED to serve a notice of appearance on the *Plaintiff/ Plaintiff's Attorney(s)* within twenty (20) days after the service of this summons, exclusive of the day of service (or within thirty (30) days after the service is complete if this summons is not personally delivered to you with the State of New York); and in case of your failure to appear, judgment will be taken against you by default for the relief demanded in the notice set forth below.

Dated_____

Attorney(s) for Plaintiff
Address:

Phone No:

NOTICE: The nature of this action is to dissolve the marriage between parties, on the grounds: **DRL §170 subd._____-_____.

The relief sought is a judgment of absolute divorce in favor of the Plaintiff dissolving the marriage between the parties in this action. The nature of any ancillary or additional relief demanded is:

_____

_____

_____

**Insert the grounds for the divorce:

DRL §170(1) - cruel and inhuman treatment	DRL §170(4) - adultery
DRL §170(2) - abandonment	DRL §170(5) - living apart one year after judgment of separation
DRL §170(3) - confinement in prison	DRL §170(6) - living apart one year after execution of a separation agreement

SUPREME COURT OF THE STATE OF NEW YORK

COUNTY OF _____

--X

Index No:_____

Date Summons filed:_____

Plaintiff designates _____

County as the place of trial

The basis of venue is:

_____

Plaintiff

-against-

SUMMONS

Plaintiff/Defendant resides at:

_____

_____

Defendant

_____

--X

ACTION FOR A DIVORCE

To the above named Defendant:

YOU ARE HEREBY SUMMONED to answer the complaint in this action and to serve a copy of your answer on the Plaintiff/Plaintiff's Attorney(s) within twenty (20) days after the service of this summons, exclusive of the day of service, where service is made by delivery upon you personally within the state, or within thirty (30) days after completion of service where service is made in any other manner. In case of your failure to appear or answer, judgment will be taken against you by default for the relief demanded in the complaint.

Dated_____

Attorney(s) for Plaintiff

Address:

Phone No:

SUPREME COURT OF THE STATE OF NEW YORK

COUNTY OF _____

---X

                          Plaintiff   Index No:_____

    -against-

                                                       AFFIDAVIT OF SERVICE

                          Defendant

---X

STATE OF NEW YORK, COUNTY OF _____ ss.:

_____ being duly sworn, says:

1.   I am not a party to the action, I am over 18 years of age and reside at:

    _____

2.   On _____, _____, at _____a.m./p.m. at _____ _____ I served the within *summons with notice / summons and verified complaint* on _____, the Defendant named in the *summons with notice / summons and verified complaint*, by delivering a true copy of the *summons with notice / summons and verified complaint* to the Defendant personally.

3.   The notice required by the Domestic Relations Law, Section 232 — "ACTION FOR A DIVORCE"—was legibly printed on the face of the summons served on the Defendant.

4.   I knew the person so served to be the person described in the summons as the Defendant. My knowledge of the Defendant and how I acquired it is as follows: (select one)

    ❑   I have known the defendant for _____ years and _____
    _____
    _____

OR

    ❑   I identified the Defendant by a photograph annexed to this affidavit and which was given to me by the Plaintiff

OR

    ❑   Plaintiff accompanied me and pointed out the Defendant.

OR

    ❑   I asked the person served if he/she was the person named in the summons and Defendant admitted being the person so named.

5. Deponent describes the individual served as follows:

<u>Sex</u>	<u>Height</u>	<u>Weight</u>	<u>Age</u>	<u>Color</u> <u>of</u> <u>Skin</u>	<u>Color</u> <u>of</u> <u>Hair</u>
❏ Male	❏ Under 5"	❏ Under 100 Lbs.	❏ 14-20 Yrs.	Describe color:	❏ Black
❏ Female	❏ 5'0"-5'3"	❏ 100-130 Lbs.	❏ 21-35 Yrs.	_____	❏ Brown
	❏ 5'4"-5'8"	❏ 131-160 Lbs.	❏ 36-50 Yrs.	_____	❏ Blond
	❏ 5'9"-6'0"	❏ 161-200 Lbs.	❏ 51-65 Yrs.	_____	❏ Gray
	❏ Over 6"	❏ Over 200 Lbs.	❏ Over 65 Yrs.	_____	❏ Red
					❏ White
					❏ Balding
					❏ Bald

Other identifying feature, if any: _____.

6a. ❏ *At the time I served the Defendant, I asked him/her if he/she was in the military service of this state or nation or any other nation, and the Defendant responded in the negative.*

6b. ❏ *The Defendant stated that he/she is in the following military service* _____

_____.

Dated: _____   _____

                                        Server

Sworn to before me on

_____, _____

_____

Notary Public

SUPREME COURT OF THE STATE OF NEW YORK
COUNTY OF _____

---X

<table>
<tr><td>Plaintiff,</td><td>Index No.:</td></tr>
<tr><td>-against-</td><td>**VERIFIED COMPLAINT**</td></tr>
<tr><td></td><td>**ACTION FOR DIVORCE**</td></tr>
<tr><td>Defendant.</td><td></td></tr>
</table>

---X

FIRST:

Plaintiff*herein / by* _____, complaining of the Defendant, alleges that the parties are over the age of 18 years and;

SECOND:

❐ The Plaintiff has resided in New York State for a continuous period in excess of two years immediately preceding the commencement of this action.

OR

❐ The Defendant has resided in New York State for a continuous period in excess of two years immediately preceding the commencement of this action.

OR

❐ The Plaintiff has resided in New York State for a continuous period in excess of one year immediately preceding the commencement of this action, and:

    a.   the parties were married in New York State.
    b.   the Plaintiff has lived as husband or wife in New York State with the Defendant.
    c.   the cause of action occurred in New York State.

OR

❐ The Defendant has resided in New York State for a continuous period in excess of one year immediately preceding the commencement of this action, and:

    a.   the parties were married in New York State.
    b.   the Defendant has lived as husband or wife in New York State with the Plaintiff.
    c.   the cause of action occurred in New York State.

OR

❐ The cause of action occurred in New York State and both parties were residents thereof at the time of the commencement of this action.

THIRD: The Plaintiff and the Defendant were married on _____

in (city, town or village; and state or country)_____.

(Form UD-2 - Rev. 5/99)

The marriage was *not* performed by a clergyman, minister or by a leader of the Society for Ethical Culture.

(If the word "not" is deleted above check the appropriate box below).

☐ *To the best of my knowledge I have taken all steps solely within my power to remove any barrier to the Defendants remarriage.* **OR**

☐ *I will take prior to the entry of final judgment all steps solely within my power to the best of my knowledge to remove any barrier to the Defendants remarriage.* **OR**

☐ *The Defendant has waived in writing the requirements of DRL §253 (Barriers to Remarriage).*

FOURTH: ☐ There are no children of the marriage. **OR**

☐ There *is (are)* _____ child(ren) of the marriage, namely:

Name	Date of Birth	Address
_____	_____	_____
_____	_____	_____
_____	_____	_____
_____	_____	_____
_____	_____	_____

The Plaintiff resides at _____

_. The Defendant resides at _____

___.

The parties are covered by the following group health plans:

Plaintiff   **Defendant**

Group Health Plan:_____   Group Health Plan:_____
Address:_____   Address:_____
Identification Number:_____   Identification Number:_____
Plan Administrator:_____   Plan Administrator:_____
Type of Coverage:_____   Type of Coverage:_____

FIFTH: The grounds for divorce that are alleged as follows:

☐ **Cruel and Inhuman Treatment (DRL §170(1)):**

At the following times, none of which are earlier than (5) years prior to commencement of this action, the Defendant engaged in conduct that so endangered the mental and physical well-being of the Plaintiff, so as to render it unsafe and improper for the parties to cohabit (live together) as husband and wife.

(State the facts that demonstrate cruel and inhuman conduct giving dates, places and specific acts. Conduct may include physical, verbal, sexual or emotional behavior.)

_____
_____
_____

(Form UD-2 - Rev. 5/99)

188

_____
_____
_____
_____
_____

(Attach an additional sheet, if necessary).

Abandonment (DRL 170(2)):

That commencing on or about _____, and continuing for a period of more than one (1) year immediately prior to commencement of this action, the Defendant left the marital residence of the parties located at _____, and did not return. Such absence was without cause or justification, and was without Plaintiff's consent.

That commencing on or about _____, and continuing for a period of more than one (1) year immediately prior to commencement of this action, the Defendant refused to have sexual relations with the Plaintiff despite Plaintiff's repeated requests to resume such relations. Defendant does not suffer from any disability which would prevent *her / him* from engaging in such sexual relations with Plaintiff. The refusal to engage in sexual relations was without good cause or justification and occurred at the marital residence located at _____.

That commencing on or about_____, and continuing for a period of more than one (1) year immediately prior to commencement of this action, the Defendant willfully and without cause or justification abandoned the Plaintiff, who had been a faithful and dutiful *husband / wife*, by depriving Plaintiff of access to the marital residence located at_____
. This deprivation of access was without the consent of the Plaintiff and continued for a period of greater than one year.

Confinement to Prison (DRL §170(3)):

(a)   That after the marriage of Plaintiff and Defendant, Defendant was confined in prison for a period of three or more consecutive years, to wit: that Defendant was confined in_____ _____ prison on _____, and has remained confined to this date; and

(b)   not more that five (5) years has elapsed between the end of the third year of imprisonment and the date of commencement of this action.

Adultery (DRL §170(4)):

(a)   That on _____, at the premises located at _____ _,the Defendant engaged in sexual intercourse with_____, without the procurement nor the connivance of the Plaintiff, and the Plaintiff ceased to cohabit (live) with the Defendant upon the discovery of the adultery; and

(b)   not more than five (5) years elapsed between the date of said adultery and the date of commencement of this action.

(Attach a corroborating affidavit of a third party witness or other additional proof).

(Form UD-2 - Rev. 5/99)

☐ **Living Separate and Apart Pursuant to a Separation Decree or Judgment of Separation (DRL §170(5)):**

   (a)   That the _____ Court, _____ County, _____ (Country or State) rendered a decree or judgment of separation on _____, under Index Number _____; and

   (b)   that the parties have lived separate and apart for a period of one year or longer after the granting of such decree; and

   (c)   that the Plaintiff has substantially complied with all the terms and conditions of such decree or judgment.

☐ **Living Separate and Apart Pursuant to a Separation Agreement (DRL §170(6)):**

   (a)   That the Plaintiff and Defendant entered into a written agreement of separation, which they subscribed and acknowledged on _____, in the form required to entitle a deed to be recorded; and

   (b)   that the *agreement / memorandum of said agreement* was filed on _____ in the Office of the Clerk of the County of_____, wherein *Plaintiff / Defendant* resided; and

   (c)   that the parties have lived separate and apart for a period of one year or longer after the execution of said agreement; and

   (d)   that the Plaintiff has substantially complied with all terms and conditions of such agreement.

SIXTH: There is no judgment in any court for a divorce and no other matrimonial action between the parties pending in this court or in any other court of competent jurisdiction.

      WHEREFORE, Plaintiff demands judgment against the Defendant as follows: A judgment dissolving the marriage between the parties and

_____

_____

_____

_____

_____

AND

☐ equitable distribution of marital property;

OR

☐ marital property to be distributed pursuant to the annexed separation agreement / stipulation;

OR

☐ I waive equitable distribution of marital property;

and any other relief the court deems fitting and proper.

Dated:_____

Plaintiff

Attorney(s) for Plaintiff
Address:

Phone No.:

(Form UD-2 - Rev. 5/99)

STATE OF NEW YORK, COUNTY OF _____ ss:

a   I _____ (Print Name), am the Plaintiff inthe within action for divorce. I have read the foregoing complaint and know the contents thereof. The contents are true to my own knowledge except as to matters therein stated to be alleged upon information and belief, and as to those matters I believe them to be true.

Subscribed and Sworn to
before me on

_____

_____

_____
Plaintiff's Signature

_____
NOTARY PUBLIC

(Form UD-2 - Rev. 5/99)

SUPREME COURT OF THE STATE OF NEW YORK

COUNTY OF _____

---X

                        Plaintiff   Index No: _____

  -against-

                                                     SWORN STATEMENT
                                                     OF REMOVAL OF
                      Defendant   **BARRIERS TO REMARRIAGE**

---X

State of New York, County of _____ ss:

    I state under penalty of perjury that the parties' marriage was solemnized by a minister, clergyman or leader of the Society for Ethical Culture, and that;

❏ *To the best of my knowledge I have taken all steps solely within my power to remove any barrier to the Defendant's remarriage.*

❏ *The Defendant has waived, in writing, the requirements of DRL sec 253.*

Dated: _____   _____

                                           Plaintiff

Sworn to before me on

_____, _____

_____

Notary Public

Affidavit of Service

_____being sworn, says, I am not a party to the action, am over 18 years of age and I reside at _____
_____.

On _____, _____, I served the within removal of barriers statement on the Defendant

❏ *personally at* _____

OR

❏ *by depositing a true copy thereof enclosed in a post-paid wrapper, in an official depository under the exclusive care and custody of the U.S. Postal Service within New York State, addressed to the Defendant at* _____
_____

_____
Server

Sworn to before me on

_____, _____

_____
Notary Public

SUPREME COURT OF THE STATE OF NEW YORK

COUNTY OF _____

---X

Plaintiff

-against-

Defendant

Index No:

**AFFIRMATION (AFFIDAVIT)
OR REGULARITY**

---X

STATE OF NEW YORK, COUNTY OF _____ ss:

I, the undersigned attorney at law duly admitted to practice law in the State of New York, respectfully show:

The undersigned, being duly sworn, deposes and says:

I am *the attorney for* the Plaintiff herein.

This is a matrimonial action.

The Summons *with Notice was / and verified complaint were* personally served upon the Defendant herein, *within / outside* the State of New York as appears in the affidavit of service submitted herewith.

Defendant has appeared on his or her own behalf / by the firm of: _____ _____*and executed an affidavit agreeing that this matter be placed on the matrimonial calendar immediately.*

Defendant is in default for failure to serve a notice of appearance or failure to answer the complaint served in this action in due time, and the time to answer has not been extended by stipulation, court order, or otherwise.

WHEREFORE, I respectfully request that this action be placed on the undefended matrimonial calendar for trial.

I state under the penalties of perjury that the statements herein made are true, except as to such statements as are based on information and belief, which statements I believe to be true.

Dated: _____

_____
Attorney/Plaintiff:

Sworn to before me on

_____, _____

_____
Notary Public

SUPREME COURT OF THE STATE OF NEW YORK

COUNTY OF _____

--X

_____ ,

Plaintiff,

-against-

Index No.:

STATEMENT OF
NET WORTH, FINANCIAL
AFFIDAVIT
(Section 236 DRL)

_____ ,

Defendant.

--X

Action Commencement
Date:_____

STATE OF NEW YORK   COUNTY OF _____ss.:

_____ , the Plaintiff herein, being duly sworn, deposes and says that the following is an accurate statement as of_____ , of my net worth (assets of whatsoever kind and nature and wherever situated minus liabilities), statement of income from all sources, and statement of assets transferred of whatsoever kind and nature and wherever situated:

1. FAMILY DATA

(a) Husband's Age: Wife's Age:

(b) Husband's Place of Birth: Wife's Place of Birth:

(c) Date Married:

(d) Date of Separation:

(e) Number of dependent children under 21 Years:

(f) Names, Ages and Dates of Birth of Children:

(g) Custody of Children is with (H/W/J):

(h) Minor Children of Prior Marriage: Husband: Wife:

(i) Support for children of Prior Marriage (amount and to whom paid or paid by):

(j) Custody of Children of Prior Marriage: (Name and Address of Custodial Parent)

(k) The marital residence is occupied by (H/W/Both):

(l) Husband's present Address:

Wife's present Address:

(m) Occupation of Husband:
Occupation of Wife:

(n) Husband's Employer:

(o) Wife's Employer:

(p) Education, training & skills: (Include dates of attainment of degree, etc.)
Husband:
Wife:

(q) Husband's Health:

(r) Wife's Health:

(s) Children's Health:

II. EXPENSES

(a) **Housing:**
1. Rent
2. Mortgage and
   amortization
3. Real estate taxes

4. Condominium charges
5. Cooperative Apartment
   Maintenance

Total: Housing - $

(b) **Utilities:**
1. Fuel oil
2. Gas
3. Electricity

4. Telephone
5. Water

Total: Utilities - $

(c) **Food:**
1. Groceries
2. School Lunches
3. Lunches at work

4. Liquor/alcohol
5. Home entertainment
6. Other

Total: Food - $

(d) **Clothing:**
1. Husband
2. Wife

3. Children
4. Other

Total: Clothing - $

(e) **Laundry:**
1. Laundry at home
2. Dry cleaning

3. Other

Total: Laundry - $

(f) **Insurance:**
1. Life
2. Homeowner's/tenant's
3. Fire, theft, and
   liability
4. Automotive
5. Umbrella policy

6. Medical plan
7. Dental plan
8. Optical plan
9. Disability
10. Worker's Comp.
11. Other

Total: Insurance - $

(g) **Unreimbursed medical:**
1. Medical
2. Dental
3. Optical
4. Pharmaceutical

5. Surgical, nursing, hospital
6. Other

Total: Unreimbursed medical - $

(h) **Household maintenance**
1. Repairs
2. Furniture, furnishings
   housewares
3. Cleaning Supplies
4. Appliances including
   maintenance

5. Painting
6. Sanitation/carting
7. Gardening/landscape
8. Snow removal
9. Extermination
10. Other

Total: Household maintenance - $

(i) Household Help
1. Baby-sitter
2. Domestic (Maid, etc.)
3. Nurse
4. Other

Total: Household Help - $

(j) Automotive
1. Year: Make:
Model: Personal (Y/N):   Business: (Y/N)

1. Payments
2. Gas and Oil
3. Repairs
4. Car Wash
5. Registration/license
6. Parking and Tolls
7. Other

Total: Automotive - $

(k) Educational
1. Pre-school: Daycare:
2. Primary and secondary
3. College
4. Post-graduate
5. Religious Instruction
6. School trans.
7. School supp./books
8. Tutoring
9. School events
10. Other

Total: Educational - $

(l) Recreational
1. Summer camp
2. Vacations
3. Movies
4. Theatre, ballet, etc.
5. Video rentals
6. Tapes, CD's, etc.
7. Cable Television
8. Team Sports
9. Country/pool club
10. Health club
11. Sporting goods
12. Hobbies
13. Music/dance lessons
14. Sports lessons
15. Birthday parties
16. Other

Total: Recreational - $

(m) Income Taxes
1. Federal
2. State
3. City
4. Social Security and Medicare

Total: Taxes - $

(n) Miscellaneous
1. Beauty Parlor/Barber
2. Beauty aids/cosmetics, drug items
3. Cigarettes/tobacco
4. Books, magazines, newspapers
5. Children's allowances
6. Gifts
7. Charitable contribution
8. Religious organizations dues
9. Union and organization dues
10. Commutation and transportation
11. Veterinarian/pet exp.
12. Child support payments (prior marriage)
13. Alimony & maintenance payments
14. Loan Payments
15. Unreimbursed business expenses

Total: Miscellaneous - $

(o) Other
1.
2.
3.
4.

Total: Other

TOTAL MONTHLY EXPENSES: $

TOTAL ANNUAL EXPENSES: $

III.   GROSS INCOME (Monthly Amounts):

(a)   Salary or Wages:

        1. Salary   (+)

(b)   Monthly Deductions:

        Employer 1:

        1. Federal Tax   (-)

        2. New York State Tax   (-)

        3. Local Tax   (-)

        4. Social Security   (-)

        5. Medicare   (-)

        6. Other Payroll Deduction (Specify)   savings   (-)

                                         life insurance   (-)

(c)   Social Security Number:

(d)   Number and Names of Dependents:

(e)   Bonus, Commissions, Fringe Benefits (use of auto, memberships, etc.)   (+)

(f)   Partnerships, Royalties, Sale of Assets: (income and installment payments)   (+)

(g)   Dividends and Interest:

        1. Taxable   (+)

        2. Nontaxable   (+)

(h)   Real Estate (income only)   (+)

(i)   Trust, profit sharing, and annuity (principal distribution and income)   (+)

(j)   Pension (income only)   (+)

(k)   Awards, Prizes, Grants:

        1. Taxable   (+)

        2. Nontaxable   (+)

(l)   Income from bequests, legacies and gifts: (+)

(m)   Income from all other sources: (Including alimony, maintenance, or child support from prior marriage)   (+)

(n)   Tax preference items:

        1. Long term capital gain deduction: (-)

        2. Depreciation amortization or depletion: (-)

        3. Stock options—Excess fair market value over amount paid: (-)

(o)   Other Household Member's Income:

(p)   Social Security: (+)

(q)   Disability Benefits: (+)

(r)   Public Assistance: (+)

(s)   Other: (+)

TOTAL MONTHLY INCOME: $

TOTAL ANNUAL INCOME: $

IV. ASSETS (If any asset is held jointly with spouse or another, so state, and set forth your respective shares. Attach additional sheets if needed)

A. Cash Accounts

<u>Cash</u>

1.1   a.   Location: _____
       b.   Source of funds: _____
       c.   Other information: _____
       d.   Amount: _____   _____

<u>Checking</u>

2.1   a.   Financial Institution: _____
       b.   Account number: _____
       c.   Title holder: _____
       d.   Date opened: _____
       e.   Source of funds: _____
       f.   Other information: _____
       g.   Balance: _____   _____

2.2   a.   Financial Institution: _____
       b.   Account number: _____
       c.   Title holder: _____
       d.   Date opened: _____
       e.   Source of funds: _____
       f.   Other information: _____
       g.   Balance: _____   _____

2.3   a.   Financial Institution: _____
       b.   Account number: _____
       c.   Title holder: _____
       d.   Date opened: _____
       e.   Source of funds: _____
       f.   Other information: _____
       g.   Balance: _____   _____

<u>Savings</u>

      (Individual, joint, Totten trusts, CDs, treasury notes)

3.1   a.   Financial Institution: _____
       b.   Account number: _____
       c.   Title holder: _____
       d.   Date opened: _____
       e.   Source of funds: _____
       f.   Other information: _____
       g.   Balance: _____   _____

3.2 a. Financial Institution: _____
   b. Account number: _____
   c. Title holder: _____
   d. Date opened: _____
   e. Source of funds: _____
   f. Other information: _____
   g. Balance: _____

3.3 a. Financial Institution: _____
   b. Account number: _____
   c. Title holder: _____
   d. Date opened: _____
   e. Source of funds: _____
   f. Other information: _____
   g. Balance: _____

Security deposits (earnest money, etc.)

4.1 a. Location: _____
   b. Title owner: _____
   c. Type of Deposit: _____
   d. Source of funds: _____
   f. Other information: _____
   g. Amount: _____

Other

5.1 a. Location: _____
   b. Title owner: _____
   c. Type of Deposit: _____
   d. Source of funds: _____
   e. Date of deposit: _____
   f. Other information: _____
   g. Amount: _____

B. **Securities**

Bonds, notes, mortgages

1.1 a. Description of Security: _____
   b. Title holder: _____
   c. Location: _____
   d. Date of acquisition: _____
   e. Original price or value: _____
   f. Source of funds to acquire: _____
   g. Other information: _____
   h. Current value: _____

Stocks, options, etc.

2.1   a Description of Security: _____
         b. Title owner: _____
         c. Location: _____
         d. Date of acquisition: _____
         e. Original price or value: _____
         f. Source of funds to acquire: _____
         g. Other information: _____
         h. Current value: _____

2.2   a. Description of Security: _____
         b. Title owner: _____
         c. Location: _____
         d. Date of acquisition: _____
         e. Original price or value: _____
         f. Source of funds to acquire: _____
         g. Other information: _____
         h. Current value: _____

2.3   a. Description of Security: _____
         b. Title owner: _____
         c. Location: _____
         d. Date of acquisition: _____
         e. Original price or value: _____
         f. Source of funds to acquire: _____
         g. Other information: _____
         h. Current value: _____

2.4   a. Description of Security: _____
         b. Title owner: _____
         c. Location: _____
         d. Date of acquisition: _____
         e. Original price or value: _____
         f. Source of funds to acquire: _____
         g. Other information: _____
         h. Current value: _____

Broker Margin Accounts

3.1   a. Name and address of Broker: _____

         b. Title holder: _____
         c. Date account opened: _____
         d. Original value of account: _____
         e. Source of funds: _____
         f. Other information: _____
         g. Current value: _____

C. **Loans & Accts Receivable**

1.1　　a. Debtor's name and address　　_____
　　　　　　　　　　　　　　　　　　_____
　　　　b. Original amount of loan or debt: _____
　　　　c. Source of funds from which
　　　　　　loan made or origin of debt:　_____
　　　　d. Date payment(s) due:
　　　　e. Other information:　　　　　　_____
　　　　f. Current amount due:

1.2　　a. Debtor's name and address:　　_____
　　　　　　　　　　　　　　　　　　_____
　　　　b. Original amount of loan or debt: _____
　　　　c. Source of funds from which
　　　　　　loan made or origin of debt:　_____
　　　　d. Date payment(s) due:　　　　_____
　　　　e. Other information:　　　　　_____
　　　　f. Current amount due:
　　　　　　　　　　　　　　　　　　　　　　　　　　_____

D. **Business Interests**

1.1　　a. Business name and address:　　_____
　　　　　　　　　　　　　　　　　　_____
　　　　b. Type of business (corporate,
　　　　　　partnership, sole
　　　　　　proprietorship, or other):　_____
　　　　c. Your capital contribution:　　_____
　　　　d. Your percentage of interest:　_____
　　　　e. Date of acquisition:　　　　_____
　　　　f. Original price or value:　　　_____
　　　　g. Source of funds to acquire:　_____
　　　　h. Method of valuation:　　　　_____
　　　　i. Other relevant information:　_____
　　　　j. Current net worth of business:
　　　　　　　　　　　　　　　　　　　　　　　　　　_____

1.2　　a. Business name and address:　　_____
　　　　　　　　　　　　　　　　　　_____
　　　　b. Type of business (corporate,
　　　　　　partnership, sole
　　　　　　proprietorship, or other):　_____
　　　　c. Your capital contribution:　　_____
　　　　d. Your percentage of interest:　_____
　　　　e. Date of acquisition:　　　　_____
　　　　f. Original price or value:　　　_____
　　　　g. Source of funds to acquire:　_____
　　　　h. Method of valuation:　　　　_____
　　　　i. Other relevant information:　_____
　　　　j. Current net worth of business:
　　　　　　　　　　　　　　　　　　　　　　　　　　_____

E. **Life Insurance Cash Value**

1.1   a. Insurer's name and address: _____

        b. Name of insured: _____
        c. Policy Number: _____
        d. Face amount of policy: _____
        e. Policy owner: _____
        f. Date of acquisition: _____
        g. Source of funds to acquire: _____
        h. Other information: _____
        i. Current cash surrender value: _____

1.2   a. Insurer's name and address: _____

        b. Name of insured: _____
        c. Policy Number: _____
        d. Face amount of policy: _____
        e. Policy owner: _____
        f. Date of acquisition: _____
        g. Source of funds to acquire: _____
        h. Other information: _____
        i. Current cash surrender value: _____

F. **Vehicles** (automobile, boat, plane, truck, camper, etc.)

1.1   a. Description: _____
        b. Title owner: _____
        c. Date of acquisition: _____
        d. Original price: _____
        e. Source of funds to acquire: _____
        f. Amount current lien unpaid: _____
        g. Other information: _____
        h. Current fair market value: _____

1.2   a. Description: _____
        b. Title owner: _____
        c. Date of acquisition: _____
        d. Original price: _____
        e. Source of funds to acquire: _____
        f. Amount current lien unpaid: _____
        g. Other information: _____
        h. Current fair market value: _____

1.3   a. Description: _____
        b. Title owner: _____
        c. Date of acquisition: _____
        d. Original price: _____
        e. Source of funds to acquire: _____
        f. Amount current lien unpaid: _____
        g. Other information: _____
        h. Current fair market value: _____

G.   Real Estate
(including real property, leaseholds, life estates, etc.
at market value--do not deduct any mortgage)

1.1   a. Description: _____
        b. Title owner: _____
        c. Date of acquisition: _____
        d. Original price: _____
        e. Source of funds to acquire: _____
        f. Amount current lien unpaid: _____
        g. Other information: _____
        h. Estimated Current market value: _____

1.2   a. Description: _____
        b. Title owner: _____
        c. Date of acquisition: _____
        d. Original price: _____
        e. Source of funds to acquire: _____
        f. Amount current lien unpaid: _____
        g. Other information: _____
        h. Estimated Current market value: _____

1.3   a. Description: _____
        b. Title owner: _____
        c. Date of acquisition: _____
        d. Original price: _____
        e. Source of funds to acquire: _____
        f. Amount current lien unpaid: _____
        g. Other information: _____
        h. Estimated Current market value: _____

1.4   a. Description: _____
        b. Title owner: _____
        c. Date of acquisition: _____
        d. Original price: _____
        e. Source of funds to acquire: _____
        f. Amount current lien unpaid: _____
        g. Other information: _____
        h. Estimated Current market value: _____

H.   Pensions & Trusts
(pension, profit sharing, legacies, deferred compensation, etc.)

1.1   a. Description of trust: _____
        b. Location of assets: _____
        c. Title owner: _____
        d. Date of acquisition: _____
        e. Original investment: _____
        f. Source of funds: _____
        g. Amount of unpaid liens: _____
        h. Other information: _____
        i. Current value: _____

1.2   a. Description of trust: _____
          b. Location of assets: _____
          c. Title owner: _____
          d. Date of acquisition: _____
          e. Original investment: _____
          f. Source of funds: _____
          g. Amount of unpaid liens: _____
          h. Other information: _____
          i. Current value: _____

I.   Contingent Interests
(stock options, interests subject to
life estates, prospective inheritances, etc.)

1.1   a. Description: _____
          b. Location: _____
          c. Date of vesting: _____
          d. Title owner: _____
          e. Date of acquisition: _____
          f. Original price or value: _____
          g. Source of funds to acquire: _____
          h. Method of valuation: _____
          i. Other information: _____
          j. Current value: _____

J.   Household Furnishings

1.1   a. Description: _____
          b. Location: _____
          c. Title owner: _____
          d. Original price: _____
          e. Source of funds to acquire: _____
          f. Amount of lien unpaid: _____
          g. Other information: _____
          h. Current value: _____

K.   Jewelry/Art/Antiques
(only if valued at more than $500.00)

1.1   a. Description: _____
          b. Title owner: _____
          c. Location: _____
          d. Original price or value: _____
          e. Source of funds to acquire: _____
          f. Amount of lien unpaid: _____
          g. Other information: _____
          h. Current value: _____

1.2   a. Description: _____
          b. Title owner: _____
          c. Location: _____
          d. Original price: _____
          e. Source of funds to acquire: _____
          f. Amount of lien unpaid: _____
          g. Other information: _____
          h. Current value: _____

1.3   a. Description: _____

b. Title owner: _____

c. Location: _____

d. Original price: _____

e. Source of funds to acquire: _____

f. Amount of lien unpaid: _____

g. Other information: _____

h. Current value: _____

1.4   a. Description: _____

b. Title owner: _____

c. Location: _____

d. Original price: _____

e. Source of funds to acquire: _____

f. Amount of lien unpaid: _____

g. Other information: _____

h. Current value: _____

L.   Other Assets

(tax shelter investments, collections, judgments, causes of action, patents, trademarks, copyrights, and any other asset not hereinabove itemized)

1.1   a. Description: _____

b. Title owner: _____

c. Location: _____

d. Original price of value: _____

e. Source of funds to acquire: _____

f. Amount of lien unpaid: _____

g. Other information: _____

h. Current value: _____

1.2   a. Description: _____

b. Title owner: _____

c. Location: _____

d. Original price of value: _____

e. Source of funds to acquire: _____

f. Amount of lien unpaid: _____

g. Other information: _____

h. Current value: _____

V.   LIABILITIES

A.   Accounts Payable

1.1   a. Name and address of Creditor:_____

_____

b. Debtor: _____

c. Amount of original Debt: _____

d. Date of incurring Debt: _____

e. Purpose: _____

f. Monthly/other periodic pmt: _____

g. Other information: _____

h. Amount of current Debt: _____

1.2 a. Name and address of Creditor:_____

  b. Debtor:_____
  c. Amount of original Debt:_____
  d. Date of incurring Debt:_____
  e. Purpose:_____
  f. Monthly/other periodic pmt:_____
  g. Other information:_____
  h. Amount of current Debt:

                  _____

1.3 a. Name and address of Creditor:_____
  b. Debtor:_____
  c. Amount of original Debt:_____
  d. Date of incurring Debt:_____
  e. Purpose:_____
  f. Monthly/other periodic pmt:_____
  g. Other information:_____
  h. Amount of current Debt:

                  _____

1.4 a. Name and address of Creditor:_____
  b. Debtor:_____
  c. Amount of original Debt:_____
  d. Date of incurring Debt:_____
  e. Purpose:_____
  f. Monthly/other periodic pmt:_____
  g. Other information:_____
  h. Amount of current Debt:

                  _____

1.5 a. Name and address of Creditor:_____
  b. Debtor:_____
  c. Amount of original Debt:_____
  d. Date of incurring Debt:_____
  e. Purpose:_____
  f. Monthly/other periodic pmt:_____
  g. Other information:_____
  h. Amount of current Debt:

                  _____

1.6 a. Name and address of Creditor:_____
  b. Debtor:_____
  c. Amount of original Debt:_____
  d. Date of incurring Debt:_____
  e. Purpose:_____
  f. Monthly/other periodic pmt:_____
  g. Other information:_____
  h. Amount of current Debt:

                  _____

1.7 a. Name and address of Creditor:_____

  b. Debtor:_____
  c. Amount of original Debt:_____
  d. Date of incurring Debt:_____
  e. Purpose:_____
  f. Monthly/other periodic pmt:_____
  g. Other information:_____
  h. Amount of current Debt:

                  _____

1.8   a. Name and address of Creditor: _____

                        _____
b. Debtor: _____
c. Amount of original Debt: _____
d. Date of incurring Debt: _____
e. Purpose: _____
f. Monthly/other periodic pmt: _____
g. Other information: _____
h. Amount of current Debt: _____

B.   **Notes Payable**

1.1   a. Name and address
       of note holder: _____
b. Debtor: _____
c. Amount of original Debt: _____
d. Date of incurring Debt: _____
e. Purpose: _____
f. Monthly/other periodic pmt: _____
g. Other information: _____
h. Amount of current Debt: _____

1.2   a. Name and address
       of note holder: _____
b. Debtor: _____
c. Amount of original Debt: _____
d. Date of incurring Debt: _____
e. Purpose: _____
f. Monthly/other periodic pmt: _____
g. Other information: _____
h. Amount of current Debt: _____

C.   **Installment Acct. Payable** (security agreements, chattel mortgages)

1.1   a. Name and address of creditor: _____

                        _____
b. Debtor: _____
c. Amount of original Debt: _____
d. Date of incurring Debt: _____
e. Purpose: _____
f. Monthly/other periodic pmt: _____
g. Other information: _____
h. Amount of current Debt: _____

1.2   a. Name and address of creditor: _____

                        _____
b. Debtor: _____
c. Amount of original Debt: _____
d. Date of incurring Debt: _____
e. Purpose: _____
f. Monthly/other periodic pmt: _____
g. Other information: _____
h. Amount of current Debt: _____

D. **Brokers Margin Accounts**

    1.1   a. Name and address of broker: _____

                   _____

                   b. Debtor: _____
                   c. Amount of original Debt: _____
                   d. Date of incurring Debt: _____
                   e. Purpose: _____
                   f. Monthly/other periodic pmt: _____
                   g. Other information: _____
                   h. Amount of current Debt: _____

E. **Mortgages on Real Estate**

    1.1   a. Name and address of mortgagee: _____

                   b. Address of property mortgaged: _____

                   _____

                   c. Mortgagor: _____
                   d. Original Debt: _____
                   e. Date of incurring Debt: _____
                   f. Monthly/other periodic pmt: _____
                   g. Maturity Date: _____
                   h. Other information: _____
                   i. Amount of current Debt: _____

    1.2   a. Name and address of mortgagee:_____

                   b. Address of property mortgaged:_____

                   _____

                   c. Mortgagor: _____
                   d. Original Debt: _____
                   e. Date of incurring Debt: _____
                   f. Monthly/other periodic pmt: _____
                   g. Maturity Date: _____
                   h. Other information: _____
                   i. Amount of current Debt: _____

    1.3   a. Name and address of mortgagee:_____

                   b. Address of property mortgaged:_____

                   _____

                   c. Mortgagor: _____
                   d. Original Debt: _____
                   e. Date of incurring Debt: _____
                   f. Monthly/other periodic pmt: _____
                   g. Maturity Date: _____
                   h. Other information: _____
                   i. Amount of current Debt: _____

F.   **Taxes Payable**

    1.1   a. Description of tax: _____   _____
              b. Amount of tax: _____
              c. Date Due: _____
              d. Other information: _____

G.   **Loans on Life Insurance**

    1.1   a. Name and address of insurer: _____
                                               _____

              b. Amount of Loan: _____
              c. Date incurred: _____
              d. Purpose: _____
              e. Borrower: _____
              f. Monthly/other periodic pmt: _____
              g. Other information: _____
              h. Amount of current Debt: _____

H.   **Other Liabilities**

    1.1   a. Description: _____
              b. Name and Address of Creditor:_____

                                               _____
              c. Debtor: _____
               d. Amount of original Debt: _____
              e. Date incurred: _____
              f. Purpose: _____
              g. Monthly/other periodic pmt: _____
              h. Other information: _____
              i. Amount of current Debt: _____

    1.2   a. Description: _____
              b. Name and Address of Creditor:_____

                                               _____
              c. Debtor: _____
               d. Amount of original Debt: _____
              e. Date incurred: _____
              f. Purpose: _____
              g. Monthly/other periodic pmt: _____
              h. Other information: _____
              i. Amount of current Debt: _____

NET WORTH

TOTAL ASSETS: _____

TOTAL LIABILITIES: (minus)   _____

NET WORTH: _____

VI. ASSETS TRANSFERRED:

List all assets transferred in any manner during the preceding three years, or length of the marriage, whichever is shorter (transfers in the routine course of business which resulted in an exchange of assets of substantially equivalent value need not be specifically disclosed where such assets are identified in the statement of net worth).

DESCRIPTION OF PROPERTY TRANSFERRED	TO WHOM TRANSFERRED & RELATIONSHIP	DATE OF TRANSFER	VALUE
_____	_____	_____	_____
_____	_____	_____	_____
_____	_____	_____	_____
_____	_____	_____	_____
_____	_____	_____	_____
_____	_____	_____	_____
_____	_____	_____	_____
_____	_____	_____	_____
_____	_____	_____	_____
_____	_____	_____	_____

VII. SUPPORT REQUIREMENTS

[ ]   At this time, deponent is not paying or receiving support.

[ ]   Deponent is at present (paying/receiving) _____ (per week/month) _____, and prior to separation (paid/received) _____ per (week/month) _____ to cover expenses for household necessities, utilities, mortgage.

These payments are being made [ ] (voluntarily) [ ] (pursuant to court order or judgment, and there are) [ ] (no) arrears outstanding [ ] (in the sum of $_____ to date).

[ ]   Deponent requests support of each child in accordance with CSSA and half of all school expenses.

[ ]   Deponent requests for self $_____ per (week/month) _____.

[ ]   The day of the (week/month) _____ on which payments should be made is _____.

VIII. COUNSEL FEE REQUIREMENTS

[ ]   Deponent requests no counsel fees or disbursements a this time.

[ ]   Deponent requests for counsel fees and disbursements the sum of $_____.

[ ]   Deponent has paid counsel the sum _____ and has agreed with counsel concerning fees as follows: _____
_____

[ ]   There is a retainer agreement or written agreement relating to payment of legal fees. (A copy of any such agreement must be annexed).

IX. ACCOUNT AND APPRAISAL FEE REQUIREMENTS

[ ]   Deponent requests no expert fees at this time.

[ ]   Deponent requests for accountant's fees and disbursements the sum of $_____ based on a

        [ ] (hourly) [ ] (flat rate) fee.

[ ]   Deponent requests for appraisal fees and disbursements the sum of $_____ based on a

        [ ] (hourly) [ ] (flat rate) fee.

[ ]   Deponent requires the services of an accountant for the following reasons:

_____

_____

[ ]   Deponent requires the services of an appraiser for the following reasons:

_____

_____

X. OTHER DATA

Other Data Regarding the Financial Circumstances of the Parties that Should be Brought to the Attention of the Court:

_____

_____

_____

_____

    The foregoing statements [ ] and a rider of __ page(s) annexed hereto and made part hereof, have been carefully read by the undersigned who states that they are true and correct.

                                    _____

                                      Plaintiff

Sworn to before me on

_____, _____.

_____

Notary Public

CLIENT CERTIFICATION

I, _____, HEREBY CERTIFY, under penalty of perjury, that I have carefully read and reviewed the annexed document and that all information contained in that document is true and accurate in all respects to the best of my knowledge and understanding.

I, FURTHER CERTIFY, under penalty of perjury, that neither my attorney, nor anyone acting on my attorney's behalf, was the source of any of the information contained in the annexed document; that I provided all of the information contained in the annexed document to my attorney; and that I understand that my attorney, in executing the Attorney Certification required by 22 NYCRR Section 202.16 (e), is relying entirely upon the information provided by me and upon my certification that all such information is true and accurate.

I, FURTHER CERTIFY, that the annexed document includes all information which I provided to my attorney which is relevant to such document and that my attorney has not deleted, omitted or excluded any such information.

Dated: _____

_____
Plaintiff

SUPREME COURT OF THE STATE OF NEW YORK
COUNTY OF _____
---X

                        Plaintiff,   Index No.:_____

   -against-   **AFFIDAVIT OF PLAINTIFF**

                        Defendant.
---X

STATE OF _____ }
                                                ss:
COUNTY OF _____ }

_____ being duly sworn, says:

1.   The Plaintiff's address is _____
   ⸴, and social security number is_____. The Defendant's address is _____
   _____, and social security number is_____
   ⸴.

2. ☐ The Plaintiff has resided in New York State for a continuous period in excess of two years immediately preceding the commencement of this action.
                                   OR
   ☐ The Defendant has resided in New York State for a continuous period in excess of two years immediately preceding the commencement of this action.
                                   OR
   ☐ The Plaintiff has resided in New York State for a continuous period in excess of one year immediately preceding the commencement of this action, and:

        a. ☐   the parties were married in New York State.
        b. ☐ the Plaintiff has lived as husband or wife in New York State with the Defendant.
        c. ☐   the cause of action occurred in New York State.
                                   OR
   The Defendant has resided in New York State for a continuous period in excess of one year immediately preceding the commencement of this action, and:

        a. ☐   the parties were married in New York State.
        b. ☐   the Defendant has lived as husband or wife in New York State with the Plaintiff.
        c. ☐   the cause of action occurred in New York State.
                                   OR
   ☐   The cause of action occurred in New York State and both parties were residents thereof at the time of the commencement of this action.

(Form UD-6 - Rev. 5/99)

3.   I married the Defendant on _____, in the City, Town or Village of
        _____, County of _____, State or Country of _____. The
        marriage was *not* performed by a clergyman, minister or by a leader of the Society for
        Ethical Culture.

(If the word "not" is deleted, check one of the following below:)

❏ *To the best of my knowledge I have taken all steps solely within my power to remove any barrier*
   to the Defendant's remarriage.   **OR**
❏ *I will take prior to the entry of final judgment all steps solely within my power to the best of my*
   knowledge to remove any barrier to the Defendant's remarriage.   **OR**
❏ *The Defendant has waived in writing the requirements of DRL §253 (Barriers to Remarriage).*

4.   There is (are) _____ child(ren) of the marriage:

        <u>Name & Social Security Number</u>   <u>Date of Birth</u>

        _____   _____
        _____   _____
        _____   _____
        _____   _____

        The present address of each child under the age of 18 and all other places where each child
        has lived within the last five (5) years is as follows:
        <u>Child</u>   <u>Present Address</u>

        _____   _____
        _____   _____
        _____   _____
        _____   _____

        <u>Child</u>   <u>Other Address Within Last 5 years</u>

        _____   _____
        _____   _____
        _____   _____
        _____   _____

        The name(s) and present address(es) of the person(s) with whom each child under the age
        of 18 has lived within the last five (5) years is:

        _____   _____
        _____   _____
        _____   _____
        _____   _____

        I have participated in other litigation concerning the custody of the child(ren) in this or another
        state.   Yes   No
        I have information of a custody proceeding concerning the child(ren) pending in a court of this
        or another state.   Yes   No
        I know of a person who is not a party to this proceeding who has physical custody of the
        child(ren) or claims to have custody or visitation rights with respect to the child(ren).

                                                                        Yes   No

(Form UD-6 - Rev. 5/99)

215

The parties are covered by the following group health plans:

Plaintiff	**Defendant**
Group Health Plan:_____	Group Health Plan:_____
Address:_____	Address:_____
Identification Number:_____	Identification Number:_____
Plan Administrator:_____	Plan Administrator:_____
Type of Coverage:_____	Type of Coverage:_____

OR

Not Applicable.

5.　In addition to the dissolution of the marriage, I am seeking the following relief:

_____

_____

_____

AND

❏　equitable distribution of marital property;

OR

❏　marital property to be distributed pursuant to the annexed separation agreement / stipulation;

OR

❏　I waive equitable distribution of marital property;

and any other relief the court deems fitting and proper.

6.　The grounds for dissolution of the marriage are as follows:

❏　**Cruel and Inhuman Treatment (DRL §170(1)):**

At the following times, none of which are earlier than (5) years prior to commencement of this action, the Defendant engaged in conduct that so endangered the mental and physical well-being of the Plaintiff, so as to render it unsafe and improper for the parties to cohabit (live together) as husband and wife.

(State the facts that demonstrate cruel and inhuman conduct giving dates, places and specific acts. Conduct may include physical, verbal, sexual or emotional behavior.)

_____

_____

_____

_____

_____

_____

_____

(Attach an additional sheet, if necessary).

(Form UD-6 - Rev. 5/99)

❏ **Abandonment (DRL 170(2)):**

That commencing on or about _____, and continuing for a period of more than one (1) year immediatelyprior to commencement of this action, the Defendant left the marital residence of the parties located at _____, and did not return. Such absence was without cause or justification, and was without Plaintiff's consent.

That commencing on or about _____, and continuing for a period of more than one (1) year immediately prior to commencement of this action, the Defendantrefused to have sexual relations with the Plaintiff despite Plaintiff's repeated requests to resume such relations. Defendant does not suffer from any disability which would prevent *her / him* from engaging in such sexual relations with Plaintiff. The refusalto engage in sexual relations was without good cause or justification and occurred at the marital residence located at _____

_____.

That commencing on or about the _____, and continuing for a period of more than one (1) year immediately prior to commencement of this action, the Defendant willfully and without cause or justificationabandoned the Plaintiff, who had been a faithful and dutiful *husband / wife*, by depriving Plaintiff of access to the marital residence located at_____. This deprivation of access was without the consent of the Plaintiff and continued for a period of greater than one year.

❏ **Confinement to Prison (DRL §170(3)):**

(a)   That after the marriage of Plaintiff and Defendant, Defendant was confined in prison for a period of three or more consecutive years, to wit: that Defendant was confined in_____ _____ prison on _____, and has remained confined to this date; and

(b)   not more that five (5) years elapsed between the end of the third year of imprisonment and the date of commencement of this action.

❏ **Adultery (DRL §170(4)):**

(a)   That on _____, at the premises located at _____ _____, the Defendant engaged in sexual intercourse with_____, without the procurement nor the connivance of the Plaintiff, and the Plaintiff ceased to cohabit (live) with the Defendant upon the discovery of the adultery; and

(b)   not more than five (5) years elapsed between the date of said adultery and the date of commencement of this action.

(Attach a corroborating affidavit of a third party witness or other additional proof).

▢ <u>**Living Separate and Apart Pursuant to a Separation Decree or Judgment of Separation**</u>
<u>**(DRL §170(5)):**</u>

   (a)   That the _____ Court, _____ County, _____ (Country or State)
rendered a decree or judgment of separation on _____ under Index Number:
_____; and

   (b)   that the parties have lived separate and apart for a period of one year or longer after the granting
of such decree; and

   (c)   that the Plaintiff has substantially complied with all the terms and conditions of such decree or
judgment.

▢ <u>**Living Separate and Apart Pursuant to a Separation Agreement (DRL §170(6)):**</u>

   (a)   That the Plaintiff and Defendant entered into a written agreement of separation, which they
subscribed and acknowledged on _____, in the form required to entitle a deed
to be recorded; and

   (b)   that the *agreement / memorandum of said agreement* was filed on _____
in the Office of the Clerk of the County of _____, wherein *Plaintiff / Defendant*
resided; and

   (c)   that the parties have lived separate and apart for a period of one year or longer after the execution
of said agreement; and

   (d)   that the Plaintiff has substantially complied with all terms and conditions of such agreement.

7.   Defendant is not in the active military service of this state, or any other state or this
nation.

       I know this because: *he/she* admitted it to *me / the process server* on

       _____.

       I have submitted with these papers an *investigator's affidavit /*
Defendant's affidavit which states that Defendant is not in the active military
service of this state, or any other state or this nation.

8.   I am *not* receiving Public Assistance. To my knowledge the Defendant is *not* receiving
Public Assistance.

9.   No other matrimonial action is pending in this court or in any other court, and the
marriage has not been terminated by any decree of any court of competent jurisdiction.

10.   *Annexed to the "Affidavit of Service" of Summons and Complaint / Summons With*
Notice is a photograph. It is a fair and accurate representation of the Defendant.

11A. **▢**   I am not the custodial parent of the child*(ren)* of the marriage.

                      OR

11B. **▢**   I am the custodial parent of the unemancipated child*(ren)* entitled to receive child support
pursuant to DRL §236(B)(7)(b),

                      AND

      ▢   (1) I request child support services through the Support Collection Unit
which would authorize collection of the support obligation by the
immediate issuance of an income execution for support
enforcement.

                      OR

(Form UD-6 - Rev. 5/99)

☐   (2) I am in receipt of such services through the Support Collection Unit.

OR

☐   (3) I have applied for such services through the Support Collection Unit.

OR

☐   (4) I am aware of but decline such services through the Support Collection Unit at this time. I am aware that an income deduction order may be issued pursuant to CPLR §5242(c) without other child support enforcement services and that payment of an administrative fee may be required.

If (1) or (4) is selected, the following information must be included on a separate information sheet (Form UD-8a):

> Name, date of birth, address and social security number of each party; date and place of marriage; names and dates of birth of the children; and name and address of employer of the payor (non-custodial parent).

Plaintiff's   **OR**   *Defendant's*   prior surname is: _____.

WHEREFORE, I _____ (print name), respectfully request that judgment be entered for the relief sought and for such other relief as the court deems fitting and proper.

Subscribed and Sworn to
before me on

_____
Plaintiff's Signature

_____

_____
NOTARY PUBLIC

(Form UD-6 - Rev. 5/99)

SUPREME COURT OF THE STATE OF NEW YORK

COUNTY OF _____

---X

<table>
<tr><td>Plaintiff

-against-

Defendant</td><td>Index No:

**AFFIDAVIT OF DEFENDANT
IN ACTION FOR DIVORCE**</td></tr>
</table>

---X

State of New York, County of _____ss:

_____ being duly sworn, says:

I am the Defendant in the within action for divorce, and I am over the age of 18. I reside at_____.

1. I admit service of the *summons with notice/summons and complaint* for divorce on _____, _____ based upon the following grounds*: _____ _____.

2. I appear in this action. However, I do not intend to respond to the summons or answer the complaint and I waive the twenty (20) or thirty (30) day period provided by law to answer the summons. I waive the forty (40) day waiting period to place this matter on the calendar. I hereby consent to this action being placed on the uncontested divorce calendar immediately.

3. ❏ I am *not* a member of the armed forces of the United States, any State within the United States, or any other Country.

   ❏ *If in military: I am aware of my rights under the New York State Soldiers' and Sailors' Civil Relief Act; however, I consent that this matter be placed on the Uncontested Matrimonial calendar and waive any rights I may have under the Act.*

4a. ❏ I waive the service of all further papers in this action except for the Judgment of Divorce.

4b. ❏ I request service of the following documents: Note of Issue, Request for Judicial Intervention, Barriers to Remarriage Affidavit, Proposed Judgment of Divorce, Proposed Findings of Fact and Conclusions of Law, Notice of Settlement, Qualified Medical Child Support Order, and any other proposed orders.

5. I am not seeking equitable distribution *other than what was already agreed to in a written stipulation*. I understand that I may be prevented from further asserting my right to equitable distribution.

6. *I will or have taken all steps solely within my power to remove any barriers to the plaintiff's remarriage.*

7a. ❏ I am not the custodial parent of the child(ren) of the marriage

7b. ❏ I am the custodial parent of the unemancipated child(ren) entitled to receive child support pursuant to DRL sec 236(B)(7)(b),

AND 1) ❏ I request child support services through the Support Collection Unit which would authorize collection of the support obligation by the immediate issuance of an income execution for support enforcement

2) ☐   I am in receipt of such services through the Support Collection Unit.

3) ☐   I have applied for such services through the Support Collection Unit

4) ☐   I am aware of but declined such services through the Support Collection Unit at this time. I am aware that an income deduction order may be issued pursuant to CPLR sec 5242 (c) without other child support enforcement services and that payment of an administrative fee may be required.

If 1 or 4 is selected, the following information must be included on a separate information sheet:
Name, date of birth, address and social security number of each party; date and place of marriage; names and dates of birth of the children; and name and address of employer of the payor (non-custodial parent).

Dated_____

_____
                                    Defendant

Sworn to before me on

_____, _____

_____
Notary Public

**Insert the grounds for the divorce:

DRL §170(1) cruel and inhuman treatment   DRL §170(4) adultery
DRL §170(2) abandonment   DRL §170(5) living apart one year after judgment of separation
DRL §170(3) confinement in prison   DRL §170(6) living apart one year after execution of a separation agreement

©1989 by Steven L. Abel
BlumbergExcelsior, Publisher, NYC 10013

COURT

COUNTY OF _____

SAMPLE

Index/Docket No. _____

_____ Plaintiff, Petitioner

against

_____ Defendant, Respondent

CHILD SUPPORT WORKSHEETS

References are to DRL §240(1-b) and FCA §413(1)

Prepared by ....
Submitted by ☐ Plaintiff ☐ Defendant ☐ Petitioner ☐ Respondent
(All numbers used in these worksheets are YEARLY figures. Convert weekly or monthly figures to annualized numbers.)

	FATHER	MOTHER
STEP 1 MANDATORY PARENTAL INCOME *(b)(5)*		
1. Gross (total) income (as reported on most recent Federal tax return, or as computed in accordance with Internal Revenue Code and regulations): *(b)(5)(i)*.............		
The following items MUST be added if not already included in Line 1:		
2. Investment income: *(b)(5)(ii)*..		
3. Workers' compensation: *(b)(5)(iii)(A)*...................................		
4. Disability benefits: *(b)(5)(iii)(B)*...		
5. Unemployment insurance benefits: *(b)(5)(iii)(C)*....................		
6. Social Security benefits: *(b)(5)(iii)(D)*..................................		
7. Veterans benefits: *(b)(5)(iii)(E)*...		
8. Pension/retirement income: *(b)(5)(iii)(F)*..............................		
9. Fellowships and stipends: *(b)(5)(iii)(G)*.................................		
10. Annuity payments: *(b)(5)(iii)(H)*..		
11. If self-employed, depreciation greater than straight-line depreciation used in determining business income or investment credit: *(b)(5)(vi)(A)*.................		
12. If self-employed, entertainment and travel allowances deducted from business income to the extent the allowances reduce personal expenditures: *(b)(5)(vi)(B)*.....		
13. Former income voluntarily reduced to avoid child support: *(b)(5)(v)*..............		
14. Income voluntarily deferred: *(b)(5)(iii)*...............................		
A. TOTAL MANDATORY INCOME:............................		

STEP 2 NON—MANDATORY PARENTAL INCOME

These items must be disclosed here. Their inclusion in the final calculations, however, is discretionary. In contested cases, the Court determines whether or not they are included. In uncontested cases, the parents and their attorneys or mediators must determine which should be included.

	FATHER	MOTHER
15. Income attributable to non-income producing assets: *(b)(5)(iv)(A)*..................		
16. Employment benefits that confer personal economic benefits: *(b)(5)(iv)(B)* (Such as meals, lodging, memberships, automobiles, other)		
....		
....		
17. Fringe benefits of employment: *(b)(5)(iv)(C)*.........................		
18. Money, goods and services provided by relatives and friends: *(b)(5)(iv)(D)*.........		
....		
B. TOTAL NON-MANDATORY INCOME:.......................		
C. TOTAL INCOME (*add Line A + Line B*)....................		

STEP 3   DEDUCTIONS

19. Expenses of investment income listed on line 2: (b)(5)(ii) ....

20. Unreimbursed employee business expenses that do not reduce personal expenditures:
    (b)(5)(vii)(A) ....

21. Alimony or maintenance actually paid to a former spouse: (b)(5)(vii)(B)...........   ....

22. Alimony or maintenance paid to the other parent but only if child support will
    increase when alimony stops: (b)(5)(vii)(C) ....

23. Child support actually paid to other children the parent is legally obligated to
    support: (b)(5)(vii)(D) ....

24. Public assistance: (b)(5)(vii)(E)..   ....

25. Supplemental security income: (b)(5)(vii)(F)...............................   ....

26. New York City or Yonkers income or earnings taxes actually paid: (b)(5)(vii)(G) ...   .

27. Social Security taxes (FICA) actually paid: (b)(5)(vii)(H)......................   ....

D. TOTAL DEDUCTIONS:..   ―――――   ―――――

E. FATHER'S INCOME (Line C minus Line D) .... $ ―――――

F. MOTHER'S INCOME (Line C minus Line D)..................... $ ―――――

STEP 4 (b)(4)   G. COMBINED PARENTAL INCOME: *(Line E plus Line F)*...................... $ ―――――

STEP 5 (b)(3) and (c)(2)

MULTIPLY Line G (up to $80,000) by the proper percentage *(insert in Line H)*:
For 1 child ....17%   For 3 children ....29%   For 5 or more children .... 35% (minimum)
For 2 children ....25%   For 4 children 31%

H. COMBINED CHILD SUPPORT:...   ―――――

STEP 6 (c)(2)

DIVIDE the non-custodial parent's amount on Line E or Line F..............................   ....
by the amount of Line G ....
to obtain the percentage allocated
I. to the non-custodial parent:..   ....%

STEP 7 (c)(2)   J. MULTIPLY line H by Line I: ....

STEP 8 (c)(3)

**K. DECIDE the amount of child support to be paid on any combined parental income exceeding $80,000 per
year using the percentages in Step 5 or the factors in Step 11-C or both:** ....

L. ADD Line J and Line K ....   ―――――
    This is the amount of child support to be paid by the non-custodial parent to the custodial parent for all costs of the children,
except for child care expenses, health care expenses, and college, post-secondary, private, special or enriched education.

STEP 9   SPECIAL NUMERICAL FACTORS

CHILD CARE EXPENSES

M. Cost of child care resulting from custodial parent's
    □ seeking work (c)(6) [*discretionary*]   □ working   □ attending elementary education
    □ attending secondary education   □ attending higher education
    □ attending vocational training leading to employment: (c)(4)....................................   ....

N. MULTIPLY Line M by Line I: ....   ―――――
    This is the amount the non-custodial parent must contribute to the custodial parent for child care.

HEALTH EXPENSES *(c)(5)*

O. Reasonable future health care expenses not covered by insurance:..................................... _____

P. MULTIPLY Line O by Line I: ....
This is the amount the non-custodial parent must contribute to the custodial parent for health care or pay directly to the health care provider.

Q. EDUCATIONAL EXPENSE, if appropriate, see Step 11 (b) *(c)(7)* .... _____

STEP 10   LOW INCOME EXEMPTIONS *(d)*

R. Insert amount of non-custodial parent's income from Line E or Line F: .... _____

S. Add amounts on Line L, Line N, Line P and Line Q (This total is "basic child support"): .... _____

T. SUBTRACT Line S from Line R: .... _____

If Line T is more than $10,652, then the low income exemptions do not apply and child support remains as determined in Steps 8 and 9. If so, go to Step 11.

If Line T is less than $7,890†, then

U. Insert amount of non custodial parent's income from Line E or Line F:........................... _____

V. Self-support reserve:.. **($10,652)***

W. Subtract Line V from Line U: .... _____

If Line W is more than $300 per year, then Line W is the amount of basic child support. If Line W is less than $300 per year, then basic child support must be a minimum of $300 per year.

If Line T is less than $10,652* but more than $7,890†, then

X. Insert amount of non-custodial parent's income from Line E or Line F: .... _____

Y. Self-support reserve:.. **($10,652)***

Z. SUBTRACT Line Y from Line X : .... _____

If Line Z is more than $600 per year, then Line Z is the amount of basic child support. If Line Z is less than $600 per year, then basic child support must be a minimum of $600 per year.

STEP 11   NON-NUMERICAL FACTORS

(a) NON-RECURRING INCOME *(e)*

A portion of non-recurring income, such as life insurance proceeds, gifts and inheritances or lottery winnings, may be allocated to child support. The law does not mention a specific percentage for such non-recurring income. Such support is not modified by the low income exemptions.

(b) EDUCATIONAL EXPENSES *(c)(7)*

New York's child support law does not contain a specific percentage method to determine how parents should share the cost of education of their children. Traditionally, the courts have considered both parents' complete financial circumstances in deciding who pays how much. The most important elements of financial circumstances are income, reasonable expenses, and financial resources such as savings and investments.

---

* $10,652 is the self-support reserve as of April 1, 1997. This figure changes on April 1 of each year. In future years, use the current self-support reserve which is 135% of the official Federal poverty level for a single person household as promulgated by the U.S. Department of Health and Human Services.

†$7,890 is the Federal poverty level as of April 1, 1997. This figure changes on April 1 of each year. In future years, use the current Federal poverty level for a single person household as promulgated by the U.S. Department of Health and Human Services.

(c) ADDITIONAL FACTORS *(f)*

The child support guidelines law lists 10 factors that should be considered in deciding on the amount of child support for

- combined incomes of more than $80,000 per year or
- to vary the numerical result of these steps because the result is "unjust or inappropriate." However, any court order deviating from the guidelines must set forth the amount of "basic child support" (line S) resulting from the Guidelines and the reason for the deviation.

These factors are:

1. The financial resources of the parents and the child.
2. The physical and emotional health of the child and his/her special needs and aptitudes
3. The standard of living the child would have enjoyed if the marriage or household was not dissolved.
4. The tax consequences to the parents.
5. The non-monetary contributions the parents will make toward the care and well-being of the child.
6. The educational needs of the parents.
7. The fact that the gross income of one parent is substantially less than the gross income of the other parent.
8. The needs of the other children of the non-custodial parent for whom the non-custodial parent is providing support, but only (a) if Line 23 is not deducted; (b) after considering the financial resources of any other person obligated to support the other children; and (c) if the resources available to support the other children are less then the resources available to support the children involved in this matter.
9. If a child is not on public assistance, the amount of extraordinary costs of visitation (such as out-of-state travel) or extended visits (other than the usual two to four week summer visits), but only if the custodial parent's expenses are substantially reduced by the visitation involved.
10. Any other factor the court decides is relevant.

NON JUDICIAL DETERMINATION OF CHILD SUPPORT *(h)*

Outside of court, parents are free to agree to any amount of support, so long as they sign a statement that they have been advised of the provisions of the child support guidelines law, the amount of "basic child support" (line S) resulting from the Guidelines and the reason for any deviation. Further, the Court must approve any deviation, and the court cannot approve agreements of less than $300 per year. This minimum is not per child, meaning that the minimum for 3 children is $300 per year, not $900 per year. In addition, the courts retain discretion over child support.

Verification *(b)(5)(i)*   *Required if married person files joint income tax return.*

STATE OF NEW YORK, COUNTY OF   ss.:

being duly sworn, deposes and says: I am the
in this case; I have read
these Child Support Worksheets and I know their contents; they are true to my own knowledge, except as to the matters stated to be on information and belief, and as to those I believe it to be true.

Sworn to before me on

....
The name signed must be printed beneath.

CERTIFICATION BY ATTORNEY

STATE OF NEW YORK, COUNTY OF

I HEREBY CERTIFY under penalty of perjury and as an officer of the court that I have no knowledge that the substance of any of the submissions contained in this document is false.

Dated: ....
                                                    Print name beneath signature.

SUPREME COURT OF THE STATE OF NEW YORK
COUNTY OF _____
---x

                     Plaintiff,   **Index No.** _____

    -against-   **SUPPORT COLLECTION UNIT**
                                             INFORMATION SHEET

                    Defendant.
---x

      The following information is required pursuant to Section 240(1) of the Domestic Relations Law:

      PLAINTIFF: _____

           Address: _____

           Date of Birth _____ SS #: _____

      DEFENDANT: _____

           Address: _____

           Date of Birth _____ SS #: _____

Date and Place of Marriage: _____

❐ *Plaintiff* **OR** ❐ *Defendant* is the custodial parent and ❐ *is* **OR** ❐ *is not* receiving public assistance.

UNEMANCIPATED CHILDREN: <u>Name</u>   <u>Date of Birth</u>

SUPPORT: Maintenance $_____ ❐ *per week* **OR** ❐ *bi-weekly* **OR** ❐ *per month*

          Child Support $_____ ❐ *per week* **OR** ❐ *bi-weekly* **OR** ❐ *per month*

          Total Support $_____ ❐ *per week* **OR** ❐ *bi-weekly* **OR** ❐ *per month*

Support payments are to be made to ❐ *Plaintiff* **OR** ❐ *Defendant* **OR** ❐ *Third Party.*

If third party, list name and address: _____

Non-custodial parent's employer: _____

          Address: _____

Dated: _____

SUPREME COURT OF THE STATE OF NEW YORK
COUNTY OF _____
---X

                Plaintiff,   **Index No.** _____

   -against-   **NOTICE OF**
                                SETTLEMENT

                Defendant.

---X

       PLEASE TAKE NOTICE that the annexed ☐ *Proposed Judgment of Divorce,*

OR ☐ *Qualified Medical Child Support Order,* **OR** ☐ *Order:* _____

of which the within is a true copy, will be presented for signature to the Supreme Court

Clerk's Office, at _____,

on _____.

Dated: _____

                    Yours, etc.

                _____

               ☐ *Plaintiff;* ☐ *Attorney(s) for Plaintiff*
               ☐ *Defendant;* ☐ *Attorney(s) for Defendant*
               Address:_____

                   _____

                   _____

               Tel No. _____

TO: _____
     ☐ *Plaintiff;* ☐ *Attorney(s) for Plaintiff*
     ☐ *Defendant;* ☐ *Attorney(s) for Defendant*
     Address:_____

         _____

         _____

     Tel No. _____

SUPREME COURT OF THE STATE OF NEW YORK
COUNTY OF _____

---x

                                        Plaintiff,   **Index No.** _____

        -against-

                                                                INCOME DEDUCTION
                                                                ORDER

                                        Defendant. .

---x

ORDERED that the payments required by the support order issued simultaneously herewith shall be withheld by the debtor's employer from the debtor's compensation, made payable to the creditor identified below and sent to:

☐   *Direct Payment*   **OR**   ☐   *Forwarded Payment*

        Address: _____
                        _____
                        _____

Debtor: Name: _____
                Address: _____
                        _____
                Social Security No.: _____

Creditor: Name: _____
                Address: _____
                        _____
                Social Security No.: _____

Debtor's Employer: _____
                        _____
                        _____

Amount to be withheld: $_____ per _____

Date of Termination of Payments: _____

Dated: _____

                        SO ORDERED:

                        _____
                        Justice

Supreme Court

New York State Case Registry Filing Form *

For Use With Child Support Orders and Combined Child and Spousal Support Orders Payable To Other Than A Child Support Collection Unit

*Social Services Law §111-b(4)(c) and Domestic Relations Law §240(5) direct that such orders must be filed with the State Case Registry

Name of Court: _____   County Name: _____   Index Number: _____

Child Support
Payor: _____   Social Security #: _____   Date of Birth: _____
    (first)   (last)   (middle initial)   (Payor)   (Payor)

Child Support
Payee: _____   Social Security #: _____   Date of Birth: _____
    (first)   (last)   (middle initial)   (Payee)   (Payee)

Child #1 Name: _____   Social Security #: _____   Date of Birth: _____
    (first)   (last)   (middle initial)   (Child #1)   (Child #1)

Child #2 Name: _____   Social Security #: _____   Date of Birth: _____
    (first)   (last)   (middle initial)   (Child #2)   (Child #2)

Child #3 Name: _____   Social Security #: _____   Date of Birth: _____
    (first)   (last)   (middle initial)   (Child #3)   (Child #3)

(If more children, please use additional form.)

FAMILY VIOLENCE INQUIRY

Has a Temporary or Final Order of Protection been granted on behalf of either party?   ☐ yes ☐ no ☐ do not know

    If yes, which party - ☐ Payor ☐ Payee

Has a request for confidentiality of address been granted on behalf of either party?   ☐ yes ☐ no

    If yes, which party - ☐ Payor ☐ Payee

NOTE OF ISSUE - UNCONTESTED DIVORCE

For Use of Clerk

SUPREME COURT OF THE STATE OF NEW YORK

COUNTY OF _____

--X

Plaintiff

Index No.:

Calendar No.:

   -against-

Defendant

--X

NO TRIAL

FILED BY: *Plaintiff/Plaintiff's Attorney/Defendant/Defendant's Attorney*
          (Select one of the above by striking the other three)

DATE SUMMONS FILED: _____

DATE SUMMONS SERVED: _____

DATE ISSUE JOINED: **NOT JOINED -** (Circle one)

                    Waiver/Default/Stipulation or Separation Agreement

NATURE OF ACTION   UNCONTESTED DIVORCE

RELIEF: **ABSOLUTE DIVORCE**

Plaintiff:

Address:

Phone No.:

Defendant:

Address:

Phone No:

REQUEST FOR JUDICIAL INTERVENTION

UNCONTESTED DIVORCE

SUPREME COURT, _____ COUNTY

INDEX#:_____ DATE PURCHASED:_____

---X

Plaintiff

-against-

Defendant

---X

FOR CLERK USE ONLY
IAS ENTRY DATE
JUDGE ASSIGNED
RJI DATE
RJI NUMBER

....

NATURE OF JUDICIAL INTERVENTION - EX PARTE APPLICATION FOR THE DISSOLUTION OF MARRIAGE

ATTORNEY(S) FOR PLAINTIFF:

Name   Address   Phone No.

ATTORNEY(S) FOR DEFENDANT:

Name   Address   Phone No.

Parties appearing without an attorney should enter information in the space provided above the attorneys.

RELATED CASES: (If none, write "NONE" below)

Title   Index#   Court   Nature of Relationship

I affirm under penalty of perjury that, to my knowledge, other than as noted above, there are and have been no related actions or proceedings, nor has a request for judicial intervention previously been filed in this action or proceeding.

Dated: _____
                                               (Signature)

                                               _____
                                               (Print or type name)

                                               _____
                                               Attorney for

SUPREME COURT OF THE STATE OF NEW YORK
COUNTY OF_____
--X

Plaintiff,

-vs-

Affidavit Pursuant
to Domestic Relations
Law Section 75-j
INDEX No.:

Defendant.

--X

_____, being duly sworn deposes and states:

1. That I am the Plaintiff in the above-entitled action, and as such, am fully familiar with the facts and circumstances of this matter.

2. That there are _____ children of the marriage, to wit:

    <u>Name</u>   <u>Date of Birth</u>

3. That the present address of the children is _____, _____, New York _____.

4. That the residences of the children within the last _____ years are _____ _____ _____

5. That during the past _____ years, the children have lived with both parents.

6. That I have not participated as a party, witness, or in any other capacity in any other litigation concerning the custody of the same children in this or any other state.

7. That there are no presently pending, nor have there been any custody proceedings concerning the children in this State, or any State, Territory, or Country.

8. That there is no person who is not a party to the proceedings, who has physical custody of the children or claims to have custody or visitation rights with respect to the children.

9. That I have submitted this Affidavit in support of my application for a Default Judgment in the above-captioned matter.

Sworn to before me on

_____, _____.

_____   _____
Notary Public   Plaintiff

At a term of the Supreme Court of the
State of New York, held in and for the
County of_____
at _____, New York
on _____

PRESENT: Hon._____
                        Justice/Referee

Plaintiff,	Index No.:_____
-against-	**QUALIFIED MEDICAL**
	CHILD SUPPORT ORDER
Defendant.	

NOTICE: YOUR WILLFUL FAILURE TO OBEY THIS ORDER MAY, AFTER A COURT HEARING, RESULT IN YOUR COMMITMENT TO JAIL FOR A TERM NOT TO EXCEED SIX MONTHS, FOR CONTEMPT OF COURT.

Pursuant to DRL §240(1). This Qualified Medical Child Support Order (QMCSO) orders and directs that the unemancipated dependents named herein:
Name: Date of Birth: Soc. Sec.#:   Mailing Address:

are entitled to be enrolled in and receive the benefits for which the legally responsible relative named herein is eligible, under the group health plan named herein in accordance with Section 609 of the Federal Employee Retirement Income Security Act.

The Participant (legally responsible relative) is:
Name: Soc. Sec.#:   Mailing Address:

The Dependents' Custodial Parent or Legal Guardian who is to be provided with any identification cards and benefit claim forms on behalf of dependents:
Name: Soc. Sec.#:   Mailing Address:

The group health plan subject to this order is:

Name: Address: Identification No.:

The administrator of said plan is:
Name: Address:

The type of coverage provided is:

ORDERED that coverage shall include all plans covering the health, medical, dental, pharmaceutical and optical needs of the aforementioned Dependents named above for which the Participant is eligible.

ORDERED that said coverage shall be effective as of (give date) _____ and shall continue as available until the respective emancipation of the aforementioned dependents.

ENTER:

DATED:_____   _____
                                                JSC/Referee

TO: [Health Insurer]

NOTICE: Pursuant to Section 5241(g)(4) of the Civil Practice Laws and Rules, if an employer, organization or group health plan fails to enroll eligible dependents or to deduct from the debtor's income the debtor's share of the premium, such employer, organization or group health plan administrator shall be jointly and severally liable for all medical expenses incurred on behalf of the debtor's dependents named in the execution while such dependents are not so enrolled to the extent of the insurance benefits that should have been provided under such execution.

The group health plan is not required to provide any type or form of benefit or option not otherwise provided under the group health plan except to the extent necessary to meet the requirements of a law relating to medical child support described in section one thousand three hundred and ninety six g-1 of title forty-two of the United States Code.

Present:
Hon.   *Justice/Referee*

--X

                   Plaintiff,

-against-

**FINDINGS OF FACT
AND
CONCLUSIONS OF LAW**

                Defendant.

--X

Index No.:
Calendar No.:

     The issues of this action having ☐ *been submitted to* **OR** ☐ *been heard* before me as one of the *Justices/Referees* of this Court at Part _____ hereof, held in and for the County of _____ on _____, and having considered the allegations and proofs of the respective parties, and due deliberation having been had thereon.

     NOW, after ☐ *reading and considering the papers submitted* ☐ *hearing the testimony*, I do hereby make the following findings of essential facts which I deem established by the evidence and reach the following conclusions of law.

FINDINGS OF FACT

     FIRST: Plaintiff and Defendant were both eighteen (18) years of age or over when this action was commenced.

     SECOND:

     ☐ The Plaintiff has resided in New York State for a continuous period in excess of two years immediately preceding the commencement of this action.

OR

(Form UD-10 - Rev. 5/99)

❐   The Defendant has resided in New York State for a continuous period in excess of two years immediately preceding the commencement of this action.

OR

❐   The Plaintiff has resided in New York State for a continuous period in excess of one year immediately preceding the commencement of this action, and:

      a. ❐   the parties were married in New York State.
      b. ❐ the Plaintiff has lived as husband or wife in New York State with the Defendant.
      c. ❐ the cause of action occurred in New York State.

OR

The Defendant has resided in New York State for a continuous period in excess of one year immediately preceding the commencement of this action; and:

      a. ❐ the parties were married in New York State.
      b. ❐ the Defendant has lived as husband or wife in New York State with the Plaintiff.
      c. ❐ the cause of action occurred in New York State.

OR

❐   The cause of action occurred in New York State and both parties were residents thereof at the time of the commencement of this action.

THIRD: The Plaintiff and the Defendant were married on the date of_____ in the City, Town or Village of _____, County of _____, State or Country of _____; in a ❐ *civil* **OR** ❐ *religious* ceremony.

FOURTH: That no decree, judgment or order of divorce, annulment or dissolution of marriage has been granted to either party against the other in any Court of competent jurisdiction of this state or any other state, territory or country, and that there is no other action pending for divorce by either party against the other in any Court.

FIFTH: That this action was commenced by filing the ❐ *Summons With Notice* **OR** ❐ *Summons and Verified Complaint*   with the County Clerk on _____. Defendant was served ❐ *personally* **OR** ❐ *pursuant to Court order dated* _____ with the above stated pleadings. Defendant ❐ *defaulted in appearance* **OR** ❐ *appeared and waived his / her right to answer* **OR** ❐*filed an answer / amended answer withdrawing any previous pleading, and neither admitting nor denying the allegations in plaintiff's complaint, and consenting to entry of judgment.*

(Form UD-10 - Rev. 5/99)

SIXTH: That Defendant is not in the military service of the United States of America, the State of New York, or any other state. **OR** ☐ Defendant is a member of the military service of the _____ and ☐ has appeared by affidavit and does not oppose the action **OR** ☐   is in default.

SEVENTH: ☐ There are no children of the marriage. **OR** ☐ There *is/are* _____ child(ren) of the marriage. Their name(s), social security number(s), address(es) and date(s) of birth are:

Name & Social Security Number	*Date of Birth*	*Address*
_____	_____	_____
_____	_____	_____
_____	_____	_____
_____	_____	_____

EIGHTH: The grounds for divorce that are alleged in the Verified Complaint were proved as follows:

☐ <u>**Cruel and Inhuman Treatment (DRL §170(1))**</u>:

>At the following times, none of which are earlier than (5) years prior to commencement of this action, the Defendant engaged in conduct that so endangered the mental and physical well being of the Plaintiff, so as to render it unsafe and improper for the parties to cohabit (live together) as husband and wife.

>(State the facts that demonstrate cruel and inhuman conduct giving dates, places and specific acts. Conduct may include physical, verbal, sexual or emotional behavior).

>_____
>_____
>_____
>_____
>_____
>_____
>_____
>_____
>_____
>_____
>_____

(Attach an additional sheet, if necessary).

(Form UD-10 - Rev. 5/99)

☐ **Abandonment (DRL 170(2)):**

That commencing on or about _____, and continuing for a period of more than one (1) year immediately prior to commencement of this action, the Defendant left the marital residence of the parties located at _____ _____, and did not return. Such absence was without cause or justification, and was without Plaintiff's consent.

That commencing on or about _____, and continuing for a period of more than one (1) year immediately prior to commencement of this action, the Defendant refused to have sexual relations with the Plaintiff despite Plaintiff's repeated requests to resume such relations. Defendant does not suffer from any disability which would prevent *her / him* from engaging in such sexual relations with Plaintiff. The refusal to engage in sexual relations was without good cause or justification and occurred at the marital residence located at _____.

That commencing on or about _____, and continuing for a period of more than one (1) year immediately prior to commencement of this action, the Defendant willfully and without cause or justification abandoned the Plaintiff, who had been a faithful and dutiful *husband / wife*, by depriving Plaintiff of access to the marital residence located at___ _____. This deprivation was without the consent of the Plaintiff and continued for a period of greater than one year.

☐ **Confinement to Prison (DRL §170(3)):**

(a) That after the marriage of Plaintiff and Defendant, Defendant was confined in prison for a period of three or more consecutive years, to wit: that Defendant was confined in _____ prison on _____ __, and has remained confined to this date; and

(b) not more that five (5) years elapsed between the end of the third year of imprisonment and the date of commencement of this action.

☐ **Adultery (DRL §170(4)):**

(a) That on _____, at the premises located at _____ _____, the Defendant engaged in sexual intercourse with_____ , without the procurement nor the connivance of the Plaintiff and the Plaintiff ceased to cohabit (live) with the Defendant upon the discovery of the adultery.

(b) not more than five (5) years elapsed between the date of said adultery and the date of commencement of this action.

(Attach a corroborating affidavit of a third party witness or other additional proof).

☐ **Living Separate and Apart Pursuant to a Separation Decree or Judgment of Separation (DRL §170(5)):**

(a) That the _____ Court, _____ County, _____(Country or State) rendered a decree or judgment of separation on _____, under Index Number _____; and

(b) that the parties have lived separate and apart for a period of one year or longer after the granting of such decree; and

(c) that the Plaintiff has substantially complied with all the terms and conditions of such decree or judgment.

(Form UD-10 - Rev. 5/99)

☐ **Living Separate and Apart Pursuant to a Separation Agreement (DRL §170(6)):**

(a) That the Plaintiff and Defendant entered into a written agreement of separation, which they subscribed and acknowledged on _____, in the form required to entitle a deed to be recorded; and

(b) that the *agreement / memorandum of said agreement* was filed _____ in the Office of the Clerk of the County of_____, wherein *Plaintiff / Defendant* resided; and

(c) that the parties have lived separate and apart for a period of one year or longer after the execution of said agreement; and

(d) that the Plaintiff has substantially complied with all terms and conditions of such agreement.

NINTH: ☐ A sworn statement pursuant to DRL §253 that Plaintiff has taken all steps within his or her power to remove all barriers to Defendant's remarriage following the divorce was served on the Defendant.

☐ A sworn statement as to the removal of barriers to remarriage is not required because the parties were married in a civil ceremony.

☐ A sworn statement as to the removal of barriers to remarriage is not required because Defendant waived the need for the statement in his or her affidavit.

TENTH: *The parties have agreed* **OR** *the court has determined* that *Plaintiff* **OR** *Defendant* will receive maintenance of $_____ *per week* **OR** *bi-weekly* **OR** *per month* commencing on _____ pursuant to DRL §236(B)(6)(c).

ELEVENTH: The children of the marriage now reside with ☐ *Plaintiff* **OR** ☐ *Defendant* **OR** ☐ *third party*, namely_____. The ☐ *Plaintiff* **OR** ☐ *Defendant* is entitled to visitation away from the custodial residence. The ☐ *Plaintiff* **OR** ☐ *Defendant* **OR** ☐ *Third Party, namely* _____ is entitled to custody. **OR** ☐ No award of custody due to the child(ren) of the marriage not residing in New York State. **OR** ☐ Other custody arrangement (specify): _____

_____

TWELFTH: Equitable Distribution and ancillary issues shall be *in accordance with the settlement agreement* **OR** ☐ *pursuant to the decision of the court* **OR** ☐ *Equitable Distribution is not an issue.*

THIRTEENTH: ☐ There *is/are* no unemancipated child(ren). **OR** ☐ The award of child support is based upon the following:

(Form UD-10 - Rev. 5/99)

240

(A)   The children of the marriage entitled to receive support are:

Name	Date of Birth
_____	_____
_____	_____
_____	_____
_____	_____
_____	_____

(B)   (1) ☐ By order of _____ Court, _____ County, *Index/Docket No.* _____
dated _____ the *Plaintiff/Defendant* was directed to pay   the sum of
_____ per _____ for child support. Said Order shall continue.

OR

(2) ☐ The adjusted gross income of the Plaintiff who is the ☐ *custodial* **OR** ☐ *non-custodial* parent is _____ per year and the adjusted gross income of the Defendant who is the   *custodial* **OR** ☐ *non-custodial* parent is _____ per year and the combined parental annual income is _____. The applicable child support percentage is *17/25/29/31/35* %. The combined basic child support obligation attributable to both parents is _____ per year on income to $80,000 and ___ _____ per year on income over $80,000. The Plaintiff's pro rata share of the combined parental income is _____% and the Defendant's pro rata share of the combined parental income is_____%. The non-custodial parent's pro rata share of the child support obligation on combined income to $80,000 is_____per year or _____ *per week   bi-weekly   per month.* The non-custodial parent's pro rata share of the child support obligation on combined income over $80,000 is _____ _____ per year or _____   per week   bi-weekly   per month. The non-custodial parent's pro rata share of future health care expenses not covered by insurance, child care expenses, educational or other extraordinary expenses is_____%.

OR

(3) ☐ The parties entered into a *stipulation/agreement* on _____wherein the
☐   *Plaintiff* **OR** ☐ *Defendant* agrees to pay _____   *per week* **OR**
☐ *bi-weekly* **OR** ☐ *per month* child support   *directly* **OR** ☐   *through the Support Collection Unit* to   *Plaintiff* **OR** ☐ *Defendant* **OR** ☐   *Third Party, namely*
_____. The parties agree to   *waive* **OR** ☐   *apply* the Child Support Standards Act to combined income over $80,000. The parties have agreed that health care expenses not covered by insurance shall be paid by   *Plaintiff* **OR**
☐ *Defendant* in the amount of_____   *per week* **OR** ☐ *bi-weekly* **OR**
☐ *per month* **OR** ☐ ____% of the uncovered expenses. The parties have agreed

that child care expenses shall be paid by ☐ *Plaintiff* **OR** ☐ *Defendant* to ☐ *Plaintiff* **OR** ☐ *Defendant* in the amount of _____ *per week* **OR** ☐ *bi-weekly* **OR** ☐ *per month* **OR** ☐ ____% of said child care expenses. The parties have agreed that educational and extraordinary expenses shall be paid by ☐*Plaintiff* **OR** ☐ *Defendant* to ☐ *Plaintiff* **OR** ☐ *Defendant* in the amount of _____ *per week* **OR** ☐ *bi-weekly* **OR** ☐ *per month* **OR** ____% of said educational and extraordinary expenses. Said agreement reciting in compliance with DRL §2401-b(h): The parties have been advised of the Child Support Standards Act. The basic child support obligation presumptively results in the correct amount of child support. The unrepresented party, if any, has received a copy of the Child Support Standards Chart promulgated by Commissioner of Social Services pursuant to Social Services Law Section 111-I. The presumptive amount of child support attributable to the non-custodial parent is _____ ☐ *per week* **OR** ☐ *bi-weekly* **OR** ☐ *per month*. The amount of child support agreed to ☐ *conforms with the non-custodial parents' basic child support obligation* **OR** ☐ *deviates from the non-custodial parents' basic child support obligation for the following reasons:*

_____
_____
_____
_____

FOURTEENTH: The Plaintiff's address is _____,
and social security number is_____. The Defendant's address is _____
_____, and social security number is_____.

☐ There are no unemancipated children. **OR**

☐ There are no health plans available to the parties through their employment. **OR**

☐ The parties are covered by the following group health plans through their employment:

Plaintiff	**Defendant**
Group Health Plan:_____	Group Health Plan:_____
Address:_____	Address:_____
Identification Number:_____	Identification Number:_____
Plan Administrator:_____	Plan Administrator:_____
Type of Coverage:_____	Type of Coverage:_____

☐ *The parties have agreed or stipulated* **OR** ☐ *the court has determined* that the ☐ *Plaintiff* **OR** ☐ *Defendant* shall be the legally responsible relative and that the unemancipated child(ren) shall be enrolled in *his / her* group health plan as specified above *until the age of 21 years* **OR** ☐*until the child(ren) is / are sooner emancipated.*

(Form UD-10 - Rev. 5/99)

242

FIFTEENTH: The _____ Court entered the following order(s) under Index No(s). / Docket No(s).: _____

_____

SIXTEENTH: ❑ *Plaintiff* **OR** ❑ *Defendant* may resume use of the prior surname:

_____.

CONCLUSIONS OF LAW

FIRST: Residency as required by DRL §230 has been satisfied.

SECOND: ❑ *Plaintiff* **OR** ❑ *Defendant* is entitled to a judgment of divorce on the grounds of DRL §170 subd._____ and granting the incidental relief awarded.

Dated:_____

_____
J.S.C./Referee

(Form UD-10 - Rev. 5/99)

243

At the *Matrimonial/IAS* Part _____
of New York State Supreme Court at
the Courthouse, _____
County, on _____.

Present:
Hon.   *Justice/Referee*
---X

                        Plaintiff,

-against-

JUDGMENT OF DIVORCE

                        Defendant.
---X

THE FOLLOWING NOTICE IS ☐ *APPLICABLE*   **OR**   ☐ *NOT APPLICABLE*

NOTICE REQUIRED WHERE PAYMENTS THROUGH SUPPORT COLLECTION UNIT

Index No.:
Calendar No.:
Social Security No.:

NOTE: (1) THIS ORDER OF CHILD SUPPORT SHALL BE ADJUSTED BY THE APPLICATION OF A COST OF LIVING ADJUSTMENT AT THE DIRECTION OF THE SUPPORT COLLECTION UNIT NO EARLIER THAN TWENTY-FOUR MONTHS AFTER THIS ORDER IS ISSUED, LAST MODIFIED OR LAST ADJUSTED, UPON THE REQUEST OF ANY PARTY TO THE ORDER OR PURSUANT TO PARAGRAPH (2) BELOW. UPON APPLICATION OF A COST OF LIVING ADJUSTMENT AT THE DIRECTION OF THE SUPPORT COLLECTION UNIT, AN ADJUSTED ORDER SHALL BE SENT TO THE PARTIES WHO, IF THEY OBJECT TO THE COST OF LIVING ADJUSTMENT, SHALL HAVE THIRTY-FIVE (35) DAYS FROM THE DATE OF MAILING TO SUBMIT A WRITTEN OBJECTION TO THE COURT INDICATED ON SUCH ADJUSTED ORDER. UPON RECEIPT OF SUCH WRITTEN OBJECTION, THE COURT SHALL SCHEDULE A HEARING AT WHICH THE PARTIES MAY BE PRESENT TO OFFER EVIDENCE WHICH THE COURT WILL CONSIDER IN ADJUSTING THE CHILD SUPPORT ORDER IN ACCORDANCE WITH THE CHILD SUPPORT STANDARDS ACT.

(2) A RECIPIENT OF FAMILY ASSISTANCE SHALL HAVE THE CHILD SUPPORT ORDER REVIEWED AND ADJUSTED AT THE DIRECTION OF THE SUPPORT COLLECTION UNIT NO EARLIER THAN TWENTY-FOUR MONTHS AFTER SUCH ORDER IS ISSUED, LAST MODIFIED OR LAST ADJUSTED WITHOUT FURTHER APPLICATION BY ANY PARTY. ALL PARTIES WILL RECEIVE A COPY OF THE ADJUSTED ORDER.

(Form UD-11 - Rev. 5/99)

(3) WHERE ANY PARTY FAILS TO PROVIDE, AND UPDATE UPON ANY CHANGE, THE SUPPORT COLLECTION UNIT WITH A CURRENT ADDRESS, AS REQUIRED BY SECTION TWO HUNDRED FORTY-B OF THE DOMESTIC RELATIONS LAW, TO WHICH AN ADJUSTED ORDER CAN BE SENT, THE SUPPORT OBLIGATION AMOUNT CONTAINED THEREIN SHALL BECOME DUE AND OWING ON THE DATE THE FIRST PAYMENT IS DUE UNDER THE TERMS OF THE ORDER OF SUPPORT WHICH WAS REVIEWED AND ADJUSTED OCCURRING ON OR AFTER THE EFFECTIVE DATE OF THE ADJUSTED ORDER, REGARDLESS OF WHETHER OR NOT THE PARTY HAS RECEIVED A COPY OF THE ADJUSTED ORDER.

This action was submitted to ☐ *the referee* **OR** ☐ *this court* for ☐ *consideration* this _____ day of _____ **OR** for ☐ *inquest* on this _____ day of _____

The Defendant was served ☐ *personally* **OR** ☐ *pursuant to court order dated* _____ *within* **OR** ☐ *outside* the State of New York.

Plaintiff presented a *Verified Complaint and Affidavit of Plaintiff constituting facts of the matter* **OR** ☐ *Summons With Notice and Affidavit of Plaintiff constituting the facts of the matter.*

The Defendant has *not appeared and is in default* **OR** ☐ *appeared and waived his or her right to answer* **OR** ☐ *filed an answer or amended answer withdrawing any prior pleadings and neither admitting nor denying the allegations in the complaint and consenting to the entry of judgment* **OR** ☐ *the parties settled the ancillary issues by* ☐ *written stipulation* **OR** ☐ *oral stipulation on the record dated* _____ _____.

The Court accepted ☐ *written* **OR** ☐ *oral* proof of non-military status.

The Plaintiff's address is _____, and social security number is_____. The Defendant's address is _____ _____, and social security number is_____.

(Form UD-11 - Rev. 5/99)

Now on motion of _____, the ☐ *attorney for Plaintiff* **OR**

☐ *Plaintiff,* it is:

ORDERED AND ADJUDGED that the Referee's Report, if any, is hereby confirmed; and it is further

ORDERED, ADJUDGED AND DECREED that the marriage between_____

_____, plaintiff, and_____, defendant, is hereby dissolved by reason of:

(a)   the cruel and inhuman treatment of ☐ *Plaintiff by Defendant* **OR**

☐ *Defendant by Plaintiff* pursuant to DRL §170(1); and/or

(b)   the abandonment of ☐ *Plaintiff* **OR**☐ *Defendant* by ☐ *Plaintiff* **OR**

☐ *Defendant,* for a period of one or more years, pursuant to DRL §170(2); and/or

(c)   the confinement of ☐ *Plaintiff* **OR** ☐ *Defendant* in prison for a period of three or more consecutive years after the marriage of Plaintiff and Defendant, pursuant to DRL §170(3); and/or

(d)   the commission of an act of adultery by ☐ *Plaintiff* **OR** ☐ *Defendant,* pursuant to DRL §170(4); and/or

(e)   the parties having lived separate and apart pursuant to a decree or judgment of separation dated _____ for a period of one or more years after the granting of such decree or judgment, pursuant to DRL §170(5); and/or

(f)   the parties having lived separate and apart pursuant to a Separation Agreement dated _____ in compliance with the provisions of DRL §170(6); and it is further

(Form UD-11 - Rev. 5/99)

ORDERED AND ADJUDGED that ☐ *Plaintiff* **OR** ☐ *Defendant* **OR**

☐ *third party, namely:* _____ shall have custody of the minor

child(ren) of the marriage, i.e.:

Name	Date of Birth	Social Security No.
_____	_____	_____
_____	_____	_____
_____	_____	_____
_____	_____	_____

OR ☐ *There are no minor children of the marriage*; and it is further

ORDERED AND ADJUDGED that ☐ *Plaintiff* **OR** ☐ *Defendant* shall have

visitation with the minor child(ren) of the marriage ☐ *in accordance with the parties'*

settlement agreement **OR** ☐ *according to the following schedule:* _____

_____

_____

_____

_____

OR ☐ *Visitation is not applicable*; and it is further;

ORDERED AND ADJUDGED that the existing _____ County, _____

Court order(s) under ☐ *Index No..*_____ **OR** ☐ *Docket No.*_____

as to ☐ *custody* **OR** ☐ *visitation* **OR** ☐ *maintenance* shall continue, and a copy

of this judgment shall be served by ☐ *Plaintiff* **OR** ☐ *Defendant* upon the Clerk of the

_____ County _____ Court within _____ days of its entry;

OR ☐ *There are no court orders with regard to custody, visitation or maintenance to be*

continued; and it is further

(Form UD-11 - Rev. 5/99)

ORDERED AND ADJUDGED that ☐ *Plaintiff* **OR** ☐ *Defendant* shall pay

to ☐ *Plaintiff* **OR** ☐ *Defendant* **OR** ☐ *third party, namely:* _____

as and for the support of the parties' unemancipated children, the sum of $_____ per

_____, pursuant to an existing order issued by the _____ County, _____

Court, under ☐ *Index* **OR** ☐ *Docket* Number _____, the terms of which

are hereby continued. ☐ *Plaintiff* **OR** ☐ *Defendant* shall serve a copy of this

Judgment upon the Clerk of the _____ County, _____ Court within _____

days of its entry; **OR** ☐ *There are no orders from other courts to be continued*; and it is

further

ORDERED AND ADJUDGED that ☐ *Plaintiff* **OR** ☐ *Defendant* shall pay

to ☐ *Plaintiff* **OR** ☐ *Defendant* the sum of $_____ ☐ *per week* **OR**

☐ *bi-weekly* **OR** ☐ *per month* as and for maintenance commencing on_____

and thereafter on the _____ day of each ☐ *week* **OR** ☐ *bi-week* **OR** ☐ *month*

until _____; **OR** ☐ *That there is no award of maintenance*; and it is

further

ORDERED AND ADJUDGED that ☐ *Plaintiff* **OR** ☐ *Defendant* shall pay

to ☐ *Plaintiff* **OR** ☐ *Defendant* **OR** ☐ *third party, namely:* _____

as and for the support of the parties' unemancipated child(ren), namely:

Name	Date of Birth
_____	_____
_____	_____
_____	_____
_____	_____

(Form UD-11 - Rev. 5/99)

the sum of $_____ ☐ *per week* **OR** ☐ *bi-weekly* **OR** ☐ *per month,*

commencing on _____, and to be paid ☐ *directly to* ☐ *Plaintiff* **OR**

☐ *Defendant* **OR** ☐ *third party, namely:*_____, **OR**

through the _____ *County Support Collection Unit located at* _____

_____, together with such dollar amounts or

percentages for ☐ *child care* **OR** ☐ *education* **OR** ☐ *health care* as set forth below

in accordance with ☐ *the Court's decision* **OR** ☐ *the parties' Settlement Agreement.*

Such Agreement is in compliance with DRL §240(1-b)(h) because:

> The parties have been advised of the provisions of DRL Sec. 240(1-
> b); the unrepresented party, if any, has received a copy of the Child
> Support Standards Chart promulgated by the Commissioner of Social
> Services pursuant to Social Services Law Sec. 111-I;
> the basic child support obligation, as defined in DRL Sec. 240(1-b),
> presumptively results in the correct amount of child support to be
> awarded, and the agreed upon amount substantially conforms to the
> basic support obligation attributable to the non-custodial parent;
> the amount awarded is neither unjust nor inappropriate, and the Court
> has approved such award through the Findings of Fact and
> Conclusions of Law;

> ### OR

> The basic support obligation, as defined in DRL Sec. 240 (1-b),
> presumptively results in the correct amount of child support to be
> awarded, and the amount attributable to the non-custodial parent is
> $_____ per _____;
> the amount of child support agreed to in this action deviates from the
> amount attributable to the non-custodial parent, and the Court has
> approved of such agreed-upon amount based upon the reasons set

(Form UD-11 - Rev. 5/99)

forth in the Findings of Fact and Conclusions of Law, which are incorporated herein by reference; and it is further

OR ☐ *This provision is not applicable.*

ORDERED AND ADJUDGED that ☐ *Plaintiff* **OR** ☐ *Defendant* shall pay to ☐ *Plaintiff* **OR** ☐ *Defendant* **OR** ☐ *third party, namely:* _____ the sum of $ _____ ☐ *per week* **OR** ☐ *bi-weekly* **OR** ☐ *per month* as and for child care expenses, **OR** ☐ as follows: _____

_____

_____

_____,

OR ☐ *Not applicable*; and it is further

ORDERED AND ADJUDGED that ☐ *Plaintiff* **OR** ☐ *Defendant* shall pay to ☐ *Plaintiff* **OR** ☐ *Defendant* **OR** ☐ *third party, namely:* _____ the sum of $_____ ☐ *per week* **OR** ☐ *bi-weekly* **OR** ☐ *per month* as and for future reasonable health care, **OR** ☐ as follows:

_____

_____

_____

_____;

OR ☐ *Not applicable*; and it is further

ORDERED AND ADJUDGED that ☐ *Plaintiff* **OR** ☐ *Defendant* shall pay to ☐ *Plaintiff* **OR** ☐ *Defendant* **OR** ☐ *third party, namely:* _____ the sum of $_____ ☐ *per week* **OR** ☐ *bi-weekly* **OR** ☐ *per month* as and for ☐ *present* **OR** ☐ *future* **AND** ☐ *post-secondary* **OR** ☐ *private* **OR** *special* **OR** ☐ *enriched* education for the children, **OR** ☐ as follows:

(Form UD-11 - Rev. 5/99)

_____; **OR** ☐ *Not applicable*; and it is further

ORDERED AND ADJUDGED that ☐ *Plaintiff* **OR** ☐ *Defendant* is hereby awarded exclusive occupancy of the marital residence located at_____

_____, together with its contents until further order of the court, **OR** ☐ as follows: _____

_____

_____

_____; **OR** ☐ *Not applicable*; and it is further

ORDERED AND ADJUDGED that the Settlement Agreement entered into between the parties on the_____day of_____, a ☐ *copy* **OR** ☐ *transcript* of which is on file withthis Court and incorporated herein by reference, shall survive and shall not be merged into this judgment, and the parties are hereby directed to comply with all legally enforceable terms and conditions of said agreement as if such terms and conditions were set forth in their entirety herein, and this Court retains jurisdiction of this matter concurrently with the Family Court for the purposes of specifically enforcing such of the provisions of said Agreement as are capable of specific enforcement to the extent permitted by law with regard to maintenance, child support, custody and/or visitation, and of making such further judgment as it finds appropriate under the circumstances existing at the time application for that purpose is made to it, or both; and it is further

ORDERED AND ADJUDGED that a separate Qualified Medical Child Support Order shall be issued simultaneously herewith **OR** ☐ Not applicable; and it is further

(Form UD-11 - Rev. 5/99)

ORDERED AND ADJUDGED that, pursuant to the ☐ *parties' Settlement Agreement* **OR** ☐ *the courts decision* , a separate Qualified Domestic Relations Order shall be issued simultaneously herewith or as soon as practicable **OR** ☐ *Not applicable*; and it is further

ORDERED AND ADJUDGED that, ☐ *pursuant to this Courts direction* **OR** ☐ *pursuant to the parties 'agreement,* this Court shall issue an income deduction order simultaneously herewith **OR** ☐ *Not applicable*; and it is further

ORDERED AND ADJUDGED that both parties are authorized to resume the use of any former surname, and it is further

ORDERED AND ADJUDGED that ☐ *Plaintiff* **OR** ☐ *Defendant* is authorized to resume use of the prior surname _____.

ORDERED AND ADJUDGED that ☐ *Plaintiff* **OR** ☐ *Defendant* shall be served with a copy of this judgment, with notice of entry, by the ☐ *Plaintiff* **OR** ☐ *Defendant*, within _____ days of such entry.

Dated:

ENTER:

_____
J.S.C./Referee

_____
CLERK

(Form UD-11 - Rev. 5/99)

UNIFIED COURT SYSTEM DIVORCE AND CHILD SUPPORT SUMMARY FORM: SUPREME COURT   **UCS-113**
(10/94)

1. County _____

2. Case Number _____

3. Date Action Commenced: __/__/__

4. Party filling out form (circle one):
   a. Husband or Husband;s Attorney
   b. Wife or Wife's Attorney

5. Husband's Date of Birth: ___/___/___
   mm dd yy

6. Wife's Date of Birth: ____/____/____
   mm dd yy

7. Date of marriage: ____/____/____
   mm dd   yy

8. Children of the Marriage:
   [For each living child of the marriage indicate date of birth and who has physical custody (F=Father, M=Mother, J=Joint, T=Third Party)]

Child	Date of Birth	Custody
1	___/___/___ mm dd yy	_____
2	___/___/___ mm dd yy	_____
3	___/___/___ mm dd yy	_____
4	___/___/___ mm dd yy	_____
5	___/___/___ mm dd yy	_____

9. Was Husband represented by an attorney? (circle one)
   YES   NO

10. Was Wife represented by an attorney? (circle one)
    YES   NO

11. Financial arrangements (circle one):
    a. By Judge, Referee or Appellate Court
    b. By Written Agreement of Parties or Stipulation on the Record
    c. Both
    d. Other

12. Husband's Annual Gross Income:
    $ _____

13. Wife's Annual Gross Income:
    $ _____

14. Basic Child Support Award Paid to (circle one)
    a.Wife   b. Husband   c. Third Party

15. Value of Basic Child Support Payment:
    By Husband: $ _____ Annually
    By Wife: $ _____ Annually

16. Additional Child Support:
    (circle as many as appropriate)

By Husband:	By Wife:
a. Medical/Med. Ins.	a. Medical/Med. Ins.
b. Child Care	b. Child care
c. Education	c. Education
d. Other	d. Other

17. Did court make a finding that the child support award varied from the Child Support Standards Act amount? (circle one)
    YES   NO

18. If answer to #17 was yes, was the child support award higher or lower than the Child Support Standards Act amount? (circle one)
    a. Higher   b. Lower

19. If answer to #17 was yes, circle court's reason(s)
    a. Financial resources of parents/child
    b. Physical/emotional health of child: special needs or aptitudes.
    c. Child's expected standard of living had household remained intact.
    d. Tax consequences.
    e. Non-monetary contribution toward care and well-being of child.
    f. Educational needs of either parent.
    g. Substantial differences in gross income of parents.
    h. Needs of other children of non-custodial parent.
    i. Extraordinary visitation expenses of non-custodial parent.
    j. Other (specify): _____
    _____

20. Spousal Maintenance: (circle one)
    a. None   b. To Husband   c. To Wife

21. Value of Maintenance:
    $ _____Annually

22. Duration of Maintenance (circle one and provide date if appropriate):
    a.Until a specific date ___/____/____
    mm dd   yy
    b. Until death or remarriage.
    c. Other

23. Marital Home (circle one):
    a. Owned   b. Rented   c. Other

24. Marital Home Value (if owned):
    a. Value $_____
    b. Outstanding Mortgage $_____

25. Marital Home — Division:
    _____% to husband _____% to wife

26. Post divorce occupancy of marital home (circle one):
    a. By husband b. By wife c. Neither

27. Other Marital Assets Not Including Marital Home:
    $_____

28. Division of Other Marital Assets
    a. Amount to Husband $_____
    b. Amount to Wife $_____

29. Other Awards:

To Husband	To Wife	
$_____	$_____	Attorney Fees
$_____	$_____	Expert Fees
$_____	$_____	Arrears
$_____	$_____	Other

Prepared by (Attorney or Party):

_____

Print Name   Signature   Date

FOR COURT USE ONLY:
TO BE FILLED OUT BY COURT CLERK: DATE OF DECREE; ORDER; OR MODIFICATION_____/_____/_____

253

LOCAL INDEX NUMBER

New York State
Department of Health
CERTIFICATE OF DISSOLUTION OF MARRIAGE

STATE FILE NUMBER

TYPE , OR
PRINT IN
PERMANENT
BLACK INK

HUSBAND

1. HUSBAND -- NAME: FIRST MIDDLE LAST

1 A. SOCIAL SECURITY NUMBER

2. DATE OF BIRTH   Month Day Year

3. STATE OF BIRTH (COUNTRY IF NOT USA)

4.A RESIDENCE: STATE

4B. COUNTY

4C. LOCALITY (CHECK ONE AND SPECIFY)
☐ CITY OF
☐ TOWN OF
☐ VILLAGE OF

4

4D. STREET AND NUMBER OF RESIDENCE (INCLUDE ZIP CODE)

4E. IF CITY OR VILLAGE, IS RESIDENCE WITHIN CITY OR VILLAGE LIMITS?
YES ☐ NO ☐ IF NO, SPECIFY TOWN:

5A. ATTORNEY - NAME

5B. ADDRESS (INCLUDE ZIP CODE)

WIFE

6A. WIFE - NAME FIRST MIDDLE LAST

6B. MAIDEN

6C. SOCIAL SECURITY NUMBER

9

7. DATE OF BIRTH Month Day Year

8. STATE OF BIRTH (COUNTRY IF NOT USA)

9.A RESIDENCE: STATE

9B. COUNTY

9C. LOCALITY (CHECK ONE AND SPECIFY)
☐ CITY OF
☐ TOWN OF
☐ VILLAGE OF

9D. STREET AND NUMBER OF RESIDENCE (INCLUDE ZIP CODE)

9E. IF CITY OR VILLAGE, IS RESIDENCE WITHIN CITY OR VILLAGE LIMITS?
YES ☐ NO ☐ IF NO, SPECIFY TOWN:

10A. ATTORNEY - NAME

10B. ADDRESS (INCLUDE ZIP CODE)

11

11A. PLACE OF THIS MARRIAGE - CITY, TOWN OR VILLAGE

11B. COUNTY

11C. STATE (COUNTRY IF NOT USA)

12A. DATE OF THIS MARRIAGE Month Day Year

12B. APPROXIMATE DATE COUPLE SEPARATED Month Year

13A. NUMBER OF CHILDREN EVER BORN ALIVE OF THIS MARRIAGE (SPECIFY)

13B. NUMBER OF CHILDREN UNDER 18 IN THIS FAMILY (SPECIFY)

DECREE

15

14A. I CERTIFY THAT A DECREE OF DISSOLUTION OF THE ABOVE MARRIAGE WAS RENDERED ON Month Day Year

14B. DATE OF ENTRY: Month Day Year

14C. TYPE OF DECREE - DIVORCE, ANNULMENT, OTHER DISSOLUTION (SPECIFY)

14D. COUNTY OF DECREE

14E. TITLE OF COURT

23

14F. SIGNATURE OF COUNTY CLERK
>

CONFIDENTIAL INFORMATION

HUSBAND

24

15. RACE: WHITE, BLACK, AMERICAN INDIAN, OTHER (SPECIFY)

16. NUMBER OF THIS MARRIAGE - FIRST, SECOND, ETC. (SPECIFY)

17. IF PREVIOUSLY MARRIED HOW MANY ENDED BY

A. DEATH NUMBER____ NONE ☐

B. DIVORCE OR ANNULMENT NUMBER ____ NONE ☐

18. EDUCATION: INDICATE HIGHEST GRADE COMPLETED ONLY

	ELEMENTARY	HIGH SCHOOL	COLLEGE
0	1 2 3 4 5 6 7 8	1 2 3 4	1 2 3 4 5+
	00 01 02 03 04 05 06 07 08	09 10 11 12	13 14 15 16 17

WIFE

25

19. RACE: WHITE, BLACK, AMERICAN INDIAN, OTHER (SPECIFY)

20. NUMBER OF THIS MARRIAGE - FIRST, SECOND, ETC. (SPECIFY)

21. IF PREVIOUSLY MARRIED HOW MANY ENDED BY

A. DEATH NUMBER____ NONE ☐

B. DIVORCE OR ANNULMENT NUMBER ____ NONE ☐

22. EDUCATION: INDICATE HIGHEST GRADE COMPLETED ONLY

	ELEMENTARY	HIGH SCHOOL	COLLEGE
0	1 2 3 4 5 6 7 8	1 2 3 4	1 2 3 4 5+
	00 01 02 03 04 05 06 07 08	09 10 11 12	13 14 15 16 17

QR

23. PLAINTIFF - HUSBAND, WIFE, OTHER (SPECIFY)

24. DECREE GRANTED TO HUSBAND, WIFE, OTHER (SPECIFY)

25. LEGAL GROUNDS FOR DECREE (SPECIFY)

QS

26. SIGNATURE OF PERSON PREPARING CERTIFICATE
>

ATTORNEY AT LAW

NOTE: Social Security Numbers of the husband and wife are mandatory. They are required by New York State Public Health Law Section 4139 and 42 U.S.C. 666(a). They may be used for child support enforcement purposes.

DOH-2168 (5/2000)

SUPREME COURT OF THE STATE OF NEW YORK
COUNTY OF _____
---X

                        Plaintiff,

     -vs-   Index No.:

                                                      NOTICE OF ENTRY
                        Defendant.
---X
STATE OF NEW YORK   }
                                              ss.
COUNTY OF _____ }

         PLEASE TAKE NOTICE that the attached is a true copy of a judgment of divorce in

this matter that was entered in the Office of the Clerk of the Supreme Court,

_____ County, on the _____ day of _____, _____.

Date: _____

                                              _____
                                              Plaintiff
                                              _____
                                              _____
                                              _____
                                              _____
                                              Address

TO:

_____
Defendant/Attorney for Defendant

_____
_____
_____
_____
          Address

SUPREME COURT OF THE STATE OF NEW YORK

COUNTY OF_____

---X

                                         Index No.:

                Plaintiff,

NOTICE OF MOTION

-vs-   **FOR ALTERNATE**

SERVICE

              Defendant.

---X

        Please take notice that the undersigned Plaintiff will move this court at a term to be held on _____, _____, at _____a.m/p.m. upon the attached affidavits for an order

    ❏   allowing Plaintiff to have Defendant served with the Summons in this matter pursuant to CPLR §308(2), by serving a person of suitable age and discretion at Defendant's residence or place of business

    ❏   allowing Plaintiff to have Defendant served with the Summons in this matter pursuant to CPLR §308(4), by affixing a copy of the Summons to the door of Defendant's residence or place of business

    ❏   allowing Plaintiff to have Defendant served with the Summons in this matter pursuant to CPLR §316, by publication in _____ once in three successive weeks

                                     _____

                                     _____

                                     _____

To: _____

SUPREME COURT OF THE STATE OF NEW YORK
COUNTY OF_____
--X

                                                    Index No.:

                              Plaintiff,

                                                    AFFIDAVIT IN SUPPORT
-vs-   **OF MOTION**

                              Defendant.
--X

_____, being duly sworn, deposes and says:

1.   I have attempted to personally serve the Defendant on _____ occasions as follows:
_____
_____.

2.   I have been unable to serve the Defendant because _____
_____.

3.   I believe that further attempts to personally serve the Defendant will be unsuccessful.

Dated: _____

                                        _____

Sworn to before me on

_____, _____

_____

Notary Public

SUPREME COURT OF THE STATE OF NEW YORK
COUNTY OF_____

---X

Plaintiff,

-vs-

Defendant.

---X

Index No.:

ORDER DIRECTING SERVICE

Upon reading the affidavit of _____ sworn to on _____,
and of _____ sworn to on _____, and the Summons
with Notice / Summons and Verified Complaint in this action for divorce, and

❏ it appearing that the present whereabouts of the Defendant cannot be ascertained;

❏ it appearing that _____ attempts have been made to serve the Defendant personally;

it is hereby

❏ ORDERED, that the summons herein be served upon the Defendant by publication in accordance with the requirements of CPLR §316 by setting forth a copy of the summons with notice bearing the legend "Action for Divorce" and the relief sought herein and that said publication shall be made in the English language in one newspaper, namely _____, published at _____, New York, once each week on the same day for three consecutive weeks, which newspaper is most likely to give notice to the Defendant; first publication of the summons shall be made within twenty days after the granting of this order; the requirement of mailing a copy of the summons to the Defendant is dispensed with, it appearing that there is no place that can be ascertained with due diligence where Defendant would receive mail and that service as herein provided will be sufficient.

❏ ORDERED, that the summons herein be served upon the Defendant by service upon a person of suitable age and discretion at the Defendant's residence or place of business and mailing a copy to said person, pursuant to CPLR §308(2).

❏ ORDERED, that the summons herein be served by affixing a copy of it to Defendant's residence or place of business and mailing a copy to the Defendant, pursuant to CPLR §308(4).

Dated: _____

_____
J.S.C.

COUNTY OF   Supreme COURT   Index No.

}
}
Plaintiff (s) / Petitioner (s)   }AFFIDAVIT
}   OF
against   }   SERVICE
}
Defendant(s) / Respondent (s)   }

STATE OF NEW YORK, COUNTY OF   SS.:

being sworn, says: that deponent is not a party

to this action, is over 18 years of age and resides at

That on _____ 19___ at _____ .m., at   deponent served the
Within [ ] summons
[ ] Summons and complaint   [ ] summons with notice
[ ] Notice of Petition   [ ] Other
     [ ] summons and verified complaint

On

[ ] defendant } (hereinafter }
[ ] respondent}   called   } therein named
[ ] witness   }   the recipient)}

INDIVIDUAL
[ ]   by delivering a true copy *of each* to said recipient personally; deponent knew the person so served to be the person described as said recipient therein.

CORPORATION
[ ]   a _____ corporation, by delivering thereat a true copy *of each* to _____ personally, deponent knew said corporation so served to be the corporation described in said summons as said recipient and knew individual to be _____ thereof

SUITABLE AGE PERSON
[ ]   by delivering thereat a true copy *of each* to _____ a person of suitable age and discretion. Said premises is recipient's [ ] actual place of business [ ] dwelling house (usual place of abode) with the state

AFFIXING TO DOOR, ETC.
[ ]   by affixing a true copy *of each* to the door of said premises, which is recipient's [ ] actual place of business [ ] dwelling house (usual place of abode) within the state. Deponent was unable. with due diligence to find recipient or a person of suitable age and discretion, thereat, having called there

MAILING
USE WITH
[ ]   Deponent also enclosed a copy of same in a postpaid sealed wrapper properly addressed to recipient at recipient's last known residence, at _____ and deposited said wrapper in -- a post office -- official depository under exclusive care and custody of the United States Postal Service within New York State. [ ] The mailing was made by certified mail (Receipt No. _____) within one day after such delivering to such suitable person or such affixing [ ] and with return receipt requested.

DESCRIPTION OF RECIPIENT

Sex	Color	Hair		Approximate: Age	Height	Weight
[ ] Male	[ ] White Skin	[ ] Black Hair	[ ] White Hair	[ ] 14-20 Yrs.	[ ] Under 5'	[ ] Under 100 Lbs.
[ ] Female	[ ] Black Skin	[ ] Brown Hair	[ ] Balding	[ ] 21-35 Yrs.	[ ] 5'0"-5'3"	[ ] 100-130 Lbs.
	[ ] Yellow Skin	[ ] Blond Hair	[ ] Mustache	[ ] 36-50 Yrs.	[ ] 5'4"-5'8"	[ ] 130-160 Lbs.
	[ ] Brown Skin	[ ] Gray Hair	[ ] Beard	[ ] 51-65 Yrs.	[ ] 5'9"-6'0"	[ ] 161-200 Lbs.
	[ ] Red Skin	[ ] Red Hair	[ ] Glasses	[ ] Over 65 Yrs.	[ ] Over 6'	[ ] Over 200 Lbs.

Other identifying features:

WITNESS FEES
[ ] $ _____ the authorizing traveling expenses and one days' witness fee:
[ ] was paid *(tendered)* to the recipient
[ ] was mailed to the witness with subpoena copy.

MILITARY SERVICE
[ ]   I asked the person spoken to whether recipient was in active military service of the United States or of the State of New York in any capacity whatever and received a negative reply. Recipient *wore ordinary civilian clothes and no military uniform.* The source of my information and the grounds of my belief are the conversations and observations above narrated.
Upon information and belief I aver that the recipient is not in the military service of New York State or of the United States as that term is defined in either the State or in the Federal statutes.

Sworn to before me on

_____
PRINT NAME BELOW SIGNATURE

_____

SUPREME COURT OF THE STATE OF NEW YORK
COUNTY OF _____
--X

                    Plaintiff.

-vs-

                   Defendant.
--X

Index No.:_____

**NOTICE OF MOTION FOR
PERMISSION TO PROCEED
AS A POOR PERSON**

Please take notice that the undersigned Plaintiff will move this court at a term to be held on _____, _____, at _____a.m./p.m. upon the attached affidavits for an order allowing Plaintiff permission to prosecute an Action for Divorce as a Poor Person.

_____

_____

_____

To: _____

SUPREME COURT OF THE STATE OF NEW YORK
COUNTY OF _____
--X
In the Matter of the Application of

                    Plaintiff.   Index No.:_____

For Permission to Prosecute as a Poor Person   **AFFIDAVIT IN SUPPORT OF**
a Matter against   **APPLICATION TO PROCEED**
                                                         AS A POOR PERSON

                    Defendant.
--X
STATE OF NEW YORK   }
                                                    ss:
COUNTY OF _____ }

_____, being duly sworn, says:

1. I reside at _____in the City, Town
    or Village of_____, County of _____
    and State of _____, and I have resided in the State of
    _____ for the past _____ years.

2. I am about to commence a lawsuit for divorce.

    This lawsuit is based upon DRL sec 170_____–_____.

3. My sole source of income is: _____
    _____
    _____ I earn $_____ per _____.

4. My property and its value are as follows: _____
    _____
    _____
    _____

5. I make this application pursuant to Section 1101 of the Civil Practice Law and Rules upon the ground that I am unable to pay costs, fees and expenses necessary to pursue my case and am unable to obtain the funds to do so, and unless an order is entered relieving me from the obligation to pay, I will be unable to prosecute my case.

6. No other person is beneficially interested in the recovery sought herein.

7. No previous application for the same or similar relief has been made by me in this case except: _____

    _____.

    WHEREFORE, I respectfully ask for an order permitting me to prosecute an action as a poor person.

Date: _____

The foregoing statements have been carefully read by the undersigned who states that they are true and correct.

_____

Plaintiff

Sworn to before me on

_____, _____

_____

Notary Public

At the _____Office
of the Supreme Court of the State
of New York, held in and for the
County of _____ at the
Courthouse, _____
_____, on the
_____ day of _____, _____

PRESENT: HON._____

Justice of the Supreme Court

--X

In the Matter of the Application of

Index No.: _____

Plaintiff,

POOR PERSON ORDER

-against-

Defendant.

--X

Upon the annexed affidavit of _____, the verified complaint sworn to on _____, _____, *and the certificate of* _____ *Esq., dated* _____, _____;

And it being alleged that said Plaintiff has a good cause of action or claim based upon:

_____

_____

_____

_____

And it being alleged that he/she is unable to pay the costs, fees and expenses to prosecute this action, and that there is no other person beneficially interested in the action,

Now on motion of _____, Plaintiff, it is hereby

ORDERED that _____ is permitted to prosecute this action as a poor person against _____ and it is further

ORDERED that any recovery by judgment or settlement in favor of Plaintiff shall be paid to the Clerk of the Court to await distribution pursuant to court order, and it is further

ORDERED that the Clerk of this Court is directed to make no charge for costs or fees in connection with the prosecution of this case, including one certified copy of the judgment.

Dated: _____   ENTER:

_____
J.S.C.

SUPREME COURT OF THE STATE OF NEW YORK
COUNTY OF_____
---X

                         Plaintiff,

       Index No.:

-vs-   **NOTICE OF MOTION FOR TEMPORARY RELIEF**

                       Defendant.

---X

      Please take notice that the undersigned Plaintiff will move this court at a term to be held on _____ at _____a.m./p.m. upon the attached affidavit for an order

1. awarding temporary legal custody of the infant children of the parties to the Plaintiff during the pendency of this action subject to visitation rights on the part of the defendant, pursuant to Domestic Relations Law section 240;

2. Directing the Defendant to pay _____ per week/month to the Plaintiff for the support and maintenance of the infant children of the marriage during the pendency of this action pursuant to Domestic Relations Law section 240;

3. Directing the Defendant to pay the medical and dental expenses of the infant children and of the parties during the pendency of this action, pursuant to Domestic Relations Law section 236 and 240,

4. Directing the Defendant to pay _____ per week/month to the Plaintiff for his/her support and maintenance during the pendency of this action, pursuant to Domestic Relations Law section 236;

5. Directing the Defendant to bring up to date and make payments of the monthly mortgage installments and of the homeowner's insurance and to pay the utility bills for gas, electric, water and telephone service at the marital residence at _____ _____ during the pendency of this action, pursuant to Domestic Relations Law section 236 and 240;

6. Directing the Defendant to restore to Plaintiff the exclusive use of the _____ _____ vehicle and to pay for the automobile insurance, pursuant to Domestic Relations Law section 234, 236 and 240;

7. Granting to the Plaintiff during the pendency of this action, exclusive possession of the marital residence located at _____, and the contents thereof; pursuant to Domestic Relations Law section 234;

8. Granting _____;

9. Granting such other and further relief as this Court may deem just and proper.

Please take further notice that pursuant to CPLR 2214(b) all answering affidavits must be served upon the undersigned not later than seven days (twelve if by mail) before the return date of this motion as hereinabove set forth.

THIS IS A MOTION FOR MAINTENANCE AND CHILD SUPPORT

DATED:

_____   _____

                                 _____

To: _____

SUPREME COURT OF THE STATE OF NEW YORK

COUNTY OF_____

--X

                                                 Index No.:

                        Plaintiff,

                                                 AFFIDAVIT IN SUPPORT

-vs-   **OF MOTION FOR**

                                                 TEMPORARY RELIEF

                                 Defendant.

--X

_____, being duly sworn, deposes and says:

1.   I am the plaintiff in the above entitled action for divorce, am personally and fully familiar with all of the facts and circumstances hereof and make this affidavit in support of my application for _____ _____

2.   Because this application is based primarily upon the financial circumstances of the parties and the needs of the family, I shall not set forth any facts relating to the merits of this action except as they may pertain specifically to the relief herein sought.

3.   The parties were married on _____, _____. I am _____ years old and my spouse is _____ years old. We have _____ children of the marriage, named _____. We separated on _____, _____, and the children currently reside with _____.

4.   I am requesting temporary custody of the children because of the following, and visitation as follows: _____ _____.

5.   I am in urgent need of child support because: _____ _____.

6.   My spouse has the following income and assets: _____ _____ _____.

7. I have the following income and assets: _____

    _____

    _____ .

8. I am requesting spousal support because: _____

    _____ .

9. I am requesting exclusive use of _____ vehicle because:

    _____

    _____ .

10. I am requesting exclusive occupancy of the marital residence because: _____

    _____ .

11. I am requesting payment of the household bills because: _____

    _____ .

12. I am requesting _____ because:

    _____ .

No other application for the relief herein has been made to the Court, Family Court, or any other judge.

Dated: _____   _____

Sworn to before me on

_____, _____

_____
Notary Public

SUPREME COURT OF THE STATE OF NEW YORK
COUNTY OF_____
---X

                                     Plaintiff,

         Index No.:

         **ORDER TO SHOW
CAUSE**

-vs-

                                      Defendant.

---X

Upon the affidavit of _____sworn
to on _____ and upon all of the papers and proceedings herein,

Let the Defendant show cause before this court on _____.
at _____ am/pm to be held in the county of _____, in
_____ or as soon thereafter as the
parties can be heard why an order should not be made

Granting _____

_____

_____

And such other and further relief as this Court may deem appropriate and it is further

ORDERED that pending hearing of this motion and further order of this court, the defendant, his agents, employees, attorneys and representatives be restrained and enjoined form concealing, dissipating, utilizing, transferring or in any way disposing of or encumbering the assets held by the Defendant as marital property and any income, accretions, additions, accumulations and emoluments thereof including without limitations the following assets:_____

_____

Sufficient reason therefore appearing, let personal service of this order and a copy of the papers upon which it is granted, together with the summons and complaint herein upon the Defendant personally or upon the attorney for the Defendant pursuant to CPLR 2103 (b) on or before _____, be deemed sufficient and that answering affidavits if any be served at least two days before the return date of this motion.

ENTER

_____

J.S.C.

REQUEST FOR JUDICIAL INTERVENTION

SUPREME COURT, _____ COUNTY

INDEX #: _____   DATE PURCHASED _____

PLAINTIFF(S):   IAS ENTRY DATE

                                                 JUDGE ASSIGNED

DEFENDANTS(S):

                                                 R J I DATE

Date issue joined: _____   Bill of particulars served (Y/N): _____

NATURE OF JUDICIAL INTERVENTION   (check ONE box only and enter information)

[ ]   Request for preliminary conference
[ ]   Note of issue and/or certificate of readiness
[ ]   Notice of motion (return date _____) Relief sought _____
[ ]   Order to show cause (clerk enter return date _____)
             Relief sought _____
[ ]   Other ex parte application (specify_____)
[ ]   Notice of petition (return date _____) Relief sought _____
[ ]   Notice of medical or dental malpractice action (specify _____)
[ ]   Statement of net worth
[ ]   Writ of habeas corpus
[ ]   Other (specify _____)

NATURE OF ACTION OR PROCEEDING   (check ONE box only)

MATRIMONIAL
[ ] Contested   — CM
[ ] Uncontested   — UM

COMMERCIAL
[ ] Contract   — CONT
[ ] Corporate   — CORP
[ ] Insurance (where insurer is a
       party, except
       arbitration) — INS
[ ] UCC (including sales, negotiable
           instruments) — UCC
[ ] *Other Commercial — OC
       _____

REAL PROPERTY
[ ] Tax Certiorari — TAX
[ ] Foreclosure   — FOR
[ ] Condemnation— COND
[ ] Landlord/Tenant — LT
[ ] *Other Real Property — ORP
       _____

OTHER MATTERS
[ ] *_____ — OTH

       *If asterisk used, please specify further

TORTS
Malpractice
[ ] Medical/Pediatric — MM
[ ] Dental   — DM
[ ] *Other Professional — OPM
       _____
[ ] Motor Vehicle   — MV
[ ] *Products Liability — PL
       _____
[ ] Environmental   — EN
[ ] Asbestos   — ASB
[ ] Breast Implant   — BI
[ ] *Other Negligence — OTN
       _____
[ ] *Other Tort (including
       intentional)   — OT
       _____

SPECIAL PROCEEDINGS
[ ] Art. 75 (Arbitration)   — ART 75
[ ] Art. 77 (Trusts)   — ART 77
[ ] Article 78   — ART 78
[ ] Election Law   — ELEC
[ ] Guardianship
       (MHL Art 81)   — GUARD 81
[ ] *Other Mental Hygiene — MHYG
       _____
[ ] *Other Special Proceedings   —OSP
       _____

Check "YES" or "NO" for each of the following questions.

Is this action/proceeding against a

YES   NO   YES   NO

[ ]   [ ]   Municipality: [ ]   [ ]   Public Authority:

(specify _____)   (specify _____)

YES   NO

[ ]   [ ]   Does this action/proceeding seek equitable relief?
[ ]   [ ]   Does this action/proceeding seek recovery for personal injury?
[ ]   [ ]   Does this action/proceeding seek recovery for property damage?

ATTORNEY(S) FOR PLAINTIFF(S):   (NAME(S), ADDRESS(ES), PHONE NO.)

ATTORNEY(S) FOR DEFENDANT (S):   (NAME(S), ADDRESS(ES), PHONE NO.)

Parties appearing pro se (without attorney) should enter information in space provided above for attorneys.

INSURANCE CARRIERS:

RELATED CASES: (IF NONE, write "NONE" below)

Title	Index #	Court	Nature of Relationship

     I AFFIRM UNDER PENALTY OF PERJURY THAT, TO MY KNOWLEDGE, OTHER THAN AS NOTED ABOVE, THERE ARE AND HAVE BEEN NO RELATED ACTIONS OR PROCEEDINGS, NOR HAS A REQUEST FOR JUDICIAL INTERVENTION PREVIOUSLY BEEN FILED IN THIS ACTION OR PROCEEDING.

Dated: _____

                             (SIGNATURE)

                             _____

                             (PRINT OR TYPE NAME)

                             _____

                             ATTORNEY FOR

Attach rider sheets if necessary to provide required information.

NOTE OF ISSUE (Type or Print)

☐ NOTE OF ISSUE
STATEMENT OF READINESS

Calendar No. (if any)...

for use of clerk

Index No . . . .

. . . . .Court . . . . .County, N.Y.

Name of assigned judge . . . .

NOTICE OF TRIAL

☐ Trial by jury demanded

☐ of all issues

☐ of issues specified below
or attached hereto

☐ Trial without jury

Filed by attorney for . . . .

. . . .

Date summons served . . . .

Date service completed . . . .

Date issues joined . . . .

NATURE OF ACTION OR SPECIAL PROCEEDING

Tort:

    ☐   Motor Vehicle Negligence

    ☐   Medical Malpractice

    ☐   Other Tort

☐ Contract

☐ Contested Matrimonial

☐ Uncontested Matrimonial

☐ Tax Certiorari

☐ Condemnation

☐ Other (not itemized above)

    (specify) . . . .

☐ Indicate if this action is brought as a class action. If
a medical malpractice action ,indicate if panel procedures prescribed by court rules pursuant to section
14B-a of the

Judiciary Law have been completed. . . . .

Amount demanded $ . . . .

Other relief. . . . .

Insurance Carrier(s), if known: . . . .

. . . .

Special preference claimed under. . . . .
on the ground that . . . .
. . . .

Attorney(s) for Plaintiff(s), Office, P.O. Address, Telephone:

Attorney(s) for Defendant(s), Office, P.O. Address, Telephone

SUPREME COURT OF THE STATE OF NEW YORK
COUNTY OF_____
---X

                                        Index No.:
                        Plaintiff,
                                        VERIFIED ANSWER

-vs-

                        Defendant.
---X

Defendant answering complaint alleges:

First: Denies the allegations in paragraphs _____ of the complaint.

Second: Denies knowledge or information sufficient to form a belief with respect to the allegations in paragraphs _____ of the complaint.

Third: Admits the allegations in paragraphs _____ of the complaint.

Fourth: Neither admits nor denies the allegations of the complaint but consents that the plaintiff may proceed forthwith to inquest as an uncontested action.

Dated: _____   _____

                                      _____

                                      _____

Verification
STATE OF NEW YORK   )
COUNTY OF _____)

_____ being duly sworn, deposes and says that I am the defendant in the within action; I have read the foregoing answer and know the contents thereof ; that the same is true to my own knowledge, except as to matters therein stated to be alleged upon information and belief, and as to those matters therein stated to be alleged upon information and belief, and as to those matters I believe them to be true.

                                      _____

Sworn to before me on

_____, _____

_____

Notary Public

SUPREME COURT OF THE STATE OF NEW YORK
COUNTY OF_____
---X

                                    Plaintiff,   Index No.:

                                                        NOTICE OF MOTION
-vs-   **FOR SUBPOENA DUCES**
                                                        TECUM

                                    Defendant.
---X

       Please take notice that the undersigned Plaintiff will move this court at a term to be held on _____, _____, at _____a.m/p.m. upon the attached affidavit for signature by the Court of the attached Subpoenas Duces Tecum and granting such other and further relief as this Court may deem just and proper.

       Please take further notice that pursuant to CPLR 2214(b) all answering affidavits must be served upon the undersigned not later than seven days (twelve if by mail) before the return date of this motion as hereinabove set forth.

       DATED: _____

                                          _____

                                          _____

                                          _____

       To:_____

SUPREME COURT OF THE STATE OF NEW YORK
COUNTY OF_____
---X

                                    Plaintiff,   Index No.: _____

-vs-   **AFFIDAVIT IN SUPPORT**
                                                          OF MOTION

                                    Defendant.
---X

_____, being duly sworn, deposes and says:

1.   I am the Plaintiff in the above entitled action for a divorce, am personally and fully familiar with all of the facts and circumstances hereof, and make this affidavit in support of my application for signature by the Court of Subpoenas Duces Tecum for the following persons or businesses to provide me with the following records or information: _____

_____

_____

_____.

2.   It is necessary that I be provided with this information so that I may fully and competently prosecute this action for divorce.

Dated: _____

                                            _____

Sworn to before me on

_____, _____

_____
Notary Public

SUPREME COURT OF THE STATE OF NEW YORK
COUNTY OF_____
---X

                                                    Index No.:
                              Plaintiff,
                                                    SUBPOENA DUCES
-vs-   **TECUM**

                              Defendant.
---X

IN THE NAME OF THE PEOPLE OF THE STATE OF NEW YORK:

TO:

WE COMMAND YOU, that all business and excuses being laid aside to appear and attend before_____ of this court, to be held at _____, at _____ a.m./p.m., and at any recessed or adjourned dates, to give testimony in this action on the part of the plaintiff and that you bring with you, and produce at the time and place aforesaid, all of those items set forth on the rider annexed hereto, now in your custody and control and all other deeds, evidences and writings , which you have in your possession or power, concerning the annexed items..

Please take notice that compliance with this Subpoena Duces Tecum may be made by production of the item or items required to be produced certified as complete and accurate by the person in charge of said records and no personal appearance to certify such item or items shall be required unless the Court shall order otherwise.

For failure to comply, you will be deemed guilty of a contempt of Court and liable to pay all losses or damages sustained thereby by the party aggrieved, and forfeit FIFTY DOLLARS in addition thereto.

DATED: _____

                              BY ORDER OF:

                              _____
                              J.S.C.

SUPREME COURT OF THE STATE OF NEW YORK
COUNTY OF_____
---X

                                   Plaintiff,   Index No.:

-vs-   **NOTICE OF MOTION
FOR SUBPOENA FOR
APPEARANCE**

                              Defendant.
---X

Please take notice that the undersigned Plaintiff will move this court at a term to be held on _____, _____, at _____a.m/p.m. upon the attached affidavit for signature by the Court of the attached Subpoenas for Appearance and granting such other and further relief as this Court may deem just and proper.

Please take further notice that pursuant to CPLR 2214(b) all answering affidavits must be served upon the undersigned not later than seven days (twelve if by mail) before the return date of this motion as hereinabove set forth.

DATED: _____

                                          _____

                                          _____

                                          _____

To:_____

SUPREME COURT OF THE STATE OF NEW YORK
COUNTY OF_____
--X

                                        Plaintiff,   Index No.:

-vs-   **AFFIDAVIT IN SUPPORT**
                                                             OF MOTION

                                        Defendant.
--X

_____, being duly sworn, deposes and says:

1.   I am the Plaintiff in the above entitled action for a divorce, am personally and fully
familiar with all of the facts and circumstances hereof and make this affidavit in support of
my application for signature by the Court of Subpoenas for Appearance for the following
persons to present testimony regarding: _____
_____
_____
_____.

2.   It is necessary that I be provided with this information so that I may fully and
competently prosecute this action for divorce.

Dated: _____

                                             _____

Sworn to before me on

_____, _____

_____
Notary Public

SUPREME COURT OF THE STATE OF NEW YORK
COUNTY OF_____
--X

                                        Index No.:
                          Plaintiff,
                                        SUBPOENA FOR
                                        APPEARANCE
-vs-

                          Defendant.
--X

IN THE NAME OF THE PEOPLE OF THE STATE OF NEW YORK:

TO:

WE COMMAND YOU, that all business and excuses being laid aside to appear and attend before _____ of this court, to be held on _____, _____, at _____ a.m./p.m., and at any recessed or adjourned dates, to give testimony in this action on the part of the plaintiff.

For failure to comply, you will be deemed guilty of a contempt of Court and liable to pay all losses or damages sustained thereby by the party aggrieved, and forfeit FIFTY DOLLARS in addition thereto.

DATED: _____

                                        BY ORDER OF:

                                        _____
                                        J.S.C.

SUPREME COURT OF THE STATE OF NEW YORK
COUNTY OF_____
---X

            Index No.:

        Plaintiff,

             NOTICE OF APPEAL

-vs-

        Defendant.
---X

    PLEASE TAKE NOTICE that _____ hereby appeals to the
Supreme Court, Appellate Division, _____Department, from a Judgment
of the Supreme Court of the County of _____, (Hon. J._____)
entered in the _____County Clerk's office on _____,
from each and every part thereof and from each and every intermediate order therein
entered.

    Dated: _____

              _____

              _____

              _____

    To:

SEPARATION AND PROPERTY SETTLEMENT AGREEMENT

By and Between

_____

and

_____

SEPARATION AND PROPERTY SETTLEMENT AGREEMENT

THIS AGREEMENT is made the _____ day of_____, _____, by and between,_____. (hereinafter referred to as "Husband"), and. _____(hereinafter referred to as "Wife").

RECITALS

A. The parties were married on _____, _____, in the city/town/village of _____, County of_____, State of New York.

There are _____minor children born of this marriage, to wit:

Name	Date of Birth

B. Irreconcilable differences have arisen between the parties as a result of which the parties desire to live separate and apart from each other.

C. The parties desire that this Agreement constitutes a separation and property settlement agreement between them, with respect to all assets, real and personal, now owned by the parties or either of them, including any and all property acquired prior to the marriage of the parties, during the marriage, and hereafter acquired by either the Husband or the Wife; and settles any and all questions, issues, and other matters relative to the estates of the parties, and all other issues arising out of, or incidental to, the marital relationship.

D. The parties and each of them [have conferred with their respective attorneys regarding all aspects of this Agreement and the effect thereof, and said attorneys have fully and completely explained all terms and provisions of the Agreement and the applicable laws] [are aware of their right to legal counsel and do hereby waive that right], and both parties have relied upon the accuracy and completeness of the materials exchanged. The parties have also exchanged sworn 236(B) Financial Disclosure Affidavits (Statements of Net Worth), and. other financial data including, but not limited to, joint Federal and State Income Tax Returns, W-2 Wage and Tax Statements, data regarding the benefits from employment, pension information, bank statements, checking account statements, and credit card bills, as well as other miscellaneous business and personal financial data.

E. Both Husband and Wife acknowledge that this Agreement is freely and voluntarily entered into by and between them, and with full and complete understanding of all of the terms and conditions thereof, and further that there has been disclosure by each of the parties to the other as to their respective assets and earnings by means of the production of certain documents and records, and the parties are satisfied that there has been a complete good faith financial disclosure which each party has relied upon in entering into this Agreement.

F. The parties acknowledge that this Agreement shall in no respect alter, impair, modify, or constitute a waiver of either party's right to proceed with the action for divorce initiated by the Husband/Wife against the Husband/Wife, or the Husband's/Wife's right to defend said action for divorce.

G. If a divorce or separation is eventually granted at any time to either party against the other in this State or any other State having jurisdiction over the parties, it is agreed that the terms and provisions of this Agreement shall be incorporated in and become part of any such final judgment or decree of divorce or separation, but shall not merge therein (except as specifically provided for hereinafter). It is further agreed that all of the provisions of this Agreement shall survive such incorporation into any decree of divorce or separation and shall continue to be binding upon the parties hereto.

H. Each party, prior to the entry of a final Judgment of Divorce between them, shall take all steps within his or her power to remove any barriers to the remarriage of the other following a divorce and shall, in all respects, comply with the provisions of Section 253 of the Domestic Relations Law of the State of New York.

I. This Agreement, or a memorandum of this Agreement, shall be filed in the Office of the _____ County Clerk and recorded in the same manner required of a deed.

J. The parties understand that instead of entering into this Agreement they have a right to proceed with litigation and to seek a judicial determination of the issues covered by this Agreement, but notwithstanding such right, the parties desire to avoid the delay, expense, and risk of litigation, and they believe that their rights will be better served by the terms and provisions of this Agreement.

K. In negotiating, determining, and agreeing upon the provisions of this Agreement relating to maintenance, the Husband and Wife each specifically represent, warrant, and acknowledge that they have agreed upon all of the terms and conditions hereinabove set forth based in all respects upon due, deliberate, and informed consideration as to their respective property, the standard of living enjoyed by the parties during the marriage, income means and needs, as well as the ability and means of both the Husband and Wife, both at present and in the future. The parties further acknowledge that they have specifically considered the amount and duration of the payments to be made pursuant to all of the terms and provisions of this Agreement, and have further considered in all respects any and all items, questions, and other matters relating to this Agreement and each and every provision thereof, including, but not limited to, the following factors:

1. The income and property of the respective parties, including marital property distributed.

2. The duration of the marriage and the age and health of both parties.

3. The present and future earning capacity of both parties.

4. The ability of the party seeking maintenance to become self-supporting and, if applicable, the period of time and training necessary therefore.

5. The reduced or lost lifetime earning capacity of the party seeking maintenance as a result of having foregone or delayed education, training, employment or career opportunities during the marriage.

6. The presence of children of the marriage, and the respective homes of the parties.

7. The tax consequences to each party.

8. Contributions and services of the party seeking maintenance as a spouse, parent, wage earner and homemaker and to the career or career potential of the other party.

9. The wasteful dissipation of marital property by either spouse.

10. Any transfer or encumbrance of marital assets made in contemplation of a matrimonial action without fair compensation.

11. Any other factor which the Court shall expressly find to be just and proper.

L. In negotiating, determining and agreeing upon the provisions of this Agreement with respect to the distribution of any and all marital property of every form and description and wheresoever situate, whether real, personal, or mixed, the Husband and Wife specifically represent, warrant and acknowledge that they have agreed upon such distribution as is provided for in this Agreement, based upon satisfactory (formal and) informal disclosure by and between the parties, and after due deliberation of all matters pertaining thereto, including, but not limited to, the mutual waiver of verification of both the financial information and the interpretation and effect of said information, and have resolved the issues with respect to such distribution; and the parties further acknowledge that they have considered all issues and factors relating to the distribution of all marital property, including, but not limited to, the following factors:

1. The income and property of each party at the time of the marriage and at the time of commencement of this action.

2. The duration of the marriage and the age and health of both parties.

3. The need of a custodial parent to occupy or own the marital residence and to use or own its household effects.

4. The loss of inheritance and pension rights upon dissolution of the marriage as of the date of dissolution.

5. Any award of maintenance.

6. Any equitable claim or interest in a direct or indirect contribution made to the acquisition of such marital property by the party not having title, including joint efforts or expenditures and contributions and services as a spouse, parent, wage earner and homemaker and to the career or career potential of the other party.

7. The liquid or non-liquid character of all marital property.

8. The probable future financial circumstances of each party.

9. The impossibility or difficulty in evaluating any component assets or any interest in a business, corporation or profession, and the economic desirability of retaining such asset or interest intact and free from any claim or interference by the other party.

10. The tax consequences to each party.

11. The wasteful dissipation of assets by either spouse.

12. Any transfer or encumbrance of any marital action without fair compensation.

13. Any other factor which the court shall expressly find to be just and proper.

The Husband and Wife and each of them do hereby unequivocally and without any reservation whatsoever covenant and agree and specifically express as their mutual intent that all property, whether real, personal or mixed and of every sort and description, and whatsoever situated, and whether characterized as separate property or marital property, pursuant to the laws of the State of

New York (as the same now exists or in the future may be amended or enacted) now in the possession or under the control of either of them or hereafter acquired in any manner by either of them, whether prior or subsequent to the execution of this Agreement, including but not limited to any appreciation of any such property, shall except as is specifically provided for to the contrary in this agreement, be and remain the sole, separate and exclusive property of such party, free of any claim by the other, made pursuant to any provision of the law of the State of New York, including but not limited to Section 236(B) of the Domestic Relations Law.

M. The parties do hereby ratify, confirm, and adopt each and every recital hereinabove set forth and agree to be bound by all the terms, covenants, and conditions of this Agreement

ARTICLE I: SEPARATION

A. The Husband and Wife agree to live separate and apart from each other, except as limited specifically by this Agreement, free of all control, restraint, or interference, direct or indirect, by the other.

B. Neither party shall in any way harass, disturb, trouble, or annoy the other, or interfere with the peace and comfort of the other, or compel or seek to compel the other to associate, cohabit, or dwell with him or her by any means whatsoever, nor shall either of the parties commence any action or proceeding of any form or nature for the restoration of conjugal rights.

ARTICLE II: MARITAL RESIDENCE

❏ A. The parties are tenants by the entirety of the marital residence located at _____
_____, New York, County of
_____. The parties agree the home was purchased by both of them during the course of the marriage in _____ for a purchase price of $_____, and agree that said property can be currently valued between $_____ and $_____.

❏ B. The parties agree that the home shall become the sole and separate property of the Husband/Wife and he/she shall be solely responsible for the mortgage, taxes, insurance, repairs, and all other expenses relating to the home.

Upon the execution of this Agreement, the premises shall be conveyed to him/her by bargain and sale deed with covenant, duly executed and acknowledged, and recorded at his/her expense, conveying all of his/her right, title, and interest in and to said premises, subject only to the mortgage held by _____, in the approximate amount of $_____. There shall be no adjustment for taxes or mortgage payments. From the execution of the deed, the Husband/Wife shall have no right or claim to said premises. He/She agrees to take all steps possible to remove the other party's name from the mortgage note and indemnifies and holds the other harmless with regard to any current or future debt regarding the residence.

❏ C. The parties agree that the Husband/Wife shall purchase the Husband's/Wife's interest in the marital residence by refinancing the existing mortgage in his/her own name and paying Husband/Wife a sum of $_____ at the time of the refinance by bargain and sale deed with covenant, duly executed and acknowledged, and recorded at his/her expense, subject only to the refinanced mortgage.

❏ D. The parties agree that the home shall be placed up for sale no later than _____, _____. The parties shall agree at the time as to the real estate agent utilized and the listing price. Both parties must agree to accept a purchase price before it can be accepted, and the parties agree to cooperate in making these decisions and to act in a reasonable manner.

    ❏ 1. Commencing _____, _____, the Wife/Husband shall have exclusive use and occupancy, and shall pay the mortgage payment of $_____ per month until the time of sale. The Husband/Wife agrees to permit real estate agents and potential buyers into the home at reasonable times.

    ❏ 2.. The parties shall continue to reside together in the marital residence until _____, _____, at which time the Husband/Wife shall have exclusive use and occupancy until the time of sale. The Husband/Wife agrees to permit the real estate agents and potential buyers into the home at reasonable times.

❏ E. The parties shall continue to reside together in the marital residence until _____ _____, _____, at which time _____.

❏ F. Upon sale of the home, the parties shall first pay any unpaid taxes due and owing upon the home, the balance of the mortgage, and all closing costs, real estate agent commissions, and other costs of sale out of the proceeds. The remainder of the proceeds of the home shall then be shared equally by the parties.

❏ G. The Husband/Wife shall be responsible for the cost of home repairs up to the date of sale of the home.

❏ H. Each party warrants that he or she has not encumbered the title to the property other than the first mortgage and will not encumber the title before the sale.

❏ I. The parties no longer share a marital residence and each shall keep possession of his or her own residence.

❏ J. The Husband/Wife shall continue to have possession of the rented marital residence located at _____.

❏ K. Other: _____
_____
_____.

ARTICLE III: SEPARATE PROPERTY

The parties agree that the following is and shall remain the sole and separate property of the Wife:

_____
_____
_____
_____
_____
_____
_____
_____.

The parties agree that the following is and shall remain the sole and separate property of the Husband:

_____
_____
_____
_____
_____
_____
_____
_____.

ARTICLE IV: AUTOMOBILES AND VEHICLES

❑ A. The Wife shall have possession and ownership of _____

_____.

The Husband shall have possession and ownership of _____

_____.

Each party waives any right, title, or interest in and to the automobile or vehicle owned by the other, and shall hereafter consider such vehicle to be the sole and separate property of its owner. This shall be effective as of the date of this Agreement and the parties shall execute any necessary documents to effectuate this.

B. Each party will pay for the respective license renewal, upkeep, insurance, registration, and maintenance of their respective vehicles.

C. Each party assumes all liabilities associated with his or her own vehicle and shall indemnify and hold the other party harmless from any and all such liabilities.

ARTICLE V: BANK AND FINANCIAL ACCOUNTS

❑ A. Each party shall remain the sole and separate owner of his or her bank and financial accounts held in his or her name.

❑ B. The following joint accounts shall be divided as follows:

Name of Bank, Stock, Fund, etc.	Balance	New Owner

ARTICLE VI: INTERESTS IN BUSINESS

_____
_____
_____
_____.

ARTICLE VII: LIFE AND DISABILITY INSURANCE

A. The Wife shall maintain and be the sole owner of _____
_____.

B. The Husband shall maintain and be the sole owner of _____
_____.

C. The parties agree that each party is to name and maintain the other party / the child(ren) as beneficiary on his or her life insurance policy.

D. Each party shall be solely responsible for any loan against his or her life insurance policies.

ARTICLE VIII: PENSION AND RETIREMENT RIGHTS

Each party waives his or her rights to receive any payment from the other party's pension or retirement plan. The parties have disclosed to each other information regarding both pensions or retirement rights, and both parties have freely chosen not to have either valued.

ARTICLE IX: DISTRIBUTION OF PERSONALTY AND OTHER PROPERTY

❏ A. In order to effectuate a complete distribution of the parties' marital property, the parties have mutually agreed to a division of furniture, furnishings, jewelry, and clothing, as well as other items of personal property. The parties have previously divided all of these items and all items now in the possession of the Husband shall now become his sole and separate property. All items now in the possession of the Wife shall now become her sole and separate property.

❏ B. The parties agree that the marital personal property items listed on Schedule A shall be distributed according to Schedule A and shall become the sole and separate property of the party named as owner therein.

❏ C. Other marital property that is not personalty shall be divided according to Schedule B.

ARTICLE X: DEBTS

❏ A. Each party shall be solely responsible for debts held in his or her individual name.

❏ B. The parties agree that the marital debts shall be divided as described on Schedule C.

❏ C. Except as otherwise provided in this Agreement, the parties represent that neither has incurred, and will not at any time in the future incur, any debt, charge, or liability for which the other is now or may become liable. Each party further agrees at all times to indemnify the other party from, and hold that party free and harmless against, any and all debts, charges, contracts, and liabilities contracted by such party.

❏ D. The parties agree that they hold other joint credit cards including _____
_____
_____
_____

_____

_____

_____, and agree that said accounts
have no balance and agree to close said accounts or convert them to individual accounts.

ARTICLE XI: MAINTENANCE

❏ A.   Based on the fact that both parties are self-supporting and based on the division of property and all the facts and circumstances, no maintenance shall be due to either party.

❏ B.   Husband/Wife shall pay $_____ as a lump sum maintenance payment to the Husband/Wife. Such payment shall be due _____.

❏ C.   The parties have agreed that the Husband/Wife shall pay to the Husband/Wife $_____ per _____ as maintenance and that such payments are to be made each _____by personal check or as otherwise agreed, commencing _____. The parties acknowledge that said maintenance is due to the fact that the Husband/Wife _____

_____

_____

_____

_____.

❏ D.   Such maintenance payments shall cease upon the occurrence of whichever of the following shall first occur:

1.   Upon reaching _____ full years. Unless another termination event occurs, maintenance shall be paid up to and through _____.

2.   The death of either party.

3.   The remarriage of the Husband/Wife (party receiving maintenance) as herein defined. For purposes of this agreement, the term remarriage shall mean and include entering into a marriage contract or marriage ceremony, whether civil or religious, and whether or not such marriage be void or voidable and later annulled or avoided. Such remarriage shall also mean cohabitating with an unrelated adult person, whether or not they hold themselves out as Husband and Wife for a consecutive period of_____; however, should such cohabitation end during the period of maintenance under this Agreement, maintenance shall resume for the balance of the payment period. In the event of such a resumption, maintenance shall not be owed for the duration of the cohabitation.

ARTICLE XII: HEALTH CARE INSURANCE AND EXPENSES

❏ A.   The parties agree that the Husband/Wife shall continue to maintain health insurance for the minor child(ren) of the marriage as long as it is available to him/her and shall also continue to carry the Husband/Wife on said insurance until the date of divorce. The Husband/Wife shall be solely responsible for all payments of premiums. The parties acknowledge and agree that the insurance policy continues to carry the Husband/Wife even if the parties are legally separated.

❑ B. The parties agree that the Husband/Wife shall be permitted to pay for his/her health insurance, as permitted by COBRA, through the Husband's/Wife's insurance after the date of divorce if he/she so chooses, as long as it is available. This expense shall be the sole responsibility of the Husband/Wife.

❑ C. The Husband/Wife shall be responsible for his/her own co-pays, prescriptions, and uncovered medical, dental, optical, and mental health expenses up until the date of divorce and also afterwards if COBRA is elected.

❑ D. The parties agree that should health insurance no longer be available to the Husband/Wife or should the Husband/Wife have health insurance become available to him/her, the parties will renegotiate this portion of this agreement at that time. The parties agree that neither shall take any action causing the termination of the family's eligibility.

❑ E. The parties agree the Husband/Wife shall pay all of the child(ren)'s co-pays, prescriptions, and uncovered medical, dental, optical, and orthodontic expenses. The parties agree to renegotiate this clause should either party remarry (remarriage for this section is defined as a marriage recognized by the laws of New York State).

❑ F. The parties agree that the child(ren)'s co-pays and other uncovered medical, dental, optical, and orthodontic expenses shall be divided between the parties as follows: _____
_____
_____.

ARTICLE XIII: PARENTING

A. Custody and visitation shall be as follows:

_____
_____
_____
_____
_____
_____
_____
_____
_____
_____
_____
_____
_____
_____
_____
_____
_____
_____
_____
_____
_____.

B. The visitation and holiday schedule shall be as follows:

_____
_____
_____
_____
_____
_____
_____
_____
_____
_____
_____
_____
_____
_____
_____
_____
_____
_____
_____
_____.

❑ C. Each party agrees to notify the other of any change in address or telephone number.

❑ D. The parties agree to consult with and consider the opinion of their child in making living and visitation arrangements.

❑ E. The parties agree to exercise reasonable judgment regarding the introduction of and involvement with new partners as it impacts the child.

❑ F. Once a year, on the anniversary of this agreement, the parties agree to review the custody and visitation agreement and make any modifications mutually agreed upon.

❑ G. The parties agree that should the issue of relocation ever arise, they will discuss it and make good faith efforts to resolve it themselves.

❑ H. The parties agree that the Husband/Wife shall not relocate beyond a 50 mile radius of the current residence without the express written consent of the Husband/Wife or permission of the court.

❑ I. The parties agree to discuss any gift of over $100 for either of the children by either party before the purchase is made.

❑ J. The parties agree they shall have equal access to the children's school and medical records.

❑ K. Other: _____
_____
_____
_____.

ARTICLE XIV: CHILD SUPPORT

❑ A. With knowledge and understanding of the Child Support Standards Act, the parties have voluntarily entered into this Agreement, containing the provisions for child support as set forth herein. More particularly, the parties acknowledge that the Act presumptively sets the needs of the _____ child(ren) of the parties at _____% of the combined parental income up to $80,000 per year and said percentage and/or additional discretionary sum for combined parental income over $80,000 per year. Because the Husband claims an income of $_____ per year and the Wife claims an income of $_____ per year, their combined parental income exceeds/is less than $80,000 per year.

❑ **[Income is less than $80,000]**
Based upon combined parental income of $_____, the Act requires that the Husband/Wife pay to the Husband/Wife as child support the sum of $_____ per _____, which obligation is (consistent with/less than/more than) the sums provided for for in this agreement. If it is more than or less than the reasons are:

❑ **[Income is more than $80,000]**
Based upon the combined annual parental income of $_____, the child support payments required under the Act to be paid by the Husband/Wife to the Husband/Wife based upon percentage is $_____ per _____. Under the provisions of this agreement, the Husband's/Wife's obligation to the Husband/Wife is the sum of $_____ per _____ plus the obligation to pay or contribute to :

By reason of the foregoing and discretionary factors, including but not limited to transfers of property and payment of a distributive award to the Husband/Wife, for which some benefit will enure to the benefit of the children, the obligations of the Husband/Wife under this agreement comply with the requirements of the Act.

❑ B. Having considered the above factors, the parties wish to opt-out of the Child Support Standards Act for the following reasons: _____ _____ _____.

And the parties agree that based on the above reasons, child support shall be set at $_____ to be paid each _____ by the Husband/Wife to the Husband/Wife and shall be paid as follows: _____ _____.

❑ C. The Husband/Wife shall also be responsible for the following child(ren)'s expenses: _____ _____ _____ _____.

❑ D. The parties agree to assist their child(ren) with college expenses at a ratio to be determined at that time as they shall agree.

❑ E. The parties agree that child support shall be reduced each time a child reaches 18 or becomes emancipated and shall completely terminate when all of the children are 18 or older or are all emancipated.

ARTICLE XV: INCOME TAX RETURNS

❏ A. The parties agree to file as married filing jointly for the year _____. They shall share any refund on a pro rata basis based on their incomes.

❏ B. The parties agree to file as married filing separately for the year _____ and to each be solely responsible for his or her tax owed or refund received.

❏ C. The children shall be claimed as exemptions as follows: _____

_____

_____ .

ARTICLE XVI: BANKRUPTCY

The Parties have consented to the terms of this Agreement upon their reliance on the express representations made to each other that all of its terms, particularly those with respect to the maintenance payments of debts, property division, and distributive award, or any other transfers or payments to implement equitable distribution, which are to be made pursuant to the terms and provisions of this Agreement, shall not be discharged, canceled, terminated, diminished, or in any way affected by the filing of a petition in bankruptcy, or by the making of an assignment for the benefit of creditors.

Accordingly, in the event that the either party files a petition in bankruptcy or makes an assignment for the benefit of creditors, all transfers or payments provided for in this Agreement are intended to be maintenance. The party who files such petition in bankruptcy or makes such assignment for the benefit of creditors shall be liable for any resulting tax consequences.

To the extent that any obligation arising under this Agreement may be discharged, canceled, terminated, diminished, or in any way affected by the filing of a petition in bankruptcy, or by the making of an assignment for the benefit of creditors, the party adversely affected by such action shall be entitled to apply to any court of competent and appropriate jurisdiction for modification of this Agreement and any order or decree into which it may hereafter be incorporated. The party who files such petition in bankruptcy or who makes an assignment for the benefit of creditors hereby consents that in any proceeding brought by the other party pursuant to this provision, the court hearing the same may grant economic relief of any kind or nature to relieve the other party of the adverse impact of the bankruptcy or assignment, irrespective of the otherwise applicable standards for such relief, including, but not limited to, the granting of maintenance to a party who would otherwise not qualify for such relief under the criteria of the particular jurisdiction.

ARTICLE XVII: RELEASES

A. Both parties completely waive all their rights against the other's will or estate as beneficiary, distributee, administrator or executor, including the right of set-off and all rights of election in any jurisdiction. This does not constitute a bar to a cause of action against an estate arising out of a breach of the terms of this Agreement.

B. Both parties accept the terms of this Agreement as settlement in full of any and all rights under the equitable distribution law or community property law of any state, as well as all rights against pensions, retirements, stock options, Keoughs, IRAs, or other similar items. All other obligations or liabilities of the parties to each other, except those set forth herein, are forever terminated.

C. The Husband and Wife, in consideration of the terms of this Agreement, release each other from liabilities arising from any cause of action, contract, agreement, or any claim made by the other party or his or her executor, administrator, beneficiary, distributee, or legal representative, including any claim for maintenance, support, or equitable distribution, except as specifically provided in this Agreement.

D. The releases given above do not bar the parties from bringing an action as a result of a breach of the terms of this Agreement.

E. Nothing contained in this Agreement shall operate as a release or waiver of any cause or causes of action either party may have against the other for divorce, annulment, or separation, and any defenses thereto in any pending or future action.

F. Husband and Wife hereby expressly revoke their respective existing wills concerning any disposition made therein for the other and further revoke any nomination of the other party as an estate representative therefore, it being the intent of the parties that all wills made by either of them, executed prior to the acknowledgment of this Agreement, shall be read as if the other party had pre-deceased them for purposes of distribution of their respective estates. The same shall further apply to any testamentary substitutes not passing under a will. Each of the parties expressly renounces, covenants, and warrants to renounce, any right of administration upon the estate of the other or nomination by the other as estate representative, as required by the laws or practices of any jurisdiction whatsoever. Any disposition to the other party and/or the other party being nominated as an estate representative in a will executed after the acknowledgment of this Agreement is specifically not revoked by this Agreement.

ARTICLE XVIII: GENERAL PROVISIONS

A. This Agreement shall be construed in accordance with the laws of the State of New York, independent of any forum where this Agreement or any terms or provisions thereof may be subjected to construction and/or enforcement.

B. Except as otherwise specifically provided for to the contrary in this Agreement, each of the parties' respective rights and obligations hereunder shall be deemed independent and may be enforced independently irrespective of any of the other rights and obligations set forth herein.

C. This Agreement and all the obligations and covenants hereunder shall bind the parties, their heirs, executors, legal representatives, administrators, and assigns.

D. No modification, recision, or amendment to this Agreement shall be effective unless in writing signed by the parties with the same formality as this Agreement.

E. This Agreement and its provisions merge prior agreements, if any, of the parties and is the complete and entire agreement of the parties, and no oral statements or prior written materials extrinsic to this Agreement shall have any force and effect whatsoever.

F. In the event that any term, provision, paragraph, or Article of this Agreement is declared illegal, void, or unenforceable, such determination shall not affect or impair the other terms, provisions, paragraphs, or Articles in this Agreement. The Doctrine of Severability shall be applied. The parties do not intend by this statement to imply the illegality or unenforceability of any term, provision, paragraph, or Article of this Agreement.

G. Each of the parties hereto, without cost to the other shall at any time and from time to time hereafter, execute and deliver any and all further instruments and assurances and perform any acts that the other party may reasonably request for the purposes of giving full force and effect to the provisions of this Agreement.

H. No representation or warranties have been made by either party to the other or by anyone else except as expressly set forth in this Agreement, and this Agreement is not being executed in reliance upon any representation or warranty not expressly set forth herein.

I. The Husband and Wife each acknowledge that they have read the foregoing Agreement prior to the signing thereof.

J. The failure of either the Husband or Wife in any one or more instances to insist or require strict performances of any of the terms or conditions of this Agreement shall not be construed as a waiver of any subsequent default of the same or similar nature, nor shall the failure by either party to exercise any option or make any election herein provided for be construed as a waiver or relinquishment for the future of any such term, option, or election and all of the terms and conditions of this Agreement shall continue in full force and effect. No waiver or relinquishment shall be deemed to have been made by either party unless in writing duly signed and acknowledged by such party.

K. The descriptive Article headings contained herein are for convenience and identification only and are not intended to limit or conclusively define all the subject matter in the paragraphs accompanying such headings, and, accordingly, such headings should not be resorted to for purposes of interpretation of this Agreement.

L. This Agreement has been executed in _____ duplicate original counterparts, each of which is deemed by the parties to be an original.

M. This Agreement shall not be invalidated, terminated, canceled, otherwise affected by a reconciliation between the parties or by resumption of cohabitation or marital relations between them, unless such reconciliation or such resumption is conformed by a written document which expressly invalidates, terminates, cancels or otherwise alters this Agreement and which is executed and acknowledges with the same degree of formality as this Agreement or unless stipulated to by the parties upon the record of a court of competent jurisdiction.

N. In addition to any other grounds for divorce which either party may presently have or may hereafter acquire, the parties agree that the execution of this agreement and the filing of it, or a memorandum of it, in the Office of the County Clerk, in the county where either party resides, may give rise to a grounds for divorce which may be asserted by either party if they live separate and apart for a period of one or more years and if the party who seeks such divorce has substantially performed his or her obligations under this agreement.

ARTICLE XIX: AGREEMENT TO MEDIATE

The parties agree that should any questions, disputes, or disagreements develop with regard to the terms of this Agreement, the parties will mediate and make a good faith attempt at resolving any issues through mediation before litigating the issue. The cost of such mediation shall be paid one-half by each party.

ARTICLE XX: ATTORNEY FEES AND COURT AND RELATED COSTS

- ❏ A. Each party agrees to be solely responsible for paying his or her own attorney fees.

- ❏ B. It is the intent of the parties that the Husband/Wife shall initiate an action for divorce and the parties agree that all costs and attorney's fees incurred by the Husband/Wife associated with the action shall be the sole responsibility of the Husband/Wife.

- ❏ C. The Husband/Wife shall pay to the Husband/Wife the sum of $_____ for his/her attorney's fees.

ARTICLE XXI: OTHER AGREEMENTS

❏ Additional agreements of the parties are included on _____ pages attached hereto.

IN WITNESS WHEREOF, the parties have hereunto set their signatures on the day and year first above written. EACH OF THE PARTIES REPRESENTS AND WARRANTS THAT THEY HAVE CAREFULLY READ THIS AGREEMENT AND EACH AND EVERY PAGE THEREOF (INCLUDING THE TITLE PAGE, SCHEDULES, EXHIBITS, ATTACHMENTS, AND ADDENDA, IF ANY) PRIOR TO SIGNING.

_____
Husband

_____
Wife

STATE OF NEW YORK

SS.:

COUNTY OF _____

On _____, before me, the undersigned, a Notary Public, in and for the said State, personally appeared _____, personally known to me or proved to me on the basis of satisfactory evidence to be the individual whose name is subscribed to the within instrument and acknowledged to me that he/she executed the same in his/her capacity and that by his/her signature on the instrument, the individual, or the person upon behalf of which the individual acted, executed the instrument.

_____
NOTARY PUBLIC

STATE OF NEW YORK

SS.:

COUNTY OF _____

On _____, before me, the undersigned, a Notary Public, in and for the said State, personally appeared _____, personally known to me or proved to me on the basis of satisfactory evidence to be the individual whose name is subscribed to the within instrument and acknowledged to me that he/she executed the same in his/her capacity and that by his/her signature on the instrument, the individual, or the person upon behalf of which the individual acted, executed the instrument.

_____
NOTARY PUBLIC

STATE OF NEW YORK
COUNTY OF_____
---X

_____, Husband,

and

_____, Wife.
---X

**MEMORANDUM OF
SEPARATION AGREEMENT**

A. Names and Addresses of Parties:

Husband: _____   Wife: _____

           _____   _____

           _____   _____

B. Date of Marriage: _____

C. Date of Separation Agreement: _____

D. Date of Subscription to Agreement: Husband:_____ Wife:_____

_____   _____
Husband's Signature   Wife's Signature

STATE OF NEW YORK   )
COUNTY OF   ) ss.:
TOWN OF   )

On this _____ day of _____, _____, before me personally appeared
_____, to me personally known and known to me to be the same
person described in and who executed the foregoing instrument, and he/she duly acknowledged to
me that he/she executed the same.

_____
Notary Public

STATE OF NEW YORK   )
COUNTY OF   ) ss.:
TOWN OF   )

On this _____ day of _____, _____, before me personally appeared
_____, to me personally known and known to me to be the same
person described in and who executed the foregoing instrument, and he/she duly acknowledged to
me that he/she executed the same.

_____
Notary Public

INDEX

SPHINX® PUBLISHING ORDER FORM

BILL TO:		SHIP TO:	
Phone #	Terms	F.O.B. Chicago, IL	Ship Date

Charge my: ☐ VISA ☐ MasterCard ☐ American Express

☐ **Money Order or Personal Check**

Credit Card Number   Expiration Date

Qty	ISBN	Title	Retail	Ext.
		SPHINX PUBLISHING NATIONAL TITLES		
___	1-57071-342-1	Debtors' Rights (3E)	$14.95	___
___	1-57248-139-0	Grandparents' Rights (3E)	$24.95	___
___	1-57248-087-4	Guia de Inmigracion a Estados Unidos (2E)	$24.95	___
___	1-57248-103-X	Help Your Lawyer Win Your Case (2E)	$14.95	___
___	1-57071-164-X	How to Buy a Condominium or Townhome	$19.95	___
___	1-57071-223-9	How to File Your Own Bankruptcy (4E)	$19.95	___
___	1-57248-132-3	How to File Your Own Divorce (4E)	$24.95	___
___	1-57248-100-5	How to Form a DE Corporation from Any State	$24.95	___
___	1-57248-083-1	How to Form a Limited Liability Company	$22.95	___
___	1-57248-101-3	How to Form a NV Corporation from Any State	$24.95	___
___	1-57248-099-8	How to Form a Nonprofit Corporation	$24.95	___
___	1-57248-133-1	How to Form Your Own Corporation (3E)	$24.95	___
___	1-57071-343-X	How to Form Your Own Partnership	$22.95	___
___	1-57248-119-6	How to Make Your Own Will (2E)	$16.95	___
___	1-57071-331-6	How to Negotiate Real Estate Contracts (3E)	$18.95	___
___	1-57071-332-4	How to Negotiate Real Estate Leases (3E)	$18.95	___
___	1-57248-124-2	How to Register Your Own Copyright (3E)	$21.95	___
___	1-57248-104-8	How to Register Your Own Trademark (3E)	$21.95	___
___	1-57071-349-9	How to Win Your Unemployment Compensation Claim	$19.95	___
___	1-57248-118-8	How to Write Your Own Living Will (2E)	$16.95	___
___	1-57071-344-8	How to Write Your Own Premarital Agreement (2E)	$21.95	___
___	1-57071-333-2	Jurors' Rights (2E)	$12.95	___
___	1-57071-400-2	Legal Research Made Easy (2E)	$14.95	___
___	1-57071-336-7	Living Trusts and Simple Ways to Avoid Probate (2E)	$22.95	___
___	1-57071-345-6	Most Valuable Bus. Legal Forms You'll Ever Need (2E)	$19.95	___
___	1-57071-346-4	Most Valuable Corporate Forms You'll Ever Need (2E)	$24.95	___

Qty	ISBN	Title	Retail	Ext.
___	1-57248-130-7	Most Valuable Personal Legal Forms You'll Ever Need	$19.95	___
___	1-57248-098-X	The Nanny and Domestic Help Legal Kit	$22.95	___
___	1-57248-089-0	Neighbor v. Neighbor (2E)	$16.95	___
___	1-57071-348-0	The Power of Attorney Handbook (3E)	$19.95	___
___	1-57071-337-5	Social Security Benefits Handbook (2E)	$16.95	___
___	1-57071-399-5	Unmarried Parents' Rights	$19.95	___
___	1-57071-354-5	U.S.A. Immigration Guide (3E)	$19.95	___
___	1-57248-138-2	Winning Your Personal Injury Claim (2E)	$24.95	___
___	1-57248-097-1	Your Right to Child Custody, Visitation and Support	$22.95	___
		CALIFORNIA TITLES		
___	1-57248-150-1	CA Power of Attorney Handbook (2E)	$18.95	___
___	1-57248-151-X	How to File for Divorce in CA (3E)	$26.95	___
___	1-57071-356-1	How to Make a CA Will	$16.95	___
___	1-57248-146-3	How to Start a Business in CA	$18.95	___
___	1-57071-358-8	How to Win in Small Claims Court in CA	$16.95	___
___	1-57071-359-6	Landlords' Rights and Duties in CA	$21.95	___
		FLORIDA TITLES		
___	1-57071-363-4	Florida Power of Attorney Handbook (2E)	$16.95	___
___	1-57248-093-9	How to File for Divorce in FL (6E)	$24.95	___
___	1-57071-380-4	How to Form a Corporation in FL (4E)	$24.95	___
___	1-57248-086-6	How to Form a Limited Liability Co. in FL	$22.95	___
___	1-57071-401-0	How to Form a Partnership in FL	$22.95	___
___	1-57248-113-7	How to Make a FL Will (6E)	$16.95	___
___	1-57248-088-2	How to Modify Your FL Divorce Judgment (4E)	$24.95	___
___	1-57248-081-5	How to Start a Business in FL (5E)	$16.95	___
___	1-57071-362-6	How to Win in Small Claims Court in FL (6E)	$16.95	___
___	1-57248-123-4	Landlords' Rights and Duties in FL (8E)	$21.95	___

Form Continued on Following Page   **SUBTOTAL**

To order, call Sourcebooks at 1-800-432-7444 or FAX (630) 961-2168 (Bookstores, libraries, wholesalers—please call for discount)

Prices are subject to change without notice.

SPHINX® PUBLISHING ORDER FORM

Qty	ISBN	Title	Retail	Ext.
		GEORGIA TITLES		
____	1-57248-137-4	How to File for Divorce in GA (4E)	$21.95	____
____	1-57248-075-0	How to Make a GA Will (3E)	$16.95	____
____	1-57248-140-4	How to Start a Business in Georgia (2E)	$16.95	____
		ILLINOIS TITLES		
____	1-57071-405-3	How to File for Divorce in IL (2E)	$21.95	____
____	1-57071-415-0	How to Make an IL Will (2E)	$16.95	____
____	1-57071-416-9	How to Start a Business in IL (2E)	$16.95	____
____	1-57248-078-5	Landlords' Rights & Duties in IL	$21.95	____
		MASSACHUSETTS TITLES		
____	1-57248-128-5	How to File for Divorce in MA (3E)	$24.95	____
____	1-57248-115-3	How to Form a Corporation in MA	$24.95	____
____	1-57248-108-0	How to Make a MA Will (2E)	$16.95	____
____	1-57248-106-4	How to Start a Business in MA (2E)	$16.95	____
____	1-57248-107-2	Landlords' Rights and Duties in MA (2E)	$21.95	____
		MICHIGAN TITLES		
____	1-57071-409-6	How to File for Divorce in MI (2E)	$21.95	____
____	1-57248-077-7	How to Make a MI Will (2E)	$16.95	____
____	1-57071-407-X	How to Start a Business in MI (2E)	$16.95	____
		NEW YORK TITLES		
____	1-57248-141-2	How to File for Divorce in NY (2E)	$26.95	____
____	1-57248-105-6	How to Form a Corporation in NY	$24.95	____
____	1-57248-095-5	How to Make a NY Will (2E)	$16.95	____
____	1-57071-185-2	How to Start a Business in NY	$16.95	____
____	1-57071-187-9	How to Win in Small Claims Court in NY	$16.95	____
____	1-57071-186-0	Landlords' Rights and Duties in NY	$21.95	____
____	1-57071-188-7	New York Power of Attorney Handbook	$19.95	____
____	1-57248-122-6	Tenants' Rights in NY	$21..95	____
		NORTH CAROLINA TITLES		
____	1-57071-326-X	How to File for Divorce in NC (2E)	$22.95	____
____	1-57248-129-3	How to Make a NC Will (3E)	$16.95	____
____	1-57248-096-3	How to Start a Business in NC (2E)	$16.95	____
____	1-57248-091-2	Landlords' Rights & Duties in NC	$21.95	____
		OHIO TITLES		
____	1-57248-102-1	How to File for Divorce in OH	$24.95	____
		PENNSYLVANIA TITLES		
____	1-57248-127-7	How to File for Divorce in PA (2E)	$24.95	____
____	1-57248-094-7	How to Make a PA Will (2E)	$16.95	____
____	1-57248-112-9	How to Start a Business in PA (2E)	$18.95	____
____	1-57071-179-8	Landlords' Rights and Duties in PA	$19.95	____
		TEXAS TITLES		
____	1-57071-330-8	How to File for Divorce in TX (2E)	$21.95	____
____	1-57248-114-5	How to Form a Corporation in TX (2E)	$24.95	____
____	1-57071-417-7	How to Make a TX Will (2E)	$16.95	____
____	1-57071-418-5	How to Probate an Estate in TX (2E)	$22.95	____
____	1-57071-365-0	How to Start a Business in TX (2E)	$16.95	____
____	1-57248-111-0	How to Win in Small Claims Court in TX (2E)	$16.95	____
____	1-57248-110-2	Landlords' Rights and Duties in TX (2E)	$21.95	____

SUBTOTAL THIS PAGE ____

SUBTOTAL PREVIOUS PAGE ____

Shipping — $5.00 for 1st book, $1.00 each additional ____

Illinois residents add 6.75% sales tax ____

Connecticut residents add 6.00% sales tax ____

TOTAL ____

To order, call Sourcebooks at 1-800-432-7444 or FAX (630) 961-2168 (Bookstores, libraries, wholesalers—please call for discount)

Prices are subject to change without notice.